The Poetics of Piracy

The Poetics of Piracy

Emulating Spain in English Literature

Barbara Fuchs

PENN

UNIVERSITY OF PENNSYLVANIA PRESS

PHILADELPHIA

A volume in the Haney Foundation Series, established in
1961 with the generous support of Dr. John Louis Haney.

Published by
University of Pennsylvania Press
Philadelphia, Pennsylvania 19104-4112

Printed in the United States of America on acid-free paper
10 9 8 7 6 5 4 3 2 1

Library of Congress Cataloging-in-Publication Data
Fuchs, Barbara, 1970–
    The poetics of piracy : emulating Spain in English
literature / Barbara Fuchs — 1st ed.
        p. cm. — (Haney Foundation series)
    ISBN 978-0-8122-4475-5 (hardcover ; alk. paper)
    Includes bibliographical references and index
        1. English literature—Spanish influences. 2. English
literature—Early modern, 1500–1700—History and
criticism. 3. Imitation in literature. I Title. II. Series: Haney
Foundation series.
PR129.S7 F83   2013
820.9'35846   2012031344

For Marshall Brown, who was on the lookout for Spain

Contents

The Poetics of Piracy

Introduction

Imagine for a moment that we found, in some dusty attic, the late, lost play *Cardenio* by William Shakespeare and John Fletcher, based on the unhinged lover-turned-wild-man in the first part of *Don Quijote*. Shakespeare scholars would be beside themselves with joy. A flurry of papers, conferences, publications would follow hard upon. But what would the discovery of *Cardenio* do for the shape of the discipline? Would English studies look any different if we miraculously recovered the lost play?

For scholars of Anglo-Spanish relations, the lost *Cardenio* looms large. The play is the absent center, the purloined letter, the missing link, the huge gaping O. Exhibit A for the connection between the two foremost representatives of early modern English and Spanish literature—Shakespeare and Miguel de Cervantes—has gone missing, leaving in its stead a tantalizing title and the thought of what might have been. The recent surge of interest in this lost play, including several reconstructions both scholarly and theatrical, as well as an edition of its eighteenth-century redaction in the prestigious Arden Shakespeare series, mark it as a crucial missing piece in our conception of early modern English culture. By recovering the Spanish connection that makes sense of *Cardenio*, this book demonstrates how the play's absent presence has conditioned our understanding of Anglo-Spanish cultural relations in the early modern period and beyond. Beyond charting the lively debates around *Cardenio*'s absence, *The Poetics of Piracy* shows how rich the Spanish vein proved for early modern English writers, and analyzes the occlusion of that debt in their time as in ours.

Early modern English writers turned frequently to Spain for literary models, even at the times of greatest rivalry between the two nations. Spain's position as the dominant European power of the period, as well as the huge explosion in Spanish prose and dramatic writing across a wide variety of genres in the sixteenth and early seventeenth centuries made it an irresistible literary source. The frequent English translations from the Spanish, even during the

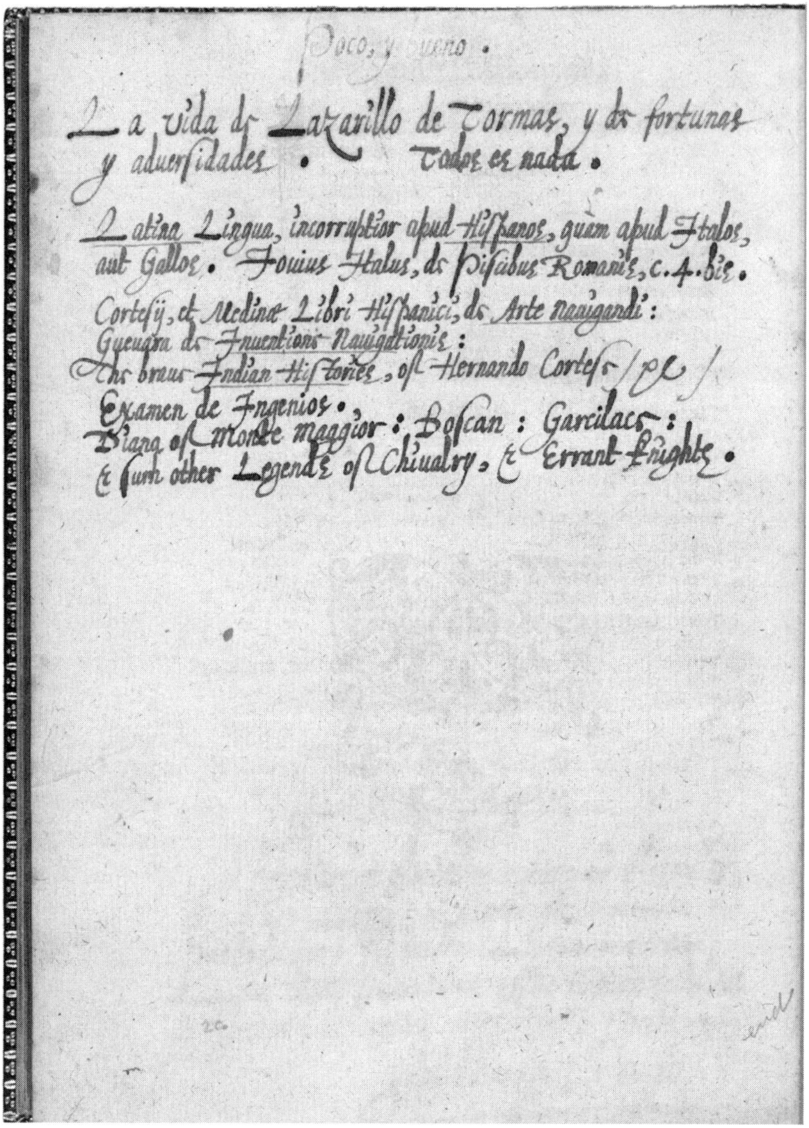

Poco, y bueno.

La vida de Lazarillo de Tormes, y de fortunas y aduersidades. Todos es nada.

Latina Lingua, incorruptior apud Hispanos, quam apud Italos, aut Gallos. Jouius Italus, de piscibus Romanis, c. 4. bis.

Cortesij, et Medinæ Libri Hispanici, de Arte nauigandi:

Gueuara de Inuentione Nauigationis:

The braue Indian Histories, of Hernando Cortes.

Examen de Ingenios.

Diana of Monte maggior: Boscan: Garcilaço:

& such other Legends of Chiualry, & Errant Knights.

Figure 1. Gabriel Harvey's reading list, from the flyleaf of his copy of Antonio de Corro and John Thorius, *The Spanish Grammar* (1590). Huntington Library.

long period of war under Elizabeth, provide evidence of a sustained fascination, from the bawdy *Celestina* (1499, translated by John Rastell in 1525 and by James Mabbe in 1631), to the picaresque *Lazarillo* (1554, translated c.1586 by David Rowland, among others), the pastoral *Diana*, with its interpolated Moorish novella *Abencerraje y Jarifa* (1559, trans. 1598 by Bartholomew Yong, among others), the romances of chivalry translated by Anthony Munday and Margaret Tyler in the 1580s and 1590s, and the early seventeenth-century translations of Cervantes and Mateo Alemán by Thomas Shelton and Mabbe. A broad variety of signal Spanish texts, many of them chefs-d'oeuvre for entire European traditions in poetry and prose—chivalric, sentimental, and maurophile romance, as well as picaresque, pastoral, and novella—thus made their way into English, even as the political situation between the two nations deteriorated in the wake of the Reformation and imperial rivalries. As philologists have long noted, Spanish sources, whether in the original or in intermediary versions, provided material for such central figures as Sidney, Spenser, and Shakespeare,[1] while England's extensive experience of sixteenth-century Spanish prose counters those histories of the novel that offer a proprietary, exclusively English version of its origins in the eighteenth.[2]

By the 1590s, large numbers of Englishmen were learning Spanish with the aid of new language manuals, whether for commercial, military, or literary purposes. In his copy of Antonio de Corro's *The Spanish Grammar* (1590), Gabriel Harvey noted: "Praecipue Linguae hodiernarum Negotiationum Anglicarum; Francica et Hispanica" [The main languages of today for English commerce are French and Spanish].[3] Harvey also kept in his Spanish textbook a running list of the best-sellers that he was presumably looking forward to reading in the original once he had mastered the language, many of which he may have first encountered in English translation.[4] Harvey's reading list includes the pragmatic: accounts of the New World, guides to navigation. Yet much of it would still belong on a master's exam in Spanish Golden Age literature: the anonymous picaresque *Lazarillo*, the psychological treatise *Examen de ingenios para las ciencias* by Juan Huarte de San Juan, Montemayor's *Diana*, and the Petrarchan poetry of Boscán and Garcilaso, as well as "other legends of chivalry and errant knights."[5]

Beyond charting his own fascination with Spanish, Harvey admires Spain's potency, and the role of language in its imperium: "Suo potentior, et gloriosior natio: eô florentior, et nobilior Lingua. Certè, vt Monarchia praedominatur: sic tandem Lingua. Et ea Lingua dianissima; cuius Vsus maximè catholicus in genere; aut maximè necessarius in specie" [The nation itself {is} stronger and more glorious, the language more blooming and more noble. Certainly, wherever their monarchy has ruled, their language has done the same. And this is a most famous language; used in the highest degree among Catholic peoples, or at least exceedingly indispensable in appearance].[6] Appreciation for the language is closely tied with admiration for Spain itself.

Yet while the English turn to Spain has been periodically noted—most fully in Dale Randall's 1963 classic, *The Golden Tapestry*—traditional literary history has managed neither wholly to insert Spain into English studies, nor convincingly to explain the ongoing disavowal of Spain in the field.[7] As I argue here, the reason is twofold. First, the English turn to Spain appears paradoxical, given the religious and political enmity between the two nations. Second, and more important, the early modern English rivalry with Spain has largely colored our own cultural and intellectual histories, limiting our view of the Spanish connection. The challenge lies in recognizing that the often vociferous rhetorical denunciation of Spain in the period and beyond did not impede literary traffic. Certainly, the increasing acrimony between the two nations, which came to a head with the attempted invasion by the Spanish Armada in 1588, raised the stakes for the English *imitatio* of Spain, placing literary transmission in a fundamental tension with religious and political conflicts, never fully resolved even when James declared peace with Spain in 1604. Yet transmission there was, from translation, to reelaboration, to occasional citation—all versions of a sustained fascination with Spanish matter. I thus offer in this book a reading of *imitatio* as a historically situated practice, coterminous with imperial competition and national self-definition.

While the interdependence of empire and culture was a central assumption for humanists charting their own descent from Rome and their role in *translatio imperii studiique*, scholarship has only begun to grapple with the extent to which a fully contemporary imperial and cultural competition undergirds the complex relations between England and Spain in the early modern period. The work of Richard Helgerson and Roland Greene has illuminated these complex interrelations primarily in terms of imperial rivalry; my aim here is to consider more broadly how Spanish influence is negotiated, and how it makes its way to the English stage.[8] I argue that translation and appropriation are loaded practices in an era that includes both the exacerbation of imperial rivalries and national differences on the one hand, and the emergence of commercial authorship, with the attendant anxieties about originality, on the other.[9] *The Poetics of Piracy* traces the emergence of a national canon for England in the context of its rivalry with Spain—a model constantly emulated even as it was disavowed. I juxtapose texts on Spain or translated from Spanish sources with early claims for England's literary eminence, often expressed in a heightened rhetoric of violent competition. My focus is on central figures of the Anglo-Spanish literary exchange, who either took from Spain for their own texts or reflected on the vexed relation to Spain that characterized English letters, particularly on the stage: Ben Jonson, William Shakespeare, Francis Beaumont, John Fletcher, and Thomas Middleton. Together, they paint a complex picture of the literary fascination with Spain, and of how entangled it became in questions of national and religious identity.

These writers are also, of course, among the most important figures of the English Renaissance, intimately tied to the development of English drama and vernacular letters. While the violent rhetoric of appropriation used to inflate the English vernacular has been well charted, as I discuss in Chapter 1, this book goes beyond language and source study to examine how English authors negotiated their debts to Spain, across a wide range of texts and genres. My point is not a course of revanchist philology, to settle scores or right literary-historical wrongs. Instead, I historicize literary borrowings, charting how productive appropriation proved in an English context. The appropriation in which these writers engaged, I argue, must be understood as an ideologically and historically situated phenomenon; for early modern England, the vectors of translation carried political freight that was often at odds with the literary dependence on Spanish sources. As the "Englished" works negotiate their paradoxical cultural reliance on a political enemy, they evince the textual marks of that contradiction.

Yet while it is critical to historicize the Anglo-Spanish exchange, the emphasis on political rivalry in the period has run the risk of occluding the significant literary and cultural contacts between the two nations.[10] Thus while England's connections to Italy and France have been widely recognized in the work of such scholars as Karen Newman, Margaret Ferguson, Susanne Wofford, and Jane Tylus, the profound debt of English letters to Spain has received far less critical attention, and, in many instances, been loudly denied. The contemporary erasure of Spain thus rehearses the early modern disavowal of the Spanish connection. Rather than establishing the sources for and influence of Spanish texts in England, however, I focus on analyzing the ideological vectors of *translatio*, both in the early modern period and in our own. My goal is to demonstrate the constructedness of a literary history that glorifies conflict while minimizing influence, and to assess what is at stake in how *translatio* is imagined. *The Poetics of Piracy* argues that English literature was deeply transnational, even in the period most associated with the birth of a national literature, and demonstrates how productive it proved, in this period as in subsequent ones, to cast borrowings from Spain as a triumphal taking.

My readings foreground what I call *partial historicity*, in both senses of the word. Although the texts I read are obviously deeply embedded in their political and historical context, they exhibit a certain independence from what ideology might seem to mandate: early modern taste does not rigidly follow religious or political conviction, and the most staunch defenders of England against Spain are nonetheless seduced by Spanish imaginary, language, or plots. Hence the texts' partial historicity: a historical context of anti-Spanish sentiment does not negate the appeal of Spanish sources. At the same time, the texts I analyze are partial in how they English their sources, furnishing domesticated or jingoistic versions of their originals, particularly where the history of Anglo-Spanish encounters is concerned. Together, these two forms of partial historicity give rise to a series of rhetorical operations: domestication, disavowal, or occlusion of Spanish sources, efforts to overgo or trump the original, and freeze-framing of Spain into stereotype or allegory.

English literary history, I argue, is deliberately shaped as an exclusive national property. Focusing on the Spanish connection, I trace the dynamics of appropriation—the proprietary "Englishing" that characterizes the movement of texts into the English sphere—as it works cumulatively to form an aggregate of national tradition.[11] Although I do not advocate a return to source-hunting, I want to mark the critical sleight-of-hand—the evasion and disavowal—that often operates when we claim no interest in primacy or origins. The *locus classicus* of this is Goethe's claim that "national literature is now a rather unmeaning term; the epoch of world literature is at hand."[12] For the early modern period, when national identities and literary corpora were coalescing in a context of imperial competition, such magnanimous attributions to the "world" generally involved a deliberate erasure of origins. Thus, for example, the striking prefatory poem, which I discuss in Chapter 1, in which Ben Jonson claims that Mateo Alemán's best-selling picaresque, *Guzmán de Alfarache*, "Englished" by Mabbe as *The Rogue*, "though writ / But in one tongue, was form'd with the worlds wit."[13] Clearly, Jonson's attribution to "the world" is a disavowal of the Spanish source, its "one tongue" superseded by universal possession. His gesture is symptomatic of the conflictive relationship of English literature to its Spanish sources. Even as Spanish texts and genres proved wonderfully productive for English authors, the always charged, when not openly combative, relation between the two nations made such debts difficult to acknowledge.

In a context where international literary borrowing was a given, Spain was by no means the only source for English texts, and both Spain and England participated in a longer tradition of engaging with Italian and classical models. Yet although England turned often to Italian sources, as to the classics, borrowing from them did not elicit the same competitiveness or frank aggression as borrowing from Spain. English drama, in particular, makes its Italian debts patent in Italian settings and characters. Yet while Italy, like Spain, was Roman Catholic, it was politically weak and divided, and did not pose a threat to England, as Spain did for most of Elizabeth's reign. More important, early modern Italy did not offer the imperial or military models that made Spain so attractive and unavoidable for the English, however deep the political and religious rifts between the two nations. Literary borrowing from Spain must thus be considered in this larger context of imperial rivalry and emulation. Though by no means a unique source, Spain was uniquely occluded, given the ideological context of the original appropriations and their subsequent elaboration into a narrative of national and imperial distinction.

By reading both specific English reworkings of Spanish originals and larger debates about Spain, *The Poetics of Piracy* shows how English writers constructed a pugnacious rhetorical apparatus, modeled on military rivalry, in an effort to reframe their profound debt to Spanish sources. The recurring metaphor of piracy, I argue, acknowledges taking from Spain even as it glorifies the supposedly forcible use of Spanish material. Pirates and piracy are everywhere in the corpus I present here, whether metaphorically, as in Jonson's commendatory poems to translations, or more concretely, as in the unexpected appearance of Barbarossa in Beaumont's *The Knight of the Burning Pestle* or the insistent references to Francis Drake in Fletcher's *Rule a Wife and Have a Wife*. More broadly, the retrospective construction of the Elizabethan period as a moment of twinned literary and military glory leads to the nostalgic evocation of privateering as itself a cultural treasure, both during the peace with Spain sought by James I, and at later moments of imperial rivalry, such as the mid-eighteenth-century era of "political Elizabethanism" that recreated a pugnacious Shakespeare.[14] Crucially, the metaphorics of piracy can invoke either the transnational threat of an unmoored, renegade subject, or, conversely, the patriotic privateer.[15] In the literary sphere, I propose, this ambivalence is resolved by conceptualizing *translatio* as an act of successful looting.

Although one would not have expected Jacobean playwrights, working within a regime of intellectual property quite different from our own, to acknowledge their precise sources, the notion of a *pirated* national corpus nonetheless remains useful: the term brings together issues of national and intellectual property, the historical antagonism between England and Spain, and the actual content of a number of the texts in question. Moreover, the figuration of *translatio* as piracy also provides a conceptual bridge between Renaissance notions of *imitatio* and our idea of intellectual piracy. In his capacious survey of the latter, Adrian Johns explains that "[intellectual] piracy has always been a matter of place—of territory and geopolitics—as well as time," and notes how it "therefore became a vehicle for national, and nationalist, passions."[16] Yet Johns's own brief account of the early seventeenth century considers intellectual property in a domestic rather than an international context. Moreover, he locates the first usages of "piracy" to denote an intellectual crime at the end of the seventeenth century, claiming of the period that concerns me here: "In around 1600 piracy seems not to have carried this meaning at all, except on a few isolated occasions as a metaphor."[17] In this book, I explore the extent and import of this metaphorics in the Elizabethan and Jacobean periods, providing a prehistory for the later dynamics that Johns analyzes and establishing the transnational dimension of intellectual piracy in an era when England turned to *actual* piracy as a central strategy for negotiating its imperial, military, and cultural belatedness. Rather than the legal status of imitation, I am interested in the cultural work it performs, at a moment when, as Joseph Loewenstein puts it, "commerce and competition threatened to convert that venerable practice into plagiarism."[18]

This book attempts both to recover the full complexity of transnational literary relations in early modern England and to explore how our own cultural landscape has been marked by the long-term occlusion and disavowal of Spanish influence. My goal is to historicize frequent unthinking prejudices about Spain, by showing how certain habits of thought— the supposed "obscurantism" of Spain, the impoverishment of Spanish cultural life as a result of the Inquisition, Spain's long decline—have created a kind of intellectual "Black Legend." Richard Kagan's work on historiography has traced how the United States has largely inherited English prejudices against Spain, and added to them a narrative of counter-exceptionalism, with Spain as the dark double to U.S. imperial glories.[19] In the realm of literary history, early critics from Schlegel to Ticknor largely denied any Spanish influence on English drama. By the turn of the twentieth century philologists recognized, however grudgingly, the "English debt" to Spain, but insisted on minimizing it. *Don Quijote*, whose influence is so patent, was made in this vision an honorary citizen of the world, in a move Jonson would surely approve: "Though full of contemporary Spain, *Don Quixote* is one of those immortal books which become the property of the world rather than of any particular country."[20] Spanish theater, for its part, was reduced to "types," far from the complexity and originality of Shakespeare, and the unparalleled quality of the Bard offered as evidence for the lack of Spanish influence.[21] In a symptomatic moment, the philologist Rudolf Schevill summarizes the a priori inconsequential scope of any influence that might nonetheless be traced:

> Nor could English literature for its part be more than superficially affected by writings which to the very core were the expression of a wholly different social order, of an uncongenial faith, of an antagonistic traditional training. These had been instrumental at least in making that type of Spaniard best known to the English, namely, a man whose real character was veiled and inscrutable and whose bearing invited chiefly caricature and ridicule among those who could not penetrate his uncongenial exterior. Under the circumstances it can hardly be profitable to look for English works saturated with genuine Spanish feeling. Fiction and the drama during the Renaissance, both in England and Spain are spontaneous and unconscious expressions of a very local, national spirit characteristic of the epoch.[22]

Schevill goes on to demonstrate the supposed impossibility of any connection, via broad detours into the Spanish national character, Spain's Moorishness, and the hollowness of Spain's imperial power, all placed in contradistinction to English might: "[The Spaniard's] bragging must have appeared unreasonable to the English who were constantly defeating him and making his boasted rule over the sea an extremely uncomfortable one."[23]

In an effort to undo these thought-habits, *The Poetics of Piracy* shows how the military and imperial rivalry between England and Spain in the early modern period—what one might call the "Armada paradigm"—has long furnished a conceptual model for thinking through Anglo-Spanish relations in the literary sphere. In fact, as I demonstrate, literary relations before, during, and after the Elizabethan conflict with Spain were ongoing and fruitful, despite the "national spirit" Schevill invokes, as English writers turned to Spain for its multiplicity of new forms, genres, and plots. The cultural fascination with Spain never waned, even when it was most inconvenient in military or religious terms.

My introductory chapter, "Forcible Translation," surveys Elizabethan debates on the relative poverty of English letters, which both translators and readers addressed by imaginatively enriching their native tongue in bold acts of appropriation. I show how the humanist longing to enrich the English language under Elizabeth is intimately connected to contemporary attempts to emulate Spain's empire. Literary *translatio*, I suggest, comes to share the pugnaciousness of the many translations of military manuals, guides to navigation, and other highly sensitive texts in the period. By envisioning and encouraging translation as an act of piracy, figures such as Ben Jonson tout literary appropriation as a national victory, foregrounding an English canon born of truculent competition.

Subsequent chapters turn to the larger workings of appropriation on the Jacobean stage, by charting how English dramatists take up and transform the texts of their Spanish contemporaries. Chapters on Beaumont, Middleton, and Fletcher explore how Spanish sources were put to anti-Spanish purposes. The great appeal of the Spanish plots to which these writers turned time and again overrides their suspicion of "plotting Spaniards," and produces a series of fascinating plays that take Spain against Spain. By exploring the uses of Spain in these plays, I restore texts constructed in a transnational, ideologically complex setting to their original contexts, recuperating influence and transmission as ideological vectors. When the meaning of a play is changed in translation or adaptation, what particular ideological charge does that transformation carry? How is appropriation itself coded in relation to the national project? How are local histories transformed as a text travels? My larger goal is to produce a new kind of literary history, more attuned to the deliberate exclusions and erasures, as well as the appropriations, that make up the national.

Chapter 2, "Knights and Merchants," reads Beaumont's *The Knight of the Burning Pestle* and its editorial history as a case-study in the disavowal of Spanish influence, in this case most clearly of Cervantes's *Don Quijote*. I argue that, despite its foreign sources, the play foregrounds a logic of the local and the mercantile, domesticating romance for local consumption. It thereby aligns itself with contemporary comedies centered on the city of London, rejecting both the exotic geographies of romance and colorful foreign threats that range from pirates to syphilis. In this highly self-conscious play, plots from Spain paradoxically serve to populate a local, "English" landscape and to repudiate the foreignness of romance.

Chapter 3, "Plotting Spaniards, Spanish Plots" explores how Spanish sources animate and complicate a variety of plays on the Jacobean stage, even those that seem most virulently anti-Spanish. Middleton's *A Game at Chess*, the most notorious anti-Spanish play of the period, is here contextualized in relation to the playwright's broader engagement with Spain. With its vision of Spanish ambition and Jesuit conspiracy, Middleton's play mobilizes anti-Spanish paranoia to great effect, giving literary life to political cliché. Yet despite the loud denunciations of plotting Spaniards both in this play and in the abundant pamphlet literature on which Middleton drew, English dramatists remained fascinated by Spanish plots. By juxtaposing a series of intricately plotted plays with Spanish sources to the more notorious *A Game at Chess*, this chapter shows how productive Spain proved for the English stage, despite the frequent portrayal of Spaniards as plotters and Machiavellians. The chapter then turns to Fletcher's pugnacious appropriation of Spanish materials in *Rule a Wife and Have a Wife*, a play I read in relation to the tremendous English anxiety about the possibility of a "Spanish Match" between Charles I and the Infanta of Spain in the early 1620s. These tensions are paradoxically addressed via a comedy based on Spanish sources, as the English discomfiture at the possible union is transformed into the textual comeuppance of a Spanish wife. Fletcher's *translatio* bolsters the play's jingoism with references to Drake and piracy that are nowhere to be found in his sources, as he emphasizes the cleverness of a bridegroom who can exploit a Spanish "pearl."

The Poetics of Piracy concludes by tracing the afterlives of the lost Shakespearean *Cardenio*, based on an episode in *Don Quijote*. The *Cardenio* phenomenon, I argue, exhibits the enduring critical fascination with "the hand of the Bard" and the concomitant erasure of Cervantine sources. In "Cardenio Lost and Found" I chart the peculiar reception of the lost play and its later redaction, to show how both eighteenth-century and modern readers occlude the Spanish debts of a figure revered as an English original and afforded an extraordinary status. I explore the striking critical insistence on divorcing Shakespeare from contemporary sources such as Cervantes to canonize him as the preeminent figure of English letters. The Shakespeare figured in this criticism, often expressed in praise-poetry or other paratexts, leaves all literary rivals in the dust, invoking for his eighteenth-century admirers the privateering glories of the Elizabethan era. Chapter 4 thus explores how the "Armada paradigm" frames *Double Falshood*, the 1728 "redaction" of *Cardenio* by Lewis Theobald, and then turns to the contemporary reception of the Arden edition of *Double Falsehood* (2010) as a rediscovered Shakespeare play. More broadly, it examines the long-term effects of such pugnacious canonization not just for Shakespeare studies but for the larger field of English.

I bring this discussion wholly into our own cultural arena in my final chapter, "*Cardenios* for Our Time," which explores the cultural politics of the contemporary reimagining of *Cardenio* by Stephen Greenblatt and playwright Charles Mee, on the one hand, and by Gregory Doran for the Royal Shakespeare Company, on the other. Taking my cue from Mee's website, *The (Re) making Project*, and from Greenblatt's international commissions for the rewriting of "Shakespeare's" *Cardenio*, I turn to questions of piracy, intellectual property, and cultural translation in our own era. Doran's production, for its part, provides an occasion for thinking through what it means to stage Spain, and how the long-term dynamics of appropriation impact even the most considered contemporary projects.

My larger goal is to demonstrate the productivity of the Spanish connection for English literature: Spain, I argue, is not just a rival but an irresistible source. This understanding brings us closer to a fully transnational literary history, one that recognizes the ideological coding and conditioning of all *translatio*. I also hope to underscore the impact of these historical dynamics on our own cultural politics, showing how early modern habits of erasure and disavowal have colored the long-term relation of the Anglo-American academy, and of American culture more generally, to all things Hispanic. My exploration of the poetics of piracy in English literary history is an attempt to reinscribe in our cultural imaginary the Spanish legacy that has so often been reflexively erased.

Chapter 1

Forcible Translation

IMITATIO: The third requisite in our *Poet*, or Maker, is *Imitation*, to be able to convert the substance, or Riches of another *Poet*, to his own use. To make choice of one excellent man above the rest, and so to follow him, till he grow very *He*, or, so like him, as the Copy may be mistaken for the Principal.
   —Ben Jonson, *Timber, or Discoveries*

The translators of Elizabeth's age pursued their craft in the spirit of bold adventure which animated Drake and Hawkins. It was their ambition to discover new worlds of thought and beauty. They sailed the wide ocean of knowledge to plant their colonies of intellect where they might, or to bring back to our English shores some eloquent stranger whom their industry had taught to speak with our English tongue.
   —Charles Whibley, *Literary Studies*

In the eventful century after humanist Antonio Nebrija's Spanish *Gramática* (1492) famously identified language as the companion of empire, vernacular languages became a key element of national distinction in an increasingly fragmented and belligerent Europe.[1] The development of the various vernaculars also produced great anxiety about the belatedness and relative poverty of each language in relation to both classical models and contemporary rivals. As Europe embarked on a century of exploration and expansion, linguistic and literary rivalries became an expression of imperial competition. Translation, for its part, functioned as a key site for negotiating national as well as authorial prerogatives, as self-effacing translators claimed to serve their country and prefatory poems praised the superiority of translated texts to their originals.[2] As Massimiliano Morini notes, over the course of the sixteenth century, "The English discovered that rhetorical translation also meant domestication, for the transformation of rhetorical elements of the original could be effected with an eye on the rights of the target language (and culture) rather than of the original author."[3] Yet despite the recent critical interest in early modern translation, English translation from the Spanish has not been accorded the same centrality as translation from the classics, Italian, or French, so that, for example, one recent collection on "Anglo-Continental relations" includes no mention of Spanish texts.[4]

England's anxiety about a muscular language was particularly acute, given the sense of belatedness that haunted both literary and imperial projects. In the crucial years of the later sixteenth century, a new confidence appeared among English writers, as the rich and copious language they had so longed for finally seemed to be within their grasp. This chapter charts the metaphorics of this newly confident translation, to demonstrate how it borrowed a language of rivalry and territorialization from the contemporary imperial competition with Spain.[5] While most evident in the translations of strategic works such as geographies, manuals for navigation, and military treatises, the pugnaciousness of these projects itself translates onto linguistic and literary enterprises.

From *Copia* to Loot

Humanist accounts of language routinely emphasize its richness and power. As Terence Cave explains in his famous study of Renaissance *copia*, the etymology of this rhetorical term for invention and amplification connects it to "the domains of material riches, natural plenty . . . and figurative abundance," as well as military strength.[6] Thus *copia* "confidently asserts the values of affluence, military power, and rhetorical fluency," while referencing also the source and the very stuff of abundance—the store, treasure-chest or hoard of language.[7] These associations are evident in Renaissance usages that we have inherited, such as *thesaurus* (treasury or store-house) to designate collections of words, and the related *treasury* for anthologies or encyclopedic texts, such as Pedro de Mexía's *Silva de varia lección*, translated into English as *The Treasury of Ancient and Modern Times* (1613). As Cave notes, in medieval Latin *copia* acquired an entirely different dimension of meaning, quickly taken up by the vernaculars in such words as *copy* and *copyist*. Thus in rhetorical terms *copia* simultaneously signals both the possibility of endless enrichment and expansion, and the anxiety over what might become simple iteration.

The metaphor of *copia* was taken up over and over again by early modern writers worried about the relative poverty of England's vernacular. The humanist longing to enlarge and enrich the language is a familiar story, well told in Richard Foster Jones's *The Triumph of the English Language* and, more recently, in Richard Helgerson's magisterial *Forms of Nationhood* and Paula Blank's *Broken English*.[8] The debate in the later sixteenth century over "inkhorn terms," as latinate words were despectively described, centered on their utility for enriching English. For the writer and translator George Pettie, there was no question that incorporating such terms "is in deed the way to inrich our tongue, and make it copious."[9] Following several decades of anxiety about their impoverished vernacular, by the end of the century English authors such as Richard Carew or Samuel Daniel touted a muscular version of their language in terms quite as confident as those of Nebrija. As Blank notes, for the antiquarian Carew "the 'excellency' of English lies in what he calls its 'copiousness' or wealth with respect to other languages, that is, in the extent to which English appropriates foreign words for national 'profit.'"[10] Carew envisions the enlargement of English in territorial terms: "But I must now enter into the large field of our tongs copiousnesse, and perhaps long wander up and downe without finding easie way of issue, and yet leave many parts thereof unsurveied."[11] Predictably, he surveys a landscape of triumphal English appropriation, as even the Spanish enemy, whose language is "majesticall, but fulsome, running too much on the O, and terrible like the divell in a play," is forced to yield words to the English, who "feare as little the hurte of his tongue as the dint of his sword."[12]

Though couched in a conditional, interrogative mode, these famous lines by the poet Samuel Daniel suggest that the notion of language as the companion of empire became ever more crucial as England attempted to reproduce Spain's imperial successes:

> And who in time knowes whither we may vent
> The treasure of our tongue, to what strange shores
> This gaine of our best glorie shal be sent,
> T'enrich unknowing Nations with our stores?
> What worlds in th'yet unformed Occident
> May come refin'd with th'accents that are ours?[13]

Whereas Nebrija imagines language as a companion to empire, Daniel por-
trays the English language itself as the commodity that England will "vent" to
new shores. In this vision, the English tongue has become so rich and abundant that there is plenty available for export.[14]

Following Helgerson's lead, this chapter traces how the imperial, religious,
and commercial rivalries between England and Spain in the period affect the
narrative of humanistic and national development via the vernacular.[15] These
fraught connections, I argue, made linguistic or literary appropriation from
Spain in the period much more complex, and potentially more fruitful, than
taking from the classics, France, or Italy. At the same time, the capacious-
ness of the humanist notion of *copia* allowed writers working in very different
genres, from geographies and travel writing to military manuals to defenses of
poetry, to invoke similar advantages in forcible appropriation. Only by situating these rhetorical strategies in their historical context, I suggest, can we fully
reconstruct the ideological vectors of transnational exchanges.

During the war between England and Spain (1585–1604), literary translation from Spanish into English continued unabated, with chivalric romances,
in particular, remaining very popular, as I discuss in Chapter 2. Yet the war
raised the stakes of translation, as accessing Spanish geographical and military
information became newly urgent.[16] It was one thing for prolific translator
Philemon Holland to figure translation from Latin as a belated revenge for the
Roman conquest of Britain, "subduing their literature under the dent of the
English pen, in requitall of the conquest sometime over this Island, achieved
by the edge of their sword,"[17] and a different matter entirely for the Elizabethans living in the wake of the Armada to contemplate their contemporary,
and most concrete, rivalry with a threatening Spain. In their prefatory dedications and addresses to readers, translations from the Spanish published during
these years emphasize the opportunity translation represents for England, and
the profit to be reaped from it. Taken together, these Elizabethan translations
of military manuals, accounts of voyages, and other specialized knowledges
tether the humanist longing for *copia* to an insistently nationalistic and pragmatic corpus.

Even before war was formally declared, hostilities mounted as England
encroached on Spanish possessions in the New World. Spain retaliated by providing support for the Irish uprisings against English rule, creating widespread
suspicion and anxiety. The 1582 *Compendious Treatise entitled* De Re Militari,
from an original by Luis Gutiérrez de la Vega, was translated by Nicholas Lichfield in this heightened climate. Lichfield stresses in his dedication to none

other than Philip Sidney the martial provenance of his original and the utility of the translation for the improvement of the English military: "This little Treatise (Right Worshipfull) entitled, *De re militari*: beeing lately found in the Forte in Irelande, where the Italians and Spaniards had fortified themselves, by fortune came into my hands by a Souldier of good experience, who latly served there."[18]

The source of the text bears noting: "the Forte in Irelande" was the Smerwick garrison of Dún an Óir, or the Fort of Gold, where in 1579 and 1580 two successive waves of Spanish and papal forces had landed in an effort to abet the Irish revolt, and where they retired to defend themselves from the English. The siege of the fort by the English ended in the brutal massacre of soldiers and civilians after their negotiated surrender, in an episode that was widely condemned across Europe.[19] In this light, the "little Treatise" appears as a lone survivor, after the Spanish soldiers who might have consulted it have all been killed. There is a dark irony in the treatise's careful description of military strategy and idealized formations, given its provenance in a scene of carnage that transgressed all military and civilized norms.

Abstracting himself from such contradictions, the translator emphasizes the need to improve England's own military by incorporating the Spanish innovations described in the treatise, which focuses on the nimble mixed-infantry formation known as the *tercio*. Effective imitation depends on the translation's rendering of Spanish expertise into English: "which briefe introduction (being common in our language) may be an inducement to better [sic] knowledge, and further understanding, wherby in time our servitours by good observance and imitation, may attaine the lyke perfection, that all other forreine Nations doe generally embrace." Beneath the text's prevailing triumphalism, there emerges a chagrined recognition of how short the English fall of "the lyke perfection," despite the overwhelming force of their scorched-earth policies in Ireland. Incongruously, the text places great emphasis on order: Ch. 3 is entitled "How the Souldiers shall ioyne or come together, and in what order"; Ch. 6, "How, and in what order they shall enter to the alodgement," thereby underscoring the contradiction between an ideal of carefully imitated military theory and the reality of ruthless military practice.

"Beeing . . . most ready & adventerous in all exercises of feats of warre and chivalry," as the dedication puts it, Sidney serves as the perfect audience for this rather tarnished trophy. His own multiple connections to Spain, impeccable status as a chivalric soldier-poet, and Protestant heroism render him the ideal reader for the *Compendious Treatise*. The translation resonates uncannily with Sidney's own famous contemporaneous treatise, *The Defence of Poesie* (written in 1579, and published in 1595, after Sidney's death). Replete with military imagery, the *Defence* extols the importance of imitation and exemplarity while bemoaning the relative stature of poetry in England: "That poesy, thus embraced in all other places, should only find in our time a hard welcome in England, I think the very earth lamenteth it, and therefore decketh our soil with fewer laurels than it was accustomed. For heretofore poets have in England also flourished; and, which is to be noted, even in those times when the trumpet of Mars did sound loudest."[20] Sidney implies that there is no choice to be made between arms and letters, stressing poetry's concrete effects upon subjects and polities: "substantially [poetry] worketh, not only to make a Cyrus, which had been but a particular excellency, as nature might have done, but to bestow a Cyrus upon the world to make many Cyruses, if they will learn aright why and how that maker made him."[21] Effective poetry enables imitation of the great Persian, in a multiplication of Cyruses and presumably, of their attendant empires.[22] Thus the humanist's defense of vernacular poetry and the translator's looted military manual converge in a vision of appropriation and imitation as technologies for territorialized increase.

Translation is similarly aligned with military might in the 1590 *Dialogue of the Office of a Sergeant Major*, translated from the Spanish by John Thorius. Here, translation trumps proprietary knowledge, allowing a new, English audience to profit from the Spanish original:

> And forasmuch as thys booke was written to instruct those that are professed enemyes to our estate, I thought that we might reap some profit by them, if this their Sergeant Maior were as well knowne unto our men as unto themselves; and that not so much for any poynts of pollicy which might be in their souldiers more than in ours, or for that I think them to have more knowledge in matters concerninge warfare than our English warriors, who are no whit inferior to any of them; as for that theyr orders being knowen unto us, we may the better and more easily hurte them and benefit our selues by reason of this advantage. I have therefore bestowed some pains in unarming this Spanysh Sergeant and doffing his Castilian and hostile armour, and haue clothed him in English apparel, to the end that our men may use him to theyr pleasure, and he finding him selfe metamorphosed, learne how to serue English men.[23]

Thorius's preface uneasily negotiates England's self-worth and his proposal to take from Spain: it is not that the English need to learn anything from the Spanish, he stresses, but that it may be useful to know how they do things, the better to "hurte them." The common image of translation as a new suit of clothes for the text here takes on a distinctly violent sexual cast: figured as a Spanish soldier unarmed and reclothed "in English apparel," Thorius's translation embodies its own operation, claiming for England what was once Spanish via the forcible use of the transvestite soldier.

Later translations also flirt with the pleasure of the Spanish, betraying a certain *jouissance* in the language for its own sake, even when that pleasure contrasts most markedly with the material being translated. The pragmatic *Theorique and Practise of Warre* (1597), translated by diplomat, scholar, and committed Protestant Edward Hoby, is a text profoundly imbricated in Anglo-Spanish rivalries. The original military manual was written by Bernardino de Mendoza, the much-reviled former ambassador to England whom Elizabeth expelled in 1584 for his plotting against her. The translator notes that he learned his Spanish from the prisoners taken from the English raid of Cadiz in 1595 ["de los rehenes del cativerio español"[24]], and implies that his original, too, was part of the spoils. Hoby dedicates his translation to soldier and colonial administrator George Carew, who had served in Ireland in the 1580s and would ruthlessly "pacify" it as Lord President of Munster at the turn of the century. Yet despite this belligerent context Hoby addresses Carew in Spanish, reveling in the pleasure of the enemy's language. Although the dedication is meant to serve as a testament to Hoby's skill and a mark of gratitude to the patron who had encouraged him to learn the language, the choice of medium contrasts strongly with both the text's jingoistic, combative message and its charged setting. Even if Hoby's confident command of Spanish becomes one more sign of English superiority, his pleasure in the language seems to exceed a certain national decorum.

Hoby's dedication is quite playful—he calls both himself and Carew "sr" (punning on "sir" and "señor") and his queen "Donna [Doña] Elizabeth." Yet these linguistic games pale beside the more intriguing dissolution of difference in the full title he assigns Elizabeth, referring to her as "su Sacra Cesárea Cathólica Real Magd" [her Sacred Caesarean Catholic Royal Majesty]. Elizabeth's "Catholicism," though it might surprise the modern reader, was invoked strategically to argue for the queen's dynastic rights and the universal reach of Protestantism, as in the striking 1597 composite portrait of Henry VIII, Edward VI, and Elizabeth. The portrait presents the three, in a legend across the top, as "Professors and Defendors of the True Catholicke Faythe," repurposing for the defense of Anglicanism the title Leo X had granted Henry in 1521, as a reward for his treatise against Martin Luther. As Clark Hulse notes, that title is thereby passed to Henry's children, and Christianity focused in the person of the ruler.[25] The imperial title, for its part, was usually reserved for the Holy Roman Emperor and King of Spain Charles V, while kings of Spain, such as Charles's heir Philip II, received the title "Sacra Católica Majestad." Although the 1533 Act in Restraint of Appeals had declared England an empire, neither Henry nor Elizabeth could claim "Caesarean" authority. The striking imperial *translatio* from Spain to England in Hoby's preface is hardly born of the translator's insufficiency, however, but comes from more complex rhetorical operations.

Hoby does warn his addressee that technical foreign vocabularies are virtually impossible to translate—"es de advertir que las materias y instrumentos de las milicias, por ser entre todas las naciones diferentes, según lo que acostumbra cada nación al pelear, es imposible con puntualidad exprimirlas en otra lengua, sin mezclar la propia donde fueron primeramente inventadas" [one must be warned that the matter and instruments of war, which are different for every nation, according to each nation's custom in warfare, are impossible to express precisely in another language, without mixing in the very one in which they were first invented].[26] Yet his entire project depends on the translatability of both arms and letters, and Elizabeth's own protocolary title could hardly have proved a challenge. Instead, the surprising analogy between Elizabeth I and Charles V, in a text that expresses its longing for peace between England and Spain, reveals its author as a contradictory subject, fragmented in his linguistic fluency and pleasure in the Spanish language, his allegiance to an England for which he harbors imperial ambitions, and his recollection of a time when these avocations were not at odds with each other:

> . . . que vea yo una paz entre Inglaterra y Castilla, como en el buen tiempo que mi tío Don Felipe Hoby fue embajador de la parte de Don Henrico Octavo, de pía y sancta, y felicísima memoria, padre de su SCCRM, en la Corte de Don Carlos quinto Emperador, los dos azote de la ambición y tiranía papal . . .
>
> [. . . may I see peace between England and Castile, as in those good old days when my uncle Philip Hoby was the ambassador from Henry VIII, of pious, saintly, and most happy memory, father of her Sacred Caesarean Catholic Royal Majesty {i.e., Elizabeth} to the court

Figure 2. *Henry VIII, Elizabeth I, and Edward VI* as "Professors and Defendors of the True Catholicke Faythe." Art Institute of Chicago.

of Emperor Charles V, both of them scourges of papal ambition and tyranny . . .]

In this version, the pleasure of translation adumbrates English nationalism, suggesting the possibility of a political rapprochement to match the linguistic reconciliation of their majesties.

In the translation itself, however, a more belligerent English position emerges, as the translator annotates the theoretical Spanish original with concrete examples of Spanish failings. From the margins, the translator has the last word, undermining and exploding the original's considerations on when and how Philip II should go to war. Where the translated text respectfully announces: "Your Highness going about to conquer a kingdom, state, countrey, or part of any such, which is the most secure warre for Princes," the annotation scathingly observes: "Better teach him by clemencie and pietie to recover such his grandfathers territories as his father hath loste, before he overbusie himself with other, or about the Armada." When Mendoza mentions the possibility of "great inconveniences," the translator pointedly invokes the recent experience at Cadiz, where "her sacred Majesty['s . . .] powerfull generals found 6000 of your Gallants at your owne home but Galinas [chickens]." Even more snidely, when the original warns the king against bad counsel, the note chimes in: "As to your cost your experience of 1588 tried."[27] The pleasure Hoby takes in these put-downs is palpable. In these and similar annotations to Mendoza's text, the theoretical project of translation becomes concretized into an imperial *translatio*, with England claiming precedence over Spain in such encounters as the raid of Cadiz and the defeat of the Armada, while the note's bilingual pun on "Gallants" and "Galinas" flaunts the linguistic deftness on which the commentator's ascendancy depends.

The conception of translation as a forcible technology appears not only in military manuals but in a broader range of texts that purport to offer the English the knowledge they will need to best Spain. Richard Perceval, who had translated captured Spanish dispatches for Elizabeth, dedicates his 1591 *Bibliotheca Hispanica*, an early dictionary and grammar book, to the Earl of Essex, "remembering that having employed your selfe so honorablie against the Spanyard in Flanders, Spayne & Portugal; you had gained an immortall memorie with all posteritie, & might perhaps encounter with them againe upon like occasion."[28]

Perceval's pragmatism contrasts with the heightened rhetoric of the Latin dedicatory poem by "a certain unskilled friend," which makes of the English new Jasons, inheritors to the Spaniards' power by virtue of the primer at hand:

> Hactenus Hispanis, Hispanica lingua refulsit;
> Sed reliquis, sicut nocte Diana micans.
> Latius at splendet nunc multis gentibus; alma
> Sol velut excurrens, per sua signa, die.
> Praestitit hoc Anglus, constanti pollice, scriptor,
> Ut Tartessiacae detegerentur opes.
> Non unum Typhin Graecum, sed mille Britannos
> Spe lucri accendet, nominis atque magis,
> Colchica qui levibus volitent nova regna carinis,
> Aureaque apportent vellera mille domum.[29]

[Thus far for the Spanish, the Spanish language has shone brightly; yet now they are left behind, just like Diana shivering in the night. Now it glistens uplifting many peoples, just as the nourishing sun displays itself in the day with its own signs. Here the English author stands forth, with firm promises that may sweep away the riches of the Tartessians. Not one Typhon of the Greeks but a thousand Britons he will inflame with hope of profit and also of a name of higher degree, Colchians of Carinis who swiftly fly to their new kingdoms and bring home a thousand golden fleeces.]

In this case, the text is not the loot but instead the shining tool that enables the supersession of the "Tartessians" by the "thousand Britons" who will be the new Argonauts.

For these Elizabethans, translation becomes the instrument of imperial *translatio*. These are surely the terms in which one must understand the partial, unpublished English translation of Alonso de Ercilla's *La Araucana* ((1569/1578/1589), the preeminent Spanish New World epic, on the protracted conquest of Chile. Produced around 1600 by George Carew, to whom Hoby had dedicated *Theorique and Practise of Warre*, the translation is an attempt to adapt the Spanish experience in the Americas to an Irish imperial context. As Lord President of Munster from 1597 to 1602, Carew was heavily involved in suppressing Tyrone's revolt and "pacifying" the colony. In his translation, Carew strips the epic of all poetic adornment, rendering it as a guide to conquest. His version digests Ercilla's text into a manual for conquest by which England might emulate Spain's actions in the New World. Translated from its original setting, Ercilla's description of Araucanian customs and battle lore is reduced to all-purpose instructions for defeating nomadic savages. The passages Carew translates in greatest detail are those that seem to offer instructions for how to defeat the natives, as in the following example from stanzas 23–32 in Ercilla's first canto:

> There manner of fight is in Manuples and small squadrons, minglinge or Entertyninge there pikes with bowes, the one to offend farre of, the other to defend the archer, and when any of the squadrons are broaken or beaten, another is brought vppe to mayntayne the fight: Of horse they stand in suche feare (which they never saw vntill they were invaded by the spaniardes) as when they fight itt shall ever be neare vnto boggie and Moorishe grounds, or suche places of advantage, where they may have a safe retrayte: To provoke skirmishe they turne ovt forlorne hopes with Drumes and musique vnder the Comand of daringe Leaders that

are ambitious of honnour, who are bravelye armed, paynted with divers Coullours and adornde with bewtifull plumes: vppon straytes and grounds, of advantage, they erect forts, made of great tymber, built foure square with sundrie towers, whereof one is lardge and hyghe to comande the rest, all of them full of spike holes for the vse of there archers, and in the myddest a spatious markett place to put there men in battell, they forget nott to make posternes for sallies and with out there forts (to imperille the Enemies approache) they digge deepe holes in the ground, artificiallie Covered with turfe or grasse, and in many of them they fix sharpe stakes by which stratageme we have received great losse.[30]

Here as elsewhere, Ercilla's text is "Englished" in a vocabulary that invokes the English presence in Ireland—*bog, turf,* and so forth. Thus the Chileans become the Irish, and the Spanish models their English imitators, in both poetic and imperial terms.[31] From the translation of textual loot acquired in a massacre in Ireland, to the vision of an empire via poetry in Sidney's manifesto, to the repurposing of an epic poem for military conquest, once again in Ireland, the striking interpenetration of literary and imperial *imitatio* comes full circle.

Though often in less exalted terms, translations of geographical texts also emphasize the advantage for England in accessing proprietary knowledge in Spanish. Linguistic appropriation becomes the first step to territorial expansion, as England attempts to match its rival. Editor, translator, and diplomat Richard Hakluyt's *Principal Navigations of the English Nation* (1589), perhaps the most influential volume in promoting English exploration and itself a compilation of translations and other texts, vaunts its own translations from secret Spanish texts, claiming among his sources "a secret mappe of those partes made in Mexico" and "their intercepted letters come into my hand."[32] As Donald Beecher has shown, even before Hakluyt's seminal collection Elizabethan translators from the Spanish expressed "many of the nationalist, mercantile, and explorational goals, implicit and overt," conveyed there.[33]

Beecher traces the work of John Frampton, one of the Hispanized "merchant adventurers," to Spain who had lived there in the 1550s and 1560s, before falling afoul of the Inquisition. When he was finally able to go back to England, Frampton turned to translation, producing six timely volumes in the years 1577–81.[34] He first translated the treatises of Nicholas Monardes of Seville, a kind of botanical treasury detailing the New World pharmacopoeia now available for collection and trade.[35] He also promoted English expansion more directly, with several volumes on the Far East and a manual significantly entitled *The Arte of Navigation, wherein is contained all the rules, declarations, secrets & advises, which for good Navigation are necessarie & ought to be knowen & practised* (1581).

Most striking for its pugnaciousness, perhaps, is Frampton's *A Briefe Description of the Portes, Creekes, Bayes and Havens conteyned in the West India, the originall whereof was Dedicated to the mightie Kinge, Charles the V Kinge of Castile* (1578), which suggests by its very title the imperial *translatio* it would effect, from Charles to Elizabeth and Spain to England. Published at the time of Francis Drake's piratical circumnavigation of the globe, Frampton's translation of Martín Fernández de Enciso's *Suma de geographia* was dedicated to Humphrey Gilbert, one of the many navigators who had been seeking for England the elusive "Northwest Passage" to the East that would allow it to bypass—and surpass—Spain's empire. "What might appear at first glance to be a mere travelogue or geographical account," Beecher notes, "in the hands of English buccaneers might easily be interpreted as a corsair's manual."[36]

Even though he worked from a published text, Frampton stresses that his translation discloses secret and valuable information. Although his original had been published in Spain, he notes, it was "called in aboute twentie yeares past, for that it reuealed secrets that the Spanish nation was loth to haue knowen to the worlde."[37] Yet in encouraging English travel Frampton's dedication must navigate its own awkward course, including the fact that his dedicatee (like Carew above) could actually read the original Spanish:

> And Sir, albeit this small gifte (in respect of ministring any knowledge to you your selfe) may seeme nothing, in that you doe understande the tongues, wherein this and many other knowledges of high value, lie hid from our Seamen, although not from you: yet this may for our meere English Seamen, Pilotes, Marriners, &c. not acquaynted with forrayne tongues, bring greate pleasure (if it fortune our Mariners or any other of our Nation, to be driven by winde, tempeste, currents, or by any other chaunce to any of the Ilandes, Portes, Havens, Bayes, or Forelandes mencioned in this Pamphlet,) and so it may also in the voyage, be a meane to keepe them the more from idlenesse, the Nurce of villany, and to give them also right good occasion by way of example, upon any new Discoverie, to take the Altitude and Latitude, to set downe the tracte of the Ilandes, the nature of the soyles, and to note the qualitie of the ayre, the several benefites that the Soyles and the Rivers yeelde, with all the discomodities and wantes that the same places have, and if our Countrie

men fortune the rather to be awaked out of their heavy sleepe wherein
they have long lien, and the rather hereby be occasioned to shunne
bestiall ignoraunce, and with other nations rather late than never to
make themselves shine with the brightnesse of knowledge, let them give
Sir Humphrey Gilbert the thankes, for whose sake I translated the same.

Frampton is evasive about the English agency required for imperial expansion,
first arguing that "winde, tempeste, currents, or . . . any other chaunce" just
might bring the English to the Spanish ports where they had no legal reason
to go. This evasive cover for piratical activity contrasts with the much franker
desire at the end of the passage for an end to English slothfulness, "rather late
than never." Translation is here aligned not just with a nascent imperial project
but specifically with pirating both Spanish knowledge and Spanish ports in an
effort to replicate Spain's successes. As Beecher points out, "the act of revealing to one's own nation the private cache of knowledge of an enemy nation
makes translating an act of strategic intelligencing,"[38] and the translator a full
participant in the imperial project.

If Frampton's aspirational translations are easily aligned with the project
of English empire, to what extent does their tenor characterize the broader
project of early modern translation as a whole? Clearly, not all translation was
conceived as a pugnacious extension of imperial longing—entire genres of
texts translated from Spain in the period, such as Counter-Reformation tracts,
do not participate in this dynamic. As my early examples show, however, a
broad range of texts beyond the explicitly imperial imagine translation as a
violent taking for the national good. In this shared discourse, the more openly
martial and violent figurations of translation incorporate and reiterate humanist conceptions of language's imperial potential, from Nebrija's understanding
of the role of language in the formation of empire, to the English commercial
version of Daniel. This significant overlap among the mercantile, military, and
humanist spheres extends to the actors involved: the same figures participate
in furthering the English language as the English empire, from such distinguished exemplars as Sidney to scholar-soldiers such as Hoby and Carew. In
the shared understanding of humanists and promoters of their early modern
nations, vernacularity itself produces national distinction.

In what follows, I show how the Elizabethan metaphorics of translation as
a forcible appropriation in service of the nation affects the construction of an
early modern English canon into the Jacobean period and beyond, as an emerging literary sphere adopts the same pugnacious language that characterized

translation in a context of imperial rivalry. Even after the peace with Spain, that is, the sense of translation as a site of contested cultural primacy remains, and the vexed fascination of English writers with Spanish literary materials continually renews the tensions over the terms of appropriation. I focus here on two dedicatory poems by Ben Jonson, appended to translations from the classics and from contemporary Spain, respectively. As Joseph Loewenstein notes, Jonson is a "crucial node of an encompassing economy in which intellectual possessiveness was coalescing,"[39] a central figure in the development of commercial authorship in England, expert in negotiating possession and imitation to construct poetic authority. Yet Jonson attends also to the problem of national belonging and national distinction in the literary sphere, providing a strong link between the pugnacious Elizabethan translation I have described above and the broader literary arena of the early seventeenth century and beyond.

Puffery and Piracy

Early modern commendatory poems are not often deemed worthy of critical scrutiny in their own right. Conventional wisdom tells us they are little more than conventional flattery, somewhere between flat and flatulent.[40] There are notable exceptions, to be sure. Ben Jonson's elegiac "To the Memory of my Beloved, the Author Mr. William Shakespeare," which prefaced the 1623 folio and which I discuss in Chapter 4, is perhaps the most famous commendatory poem in the language, combining as it does euphonious praise for the "sweet swan of Avon" with a remarkably successful attempt to delineate a canon of English literature in a European context. Jonson's rich reconstruction of his literary world, in praise of writing that "neither man, nor muse, can praise too much," exemplifies the possibilities of commendation for establishing standards of cultural value in a particular time and place.

A closer look at terms of praise may well afford us a more complete understanding of how poetic authority, literary competition, and international rivalries figure in calculating the value of a given early modern text. Beyond the dictates of convention, what contemporary poets choose to praise, and, more important, the metaphorics of their praise provide key insights into the valuation of literary appropriation and imitation, understood not as timeless aesthetic categories but as historical constructs deeply embedded in political and social relations, including the tradition of forcible translation I have charted above. Just as the metaphorics of translation itself is significant, the language used to praise translations provides a useful gauge of literary and national worthiness in the eyes of contemporary practitioners.

Jonson's many commendatory verses form part of his project to influence the shape and standing of English letters.[41] My focus here on translation expands the relevant contexts for Jonson's puffery from the immediate rivalries of the London literary scene to an international context of imperial rivalry. While praising translations into English of a classical Greek text and a Spanish picaresque novel, Jonson evokes imperial and economic struggles in order to portray English literary culture—original or otherwise—as a collective, national treasure.[42] If, that is, the *Epigrams* illuminate Jonson's rivalries with his English contemporaries, often accompanied by scathing comments on their imitative efforts, these two poems locate English translators—who practice a different kind of appropriation—as part of a national project in which cultural and material value are inextricably intertwined.[43]

Jonson's "To my Worthy and Honoured Friend, Mr. George Chapman, on His Translation of Hesiod's *Works and Days*" (1618) and "On the Author, Work and Translator" (1621), in praise of James Mabbe's *The Rogue*, evince the importance of translation as a gauge of England's cultural status. Both poems quite naturally focus on literary value, but do so, significantly, in terms of the nation's standing. First published along with the works they praise, they delineate quite different modes for England's engagement with classical literatures and contemporary vernacular works. The disjunction between these forms of engagement signals, I argue, the contradictions attendant upon England's position as a literary and imperial latecomer. In both cases, the resort to translation becomes an attempt to restore primacy, yet each is figured very differently by Jonson.

Jonson's poem to Chapman, along with a more extensive poem by Michael Drayton, prefaced the 1618 *Georgicks of Hesiod*, as the translator termed the *Works and Days*. The question of material value and national treasure is central to Jonson's rhetoric, and is foregrounded from the very first lines:

> Whose worke could this be, Chapman, to refine
> Olde Hesiod's ore, and give it us; but thine,
> Who hadst before wrought in rich Homer's mine?[44]

The abundant deposits of Greek culture, Jonson suggests, can be profitably mined and refined only by this English poet, whose broad previous experience extracting Greek *copia* includes translations of Homer's *Iliad* and *Odyssey*.[45] Yet, depending on how one interprets the "us" in line 2, the answer to Jonson's rhetorical question could be long and varied: there were earlier humanist "refinements" of Hesiod into both Latin and several European vernaculars, and Chapman himself seems to have mined Latin translations as often as the Greek original.[46] Chapman's novelty—and a rather delayed one at that—is rendering Hesiod (whether the original or an intermediate translation) into English to give it to an "us" of English speakers instead of to a humanist audience familiar with Latin. Jonson thus elides the first "miners" of the Greek—continental humanists of varied provenance—to praise a national achievement in the vernacular.

Whereas the first stanza imagines simply localized extraction, the second introduces the conceit of transported—or translated—riches that will prove central to the poem's project:

> What treasure has thou brought us! And what store
> Still, still, dost thou arrive with, at our shore,
> To make thy honour, and our wealth the more!

The trader, or *chapman*, brings the refined ore to England as mercantile wealth.[47] The image of a vernacular enriched by linguistic appropriation is familiar from Elizabethan sources: as Foster Jones notes, writers such as Parry, Nash, Puttenham, and Florio all emphasize the copiousness of an English tongue that has borrowed abundantly from the classical languages for some time.[48] Yet they liken industrious borrowing to production or commerce. Florio, for example, describes the "yearly increase" of words: "daily both new words are invented; and books still found, that make a new supply of old."[49] Jonson, by contrast, emphasizes treasure. As the conceit develops, his transformation of the earlier image of domestic industry into a heroic conquest of far shores becomes more pronounced:

> If all the vulgar tongues, that speake this day,
> Were askt of thy discoveries; they must say,
> To the Greek coast thine only knew the way.

> Such passage hast thou found, such returnes made,
> As, now, of all men, it is call'd thy trade:
> And who make thither else, rob, or invade.

Strikingly, these stanzas figure translation as an inaugural voyage. England, as represented by Chapman, actually discovers the one route to Greece, and claims exclusive trading privileges based on its primacy. Translation thus becomes an imperialist act of acquisition that ensures British greatness.[50] Yet the English version of the story depends on a complicated rewriting of historical events that recasts national failures as cultural successes.

Perhaps the clearest example of this rewriting is the emphasis on a "passage" in the last stanza, which suggests a very specific reference for the poem's patriotic claims: England's search for a sea-route to Cathay—the project that John Frampton had sought to aid with his translation of Spanish geographical and navigational treatises. In the middle years of the sixteenth century, the English had attempted in vain to find a Northeast passage by sailing around Muscovy.[51] From Sebastian Cabot on, they sought instead a North*west* passage to the fabled riches of the East around what is today Canada. This geographical chimera was a linchpin of the nation's imperial project in the late sixteenth and early seventeenth centuries. Though, like the eastward attempts, it proved a spectacular failure in Elizabethan times, it continued to inspire merchants and seamen well into James's reign.[52]

England had come late to the table. Because the more likely routes to the riches of the Indies had already been taken, there was no choice but to search for an unknown and improbable passage. As Richard Willes pointed out in his 1576 "Certain arguments to prove a passage by the Northwest," Iberians had taken possession of the likelier paths both East and West:

> [The Portuguese] voyage is very well understood of all men, and the
> Southeasterne way round about Afrike by the Cape of Good hope
> more spoken of, better knowen and travelled, then that it may seeme
> needfull to discourse thereof . . . The [Southwestern] way no doubt the
> Spaniardes would commodiously take, for that it lyeth neere unto their
> dominions there, could the Easterne current and levant winds as easily
> suffer them to returne.[53]

The belatedness of English expansion thus forced tenacious explorers such as Martin Frobisher and John Davis to probe the frigid waters beyond Novaya Zemlya in search of the riches of the East. Frobisher's voyages proved especially embarrassing, for he twice returned to England with a rich load of "gold ore" that turned out to be worthless pyrites. The only real treasure "mined" by England, or ever to make its way to England's shores, seems to have been the pillaged loot captured by Elizabethan privateers such as Drake, who engaged in secondary extraction from Spanish ships instead of New World mines. Needless to say, the heroic English privateers were denounced as pirates by those who suffered their ravages.

The early years of the seventeenth century saw renewed efforts to find the fabled Northwest Passage. Following Henry Hudson's seemingly auspicious discovery of the huge inlet that now bears his name (and despite the disastrous fate of his expedition), a wave of optimism led to the incorporation of the Northwest Passage Company in 1612. Its directors held the hopeful title "Governor and Company of the Merchaunts of London, Discoverers of the Northwest passage" and employed a ship named, with similar optimism, the *Discovery*. Nomenclature aside, the Company's efforts soon came to an impasse in frozen waters: William Gibbons's voyage in 1614 was a complete failure, and William Baffin's two attempts convinced that renowned navigator that there was "no passage or hope of passage" along the routes explored by his predecessors.[54] By the time Chapman's translation was published in 1618, the existence of a passage to be discovered and exploited exclusively by England seemed newly implausible.

Yet where actual voyages would not serve as models for the licit enrichment of the nation, Jonson's poem—through the alchemy of metaphor—turns pyrites into gold and mere pirates into dashing *adelantados*. The failure of proprietary discovery, whether imperial or cultural, is reimagined as an exclusive cultural triumph.[55] "Vulgar tongues"—those contemporary vernaculars that actually occupy the viable trading routes—must grant the primacy of the English passage to Greek culture, even though Chapman's achievement succeeds many other foreign translations. With their suggestion that it is others who are belated, and reduced to pirating culture, the last lines of the poem flaunt English ownership. They also make England sound suspiciously like Spain, a power bitterly resented for its restrictions on New World trade.[56] The Greek "trade," at least, here belongs to England; all others are interlopers who "rob, or invade"—pirates preying, for once, on *England*'s primacy. Thus Chapman's individual, belated project of translation, and by extension other belated British voyages, are transformed into an exceptional national achievement. The English version traduces history even as it translates empire.[57]

Englishing the Picaresque

"On the Author, Work, and Translator," Jonson's poem for Mabbe's *The Rogue* (1622), a highly popular translation of Alemán's picaresque *Guzmán de Alfarache*, presents a very different picture of literary property. Whereas the poem to Chapman lauds a heroic English vernacular exploiting the riches of Greece, these commendatory lines on Mabbe's work (which also features two dedicatory poems by "I. F.,"—John Fletcher) must justify a translation from the Spanish.[58] The questions of literary value and national standing are even more pressing in this poem, as Jonson negotiates the delicate question of the relative value of two vernaculars. If the worth of Greece is beyond question for the late Renaissance—a kind of gold standard for which the different national vernaculars vie—the idea of enriching English through a translation from the vernacular of a contemporary rival begs the question of their relative value. The poem tacitly addresses the Jacobean fascination with Spanish literature, the resultant asymmetry of Anglo-Spanish translation, and the general English unease with Spanish cultural dominance.[59] The questions become especially pressing given that the translated "work" of the title is a prime example of the picaresque, a Spanish invention that was immensely popular throughout Europe. The project here, I will argue, is both to commend and to erase the labor of translation by emphasizing the quality of the finished English product over the Spanish raw materials.[60] Whereas the praise of Chapman's Hesiod lauds the value of Greece and England's exclusive right to refine its riches, the poem to Mabbe suggests that culture cannot be proprietary. Instead, it universalizes literary value in order to allow those who come second, such as the English translator of a Spanish original, equal or even greater claim.

The poem insists on praising both author and translator, making room for two—as purported equals—where we might expect praise for one. From the title itself, which frames the "work" with the two very different kinds of labor involved, "On the Author, Work, and Translator" rejects the notion of exclusive literary property that figures so prominently in the poem to Chapman. The opening lines focus instead on a shared worth, emphasizing the value of multiplicity:

> Who tracks this Authors, or Translators Pen,
> Shall finde, that either hath read Bookes, and Men;
> To say but one, were single.[61]

The two pairs in these initial lines—author and translator, books and men—link Alemán's and Mabbe's dual labors to the literary and moral value of the work. The ambiguity of the referent in "To say but one, were single," suggests that it is impossible to disentangle one set of doubles from the other, and introduces a purely phantasmal correspondence between the two penmen and the two aspects of the text's value. The conclusion sounds like a tautology: of course, at one level, "to say but one" is "single." Yet a quick perusal of the OED yields a number of meanings that dispel the apparent redundancy and obliquely support Jonson's argument for secondary literary labors. One meaning of *single*, now obsolete, is "slight, poor, trivial." Thus in Shakespeare's *2 Henry IV* the Lord Chief Justice attacks Falstaff with: "Is not your voice broken, your winde short, your wit single . . . ?" (I. ii. 182–83).[62] Another OED example, from Daniel, suggests that *single* is also, in an apparent paradox, the opposite of *singular*: "Having married a wife of singulare beautie, but (according to the common rumour) of single honestie." The notable or exceptional *singular* is here separated from its belittled etymological cousin. If we reinsert this particular contrast into Jonson's poem, lines 1–3 seem to suggest that the *exceptional* quality of a work need not depend on its *single* authorship. Yet there remains the nagging suspicion that Jonson's lines are themselves not single—in its more positive sense of "simple, honest, sincere, single-minded; free from duplicity or deceit" (OED)—but instead hypnotize us with their oscillation between singular and plural. The separation of the singular and the single validates the labors of the translator's pen, but enacts a semantic violence that underscores the inherent duplicity of language and its manipulators.

The poem seems to relish polysemy as a way to bridge the gap between "old words" and "new times," and makes *The Rogue* a prime example:

> Then it chimes,
> When the old words doe strike on the new times,
> As in this Spanish Proteus; who, though writ
> But in one tongue, was form'd with the worlds wit . . .

The image of a Spanish Proteus marks a move from polysemy to even more complex transformations. While the *pícaro* in Alemán's novel may be a master of disguise, he is no match for Jonson himself, who here metamorphoses character into text and "one tongue" into "the world's wit." And while the translation of the Spanish original into a *lingua franca* of creativity suggests a move away from proprietary national claims, these are in fact quickly reinstated. As the rest of the poem will make clear, the supranational interlude functions simply as pretext for a reinforced English claim to the text.

The poem enacts the confusion between single and double, Spanish original and English translation, in its very terms of praise. Jonson recalls a famous Cervantine conceit in order to commend an extraordinary translator of Spanish:

> Such Bookes deserve Translators, of like coate
> As was the Genius wherewith they were wrote;
> And this hath met that one, that may be stil'd
> More than the Foster-father of this Child . . .

The image of Mabbe as more than foster-father to his translation inverts Cervantes's distancing claim, in the prologue to the first part of *Don Quijote* (1605), that although he might seem a father he is but a stepfather to his creation, and thus well aware of its faults.[63] Jonson probably knew the original, and would certainly have been familiar with Thomas Shelton's 1612 translation of Part I.[64] Shelton's version, although not an exact translation, preserves the biting Cervantine irony on literary paternity:

> It oft times befals, that a father hath a child both by birth evil-favoured
> and quite devoide of all perfection, and yet the love that he beares him
> is such, as it casts a maske over his eies, which hinders his discerning of
> the faults and simplicities thereof, and makes him rather to deeme them
> discretions and beauty, and so tels them to his friends, for witty jests and
> conceites. But I (though in shew a Father, yet in truth but a stepfather
> to Don-Quixote) will not be born away by the violent current of the
> modern custome now a daies, and therefore intreate thee, with the
> teares almost in mine eies, as many others are wont to doe (most deare
> Reader), to pardon and dissemble the faults which thou shalt discerne in
> this my sonne.[65]

Jonson's praise of Mabbe as more than foster-father to his translation thus appears quite singular, if not single. First, because it distortedly echoes a Spanish original, simultaneously appropriating it and problematizing any notion of fidelity or originality. Mabbe, for his part, no longer stands alone, as Jonson adulterates the notion of exclusive literary paternity. Second, by collapsing

Cervantes's critical distance and inverting the topos of humility in a poem of praise, the emphasis on unalienated fatherhood suggests that Mabbe himself, and certainly Jonson, may well be (willfully) blind to the translation's faults.[66]

There is a pronounced contrast in tone between Jonson's poem and Mabbe's own claims in his prologue, where he deplores his lack of skills. Although Mabbe, in a flourish of virtuosity, writes his own dedication to "Don Iuan Estrangwayes" in (a rather stilted) Spanish, he tentatively signs himself "Don Diego Puede-Ser," or James *May-be* (8). And while he claims to have clothed the *pícaro* in an English costume, he admits, "En algunos lugares, hallo mi Guzmanico escuro como la noche" [In some spots, I find my little Guzmán dark as night] (7). He follows this admission with a flat-footed pun that reminds us of the difficulty of his enterprise: "Pero, yo he hecho algunos Escolios, para quitar los Escollos" ["I have provided some schooling [notes] to remove the shoals"], and ends with a highly conventional description of his literary voyage. Nonetheless, the translator's authority as annotator is recognized by another commendatory poem to the volume, by Mabbe's friend and fellow translator Leonard Digges:

As, few, French Rablais understand; and none
Dare in our Vulgar Tongue once make him knowne:
No more our Plodding Linguists could attaine
(By turning Minshewe) to this Rogue of Spaine,
So crabbed Canting was his Authors Pen
And phrase, e'en darke to his owne Countrey-men;
Till, thankes and praise to this Translators paine,
His Margent now makes him speake English plaine.[67]

Even John Minsheu's recent *Most Copious Spanish Dictionary* (1617), Digges suggests, is not enough to render "this Rogue of Spain" legible; in fact, Mabbe's annotations often cite the contemporary Spanish dictionary of Sebastián de Covarrubias (1611) to justify his readings. Yet Digges' hyperbolic praise grants the translator the power to "make knowne" the "Rogue of Spaine," his marginal authority the last word in a text forced to speak plainly.

Despite the Spanish flourish of the dedication and his authority as bilingual editor, Mabbe turned often to Barezzo Barezzi's Italian translation of the *Guzmán*, presumably as a way to shed more light on the obscure *pícaro* or skirt the perilous shoals.[68] Thus Mabbe is often far indeed from Alemán's original—a "cozen-german," perhaps, but not an unadulterated father. The discrepancy between Jonson's praise and Mabbe's own tone and practice may well be attributable to the difference between the commender and the humble author, and the generic conventions associated with each space of enunciation, yet the contrast is so pronounced as to suggest that Jonson's larger claims for English primacy over Spanish sources themselves motivate his project of praise, regardless of Mabbe's skill.

After the internationalist interlude, Jonson's poem moves to assertions of English primacy through the metaphorics of cloth, first introduced with the reference to translators "of like coat" in line 11. Jonson turns to the conventional sartorial image for translation to emphasize the improvement of the poem in its English version:

> . . . For though Spaine gave him his first ayre and Vogue,
> He would be call'd, henceforth, the English-Rogue,
> But that hee's too well suted, in a cloth,
> Finer than was his Spanish . . .

Whereas Elizabethan instances of the clothing metaphor generally emphasize the crudeness of English—whether to condemn it as rude attire or praise it as simple homespun—Jonson here suggests that English cloth is better than Spanish.[69] In this sartorial vein, the "single" in line 3 reads as "unlined material" (OED); thus the thread of imagery runs from a poor cloth associated with the misguided effort to distinguish between author and translator, to the "like coat" of a translator well-suited to the material to, finally, the fine English cloth that rehabilitates the rogue. Paradoxically, the translation improves the original to such an extent that Jonson's proposed title becomes untenable: an *English-Rogue* would be an oxymoron because English itself ennobles the work.

Thus Jonson mobilizes the cloth industry as a powerful image of national pride, in order to "English" what was originally a Spanish possession.[70] The brief moment of humanist generosity in line 6, when the poet argues that the Spanish work actually belongs to the world, quickly gives way to an emphasis on English achievements. Free trade in Spanish texts enhances England's stature, and the end product is so thoroughly domesticated as to disguise its status as an import.

Yet the Spanish provenance of the original is not the only thing that Jonson's poem cloaks with its powerful metaphors. The cloth industry, it turns out, is an odd choice for mobilizing national pride in 1621, given that, for contemporary readers, the imagery would most likely recall the desperate straits of that industry in England. The years 1620–1624 saw, as economic historian Barry Supple puts it, "perhaps the most acute breakdown of the English economy of the first half of the seventeenth century."[71] The ill-conceived project of Alderman Cockayne to restrict exports to finished English cloth, and its relative dearness as the start of the Thirty Years' War wreaked havoc with continental currencies, essentially paralyzed the cloth industry in these years, profoundly affecting domestic well-being as well as England's economic standing vis-à-vis its European rivals. As one M.P. put it in the somber parliamentary debates of 1621: "The kingdom is hindered even within the kingdom by a decay of the trade of cloth."[72] Despite Jonson's claims for the excellence of English cloth, contemporary observers complained bitterly that it was the poor quality of the material that was causing the problem.[73] Thus the cloth industry could not prove a source of national pride in 1621; ironically, instead of the picaresque being Englished in fancy clothes, it was enacted everywhere in England through the impoverishment of large groups of unemployed laborers from the cloth trades, who suffered scarcity and dislocation.

Whereas in his praise of Chapman's translation Jonson reimagines England's failure to discover a Northwest Passage as a cultural triumph, he here disguises the economic realities of his time as a new victory for the English language. In the poetic economy of commendation, the value of all things English can rise freely, untrammeled by the setbacks of economic history. Jonson's imagery of production and exchange is gloriously free of material constraints, and value accrues for the object of commendation regardless of the historical aptness of the poet's metaphors. Poetry that thus creates value irrespective of historical circumstance—or better yet, in absolute defiance of it—is, I would suggest, a powerful tool not simply for promoting an individual work but for constructing a literary culture as an enduring and powerful source of national worth.

The dynamics of cultural production and exchange that Jonson imagines in these two poems suggests an overwhelming concern with bringing home the riches. While the classical ore of Greece is available for conquest and appropriation by (English) first-comers only, the contemporary cultural productions of rival nations should be circulated freely in order to be more effectively Englished. Whether the appropriation is achieved via cultural protectionism—Greece is ours alone—or by shady expropriation—the picaresque is the world's but, ultimately, ours—the end result is to enhance England's cultural standing, at least in its own view. Beyond the models of exemplarity and *imitatio* imagined by Sidney and his Elizabethan contemporaries, Jonson's dedications claim for poetry a central place in the production of national distinction.

Metaphors of empire and value are central to Jonson's project, since by the 1620s—and despite the crisis of the cloth industry—trade was England's preeminent source of national pride. Whether such trade be restricted or free, Jonson's poetics of acquisition provides a powerful way to reimagine cultural and material empire, in which late arrival does not bar success. More important, the cultural currency of his images, in their partial historicity, is dissociated from the specific historical circumstances of English trade and expansion—the economy of metaphor supplies any lack in actual English fortunes. The poetic project of these commendations is thus even more ambitious than the belated humanist goals Jonson sets forth in his *English Grammar* (pub. 1640), to "free our language from the opinion of rudenesse and barbarisme, wherewith it is mistaken to be diseased: we shew the copy of it, and matchablenesse with other tongues."[74] The poems also free England from the limitations of historical circumstance, as they construct a literary sphere in which the national tradition—a tradition of literary predecessors, but also of powerful myths about English greatness—itself becomes a source of value.

In Jonson's poems to Chapman and Mabbe, as in the actual translations discussed earlier, the nexus between linguistic authority and imperial conquest appears singularly charged. The empire of language comprises far more than explicit writings on empire: it includes, too, the insistent figuration of cultural authority as the conquest of poetic and material terrain, whether through translation, silent appropriation, or rewriting. The peculiar force of this piratical translation—as opposed to more heavy-handed paeans to empire—lies in its versatility, its ability to take from what is beyond the nation's experience, and to yoke together the projects of poetry and of empire. In the chapters that follow, I explore how the rich vein of poetic ore tapped by Jonson as a way to enhance England's cultural capital finds its expression on the stage, as Jacobean playwrights negotiate the complications of taking from Spain.

Chapter 2

Knights and Merchants

> . . . our *Fletcher's Knight of the Burning Pestle* was a sort of *Quixot* on
> the Stage.
>
> —Nahum Tate, *A Duke and No Duke*

The early years of James's reign provided a bonanza of Spanish materials for English readers. The end of the protracted hostilities in 1604 and the mutual peace embassies from Spain to England and England to Spain offered the occasion for English readers to encounter materials that had been harder to procure during the war. The Jacobean era is one of the richest periods for England's turn to Spain, both because it corresponds to a truly dazzling moment in Spain's own literary production, and because the peace afforded new channels of transmission. The coincidence of the English embassy to Valladolid with the 1605 publication of Cervantes's *Don Quijote*, in particular, was to make available with remarkable speed the most influential of Spanish texts, one that quickly made its way onto the London stage in a variety of guises.

If the currency and popularity of *Don Quijote* made it a source to reckon with, they also made it an irresistible target for the kind of combative *translatio* I trace through this book. This chapter analyzes how Francis Beaumont's *The Knight of the Burning Pestle*, generally dated to 1607, negotiates Spanish influences and the English taste for Spanish chivalric romances, which had been consistently translated during the war. I trace how the play attempts to domesticate *Don Quijote*, transforming it into a rumination on a national and local mercantile identity as the essence of Englishness. As a highly self-conscious and fragmented text, *The Knight of the Burning Pestle* reflects on questions of appropriation, originality, and popular reception. Yet I am interested also in how *The Knight*'s own debts have been negotiated. Exactly what the play owes to *Don Quijote* has been hotly debated from at least its first printing, and the critical negotiation of that indebtedness reveals a profound discomfort with England's larger debt to Spanish sources.

The Knight is an exceedingly complicated play, overflowing with plots and their interruption. As the play opens, a Grocer and his wife, who have come to the theater to watch *The London Merchant*, a typical city comedy of money and marriage, hijack it by insisting that the play honor their class, instead. The fourth wall is broken almost immediately, as the grocer George interrupts the Prologue to demand "something notably in honour of the commons of the city" (Induction, 25–26). As Leslie Thomson points out, George apparently enters with the gentlemen of the audience to sit on the stage, as was common in the indoors Blackfriars playhouse, suggesting the conflation of his status with theirs and further confusing the lines between reality and representation.[1] Meanwhile, his wife Nell and their apprentice Rafe muscle their way up from the audience, with Nell clamoring for room among her betters and effectively performing her social climbing as they clamber onto the stage. Dissatisfied with what the company is attempting to perform, George and Nell call for a heroic Grocer who would "kill a lion with pestle" (Induction 42–44), in a clear dig at the improbable stage romances that glorified the London trades. Undeterred by the problems with casting such a role, they offer up Rafe to play the part. Thus the self-conscious, mock-chivalric plot that recalls *Don Quijote* is only one of two plays-within-a-play, juxtaposed with the conventionality and domesticity of the much interrupted *London Merchant*.

Rafe's reading of chivalric romances, which is acted out on stage, inspires him to become a "grocer-errant" (I.262), with the burning pestle as his emblem. As the mock-knight, he mistakes an inn for a castle and refuses to pay for his lodging; encounters a barber Nick with a great red beard, whose prisoners he must release; and rejects the love of the Moldavian princess Pompiona because he has a lady of his own in Sue, the "cobbler's maid in Milk Street" (IV.96–98). The grocer and his wife (referred to in the dramatis personae as "the Citizens") spur him on to ever more spectacular feats, as they gradually lose patience with the more sophisticated play they are interrupting. By the end, these Citizens demand instead separate set-pieces: a May-Day celebration, a muster for battle, and Rafe's eloquent, speechified death as a farewell. The strange amalgam that is *The Knight of the Burning Pestle* is thus as much about the struggle for and over representation as it is about any one plot-line; perhaps the only constant is the grocer and his wife's dissatisfaction with being passive spectators and their desire instead to influence what is represented.

Quixotism

Already in the first edition of the text, published by Walter Burre in 1613, the question of the play's relation to *Don Quijote* was paramount. Burre protests in his prologue that the English play, the "unfortunate child" whom he had taken in as his foster son, came before the *Quijote*: "Perhaps it will be thought to be of the race of Don Quixote: we both may confidently swear it is his elder above a yeare, and therefore may (by vertue of his birth-right) challenge the wall of him."[2] Yet Burre's claim is qualified by the extended metaphor that governs his explanation: the text as defective son may be a commonplace, but it is one used brilliantly by Cervantes in his own prologue, where he famously refers to himself as the text's stepfather (the metaphor reprised by Jonson to describe Mabbe's translation of Alemán, as I noted in Chapter 1). Moreover, Burre moves from his combative insistence on "birth-right" to an oblique recognition of the advantage in linking his foster son to Cervantes's creation: "I doubt not but they [the two would-be knights] will meet in their adventures, and I hope the breaking of one staff will make them friends; and perhaps they will combine themselves, and travel through the world to seek their adventure" (52). Even as he denies filiation, Burre obliquely recognizes the affinities between the texts and the benefit inherent in their connection.

In general, critics have acknowledged *The Knight*'s relation to its Spanish predecessor only to discount its importance. In some cases, they claim that the two texts are merely parallel—so that parallelism takes on its own ideological weight as the *absence* of influence. Yet parallelism seems a hard argument to make given the ubiquity of *Don Quijote* in England from the time of its 1605 publication. As J. A. G. Ardila has charted, the novel "exerted a continuous and regular influence. . . from as early as 1607," with multiple written references to the text before 1610, and certainly long before the publication of Thomas Shelton's translation in 1612.[3] The English probably encountered the novel immediately on its publication, through Charles Howard's 1605 peace embassy to Spain, on which he was accompanied by six hundred Englishmen. Educated English readers, accustomed to consuming Spanish literature, would have been prepared to feast on the original, and to contribute to its immense and immediate popularity. Notably, just months after the publication of *Don Quijote*, the earl of Southampton, Shakespeare's great patron, donated one hundred pounds to the new Bodleian library for the purchase of Spanish books, in swift recognition of the opportunities the peace with Spain would afford for readers. Though the primary goal of the first librarian, Thomas James, was to acquire books of Catholic theology, in order to polemicize with them, a few historical and literary texts were purchased as well. *Don Quijote*, one of only two works of literature acquired, was catalogued on August 30, 1605.[4] The Bodleian *Quijote* and the larger donation of which it was part establish the availability of the text in England[5] and confirm the existence of a reading public perfectly capable of consuming it in the original.

Strikingly, most of the earliest references to *Don Quijote* in England come from the theater, from George Wilkins's *The Miseries of Inforst Marriage* (as early as 1607 or possibly 1606), to Middleton's *Your Five Gallants* (1607), to, in the years immediately following *The Knight*, Jonson's *Epicoene* (1610) and *The Alchemist* (1611). This theatrical currency, with allusions to fighting windmills or to the hero himself, makes it impossible to imagine a context for *The Knight of the Burning Pestle* that would not have been thoroughly saturated with an awareness of *Don Quijote*. The most recent wave of critical interest in the lost *Cardenio* may finally have established the influence of the novel on English drama of the period, so that Tiffany Stern, focusing on the *Cardenio/Double Falshood* controversy (which I turn to in Chapter 4), can refreshingly describe *The Knight*, in passing, as "a parody of *Don Quixote*."[6] Thus my point is not to try to right the record on the influence of the Spanish text, a goal now fortunately superfluous. Instead, I am interested in both the rationale for and the metaphorics of the long-term resistance to Cervantean influence on the part of Anglo-American editors and critics. Whereas Burre, writing in 1613, is most concerned with the fortunes of the singular play, and his investment in bringing it to press, later critics participate in a complex dynamic of disavowal where Spain is concerned.[7] Unthinkingly incorporating the suspicion toward Spain and Spanish properties that characterized the Elizabethan moment, these critics repeatedly attempt to contain Spanish influence in an effort to promote a national English canon that seems to depend on a refusal of influence, or its transmutation into a triumphant appropriation, as in so many of the instances I chart throughout this book.

Among modern readings of *The Knight of the Burning Pestle*, perhaps the most interesting attempt to construct a high English canon by denying a debt to Cervantes is Herbert Murch's 1908 edition, which emphasizes the play's

satire of low or middle-class tastes. Murch painstakingly goes through all possible resemblances between the play and *Don Quijote*, only to deny them:

> The objects of their satire are the same; their methods of developing a
> humorous situation—through bringing into ludicrous juxtaposition
> the common-place realities of life and the high-flying idealisms of
> knight-errantry—are the same; and, moreover, a few of the incidents
> are remarkably alike. But these similarities are the outcome of allied
> purposes in the two works; they do not of themselves argue any
> interdependence whatsoever.[8]

Murch concludes that because there is no evidence that the authors (he as-
cribes the play to Beaumont and Fletcher) knew Spanish, they could not have
worked from *Don Quijote*, and adduces the late date of Shelton's translation
as sufficient evidence for the play's "complete independence of its accredited
source."[9] There follows a list of suspiciously similar moments: seven hallmarks
of Quixotic particularity, including the inn, the barber's basin, and so forth,
some of which I have detailed above.[10] But for Murch these quintessentially
Quixotic moments betray instead the shared targets of the play and the novel.
Don Quijote and *The Knight*, Murch claims, are satirizing the same chivalric
romances: *Amadís de Gaula*, *Palmerín de Oliva*, and their like, which had been
translated into English by Anthony Munday, Margaret Tyler, and others. The
fact that these, too, are Spanish, and that they were being translated for a rav-
enous English reading public during the war with Spain, seems less important
than establishing the independence of the text at hand from its most immediate Spanish predecessor.

Murch strongly emphasizes both the originality and the Englishness of
the text, even when both Don Quijote and Rafe happen upon inns which they
mistake for castles, and where they refuse to pay for their lodging:

> It will be readily granted that, even if Beaumont did draw the idea of
> the inn-scenes from Cervantes, his development of it is independent and
> original. But what reason is there for presuming that he so derived it? Is
> not its employment a very logical issue of the conditions of the play, and
> may not the conception of it, therefore, have been wholly original with
> its author? Ralph with his squire, his dwarf, Mistress Merrythought,
> and Michael, is wandering about in the uninhabited Waltham Forest
> in search of food and a resting-place. Suddenly the party emerge into

the open, and find themselves at the end of Waltham Town, where is situated a tavern called the Bell Inn (2.393). This is a local touch which does not have the least connection with *Don Quixote*. . . . I see no reason why, in the logic of the movement, this feature of the play should not have been conceived in complete independence of *Don Quixote*. Furthermore, the ascription of the source of the scene to the novel seems nullified by the thoroughly English and local tone of the dwarf's account of the castle and its inmates.[11]

The importance of the local is also stressed by Rudolf Schevill, equally skeptical of the play's debt to *Don Quijote*, in his 1907 essay on Spanish influence in England, which touches on many of the same points as Murch's introduction. The later episodes of the play, Schevill observes, "if very carefully considered have an absolutely local, and not a borrowed flavor." He stresses that the butt of the satire, too, is purely local: "What object would there be in a satire on conditions which did not exist in England? Beaumont and Fletcher saw fit to parody merely local conditions."[12]

As I argue below, it is precisely the translation of the *Quijote* material and its relocation into a domestic sphere, marked by the specifics of place, that makes *The Knight of the Burning Pestle* such a striking example of "Englishing" in the period. By domesticating its mock-chivalric model the play offers a mercantile, London-based alternative to the transnational circulation of romance, but this ideological effect becomes invisible if we deny the parodic text's relation to its source simply because the *Quijote*'s geography has been replaced with the local. Murch and Schevill's emphasis on the English text's originality and "complete independence" as marks of literary value erase the vectors of translation along which we might trace its ideological work, promoting instead an English product unburdened by foreign debts.

Michael Hattaway's introduction to the New Mermaids edition of 1969 provides a more balanced assessment of *The Knight of the Burning Pestle*'s sources. Hattaway recognizes the Iberian origins of the chivalric romances, yet moves quickly to praise their "transmutation," and that of the *Quijote*, in the play: "But one should not stress Beaumont's debt to Cervantes too much, as *The Knight* is basically an accumulation of conventional episodes from romances and English plays as well as of elements from a native tradition of satire, all of which are welded into a splendid entertainment."[13] While Hattaway recognizes the play's multiple debts, he fails to note how its satirical take on romance aligns it most closely with *Don Quijote*. His emphasis on a "native tradition," moreover, points to the real ideological stakes of the play: to what extent can we read this *translatio* of Cervantes as an attempt to negotiate the tensions between imported fantasy and domestic carnival?

Domesticating Romance

Clearly, *The Knight* reprises not only *Don Quijote* but also the "native" apprentice-romances of Thomas Heywood and the like, in which apprentices are granted an unexpected protagonism and discovered as unlikely heroes. *The Four Prentices of London* (1594, pub. 1615) is perhaps the most obvious dramatic referent, but there is also some of the ludic spirit of Thomas Dekker's *The Shoemaker's Holiday* (1599, pub. 1600). Beaumont's text pokes fun at these earnest visions of apprentice heroics, yet it remains most concerned, I suggest, with the problem of local versus transnational attachments. In its final scenes, the play stages both the fascination with chivalric romance and its transcendence, in national, local, and class terms. Its promotion of the local, for its part, overgoes "native" plays such as Heywood's *Four Prentices*, which improbably stages distant settings and romance wanderings. For Heywood's play is hardly concerned with the local scene: its four noble protagonists, who are merely slumming as apprentices, must leave behind their London toil and join a crusade to reveal their true greatness. Conversely, *The Knight* invokes a community that ultimately rejects the individual—even solipsistic—appeal of a chivalric literature largely marked as foreign for the communal, English pleasures of May-day and local London hi-jinks. Much as in Cervantes's novel, the point is not the single addled reader and his wandering fantasy but the domestic community that serves as his cure.[14]

In *The Knight*, the pleasure in the local aligns the audience with the witty apprentice—the knowing reader—in contradistinction to his crude masters and to the improbable knights that Rafe mocks. The wily native son, closely associated with London and the dodges necessary to prosper in the city, emerges as the desirable alternative to the circulation of readerly desire beyond English borders. National allegiance trumps class difference, as the apprentice Rafe, foregrounding his *national* citizenship, steals the show from his masters, whose citizenship was conferred by the London guild. Ultimately, the promotion of the local and the national transcends the play's satire of the trades and their tastes, as the bonhomie of national belonging triumphs over differences in class and sophistication.

Moreover, the play performs a double operation of Englishing: even as the chivalric romances and the *Quijote* are transposed into the English language, the mythical geography of romance is replaced with the domesticated and familiar London of the comedy. The transformation of England from the space of romance to the locus of mercantile hi-jinks is coded in the play not as any kind of diminution or fall into realism, but as the occasion for patriotic revelry and praise of the local. Donna Hamilton has argued that the Iberian romances translated into English in the latter part of the sixteenth century promote a united Christian empire, and thus forcefully challenge the "Protestant cultural project" of Sidney, Spenser, and others.[15] Anthony Munday's translation of the Iberian *Palmerin of England*[16]—the romance Rafe is reading in *The Knight of the Burning Pestle*—engages such delicate topics as the succession to the English throne, the destruction of ancient religion, and the fate of Ireland. Given such content, it is not surprising that city comedy might offer a domestic Protestant alternative to the continental vision of England.

Part of *The Knight*'s intrinsic interest lies in the indeterminacy of the local, of what exactly counts as domestic space in the play. Janette Dillon's suggestive reading emphasizes the text's "investment in the symbolic importance of the city boundary," and its problematization of both the imaginative and the actual limits of the city.[17] Dillon astutely notes how the three plots on stage—*The London Merchant* (the play originally announced in the prologue), the adventures of Rafe as apprentice-errant, and the play that the Grocer and his wife keep trying to mount, all depend on "a tension between mobility and staying put."[18] Although Dillon elucidates the boundaries between city and suburbs in the play, these spaces actually remain quite fluid, as she herself notes. More important, London is consistently foregrounded as the synecdochal center of the nation—a city that can summon or stand in for the national. "Is not all the world Mile End?" Dillon's title, echoes the question posed in the play about the liminal space outside London proper where display battles were often held. Whereas Dillon reads this moment as a reflection on London authority and its limits, I would suggest that it signals precisely the synecdoche by which London and its environs can invoke all of England.[19]

In a brilliant reading of the erotics of domesticity in *The Knight*, Wendy Wall notes that the play, through the figure of the Citizen's exacting wife, "asks its audience to think about the potential fantasies that infiltrate domesticity— the postures of loss, mastery, dependency, and submission played out in strong form in the home regimen of kitchen physic."[20] Wall is attuned to the national inflection of the domestic in the play, arguing that it "champions domesticity as the staple of true Englishness," as home is gradually tied to patriotic ritual.[21] Yet given the connections between foreignness and chivalric romance in the play, its own "Englishing" of its sources privileges domesticity.

The play's validation of the local as a stand-in for the national must be read within a broader consideration of its foreign sources. Beyond the London/not London anxieties that Dillon recovers through her historical reconstruction of liminal spaces, and Wall's domestic regimen, the play offers a sustained relocation of errant romance into the domestic and the local bounds of Englishness. Jean Howard has argued that London-based comedies of the period "negotiate the presence of non-native Londoners and non-native commodities within the space of the city,"[22] and *The Knight of the Burning Pestle* is no exception. But it also grapples with the presence of other representations, from the Iberian chivalric romances to their reprise in *Don Quijote*, and their transnational appeal for an English reading or viewing public. For a play so invested in favoring the local, the transnational context against which it defines itself becomes key.

The tension between the foreign and the domestic pervades the play, by dint of the oxymoron implicit in the figure of the grocer-errant, with its echoes of Heywood's improbable apprentices. The contrast is more explicitly set up in Act III via an extended joke on the ravages of syphilis and piracy—twin international scourges of the age. In reading these scenes, in which the grocer-errant Rafe must fight the barber Barbarossa or Barberoso, Patricia Parker has noted the associations between Barbary, barbers, and emasculating captivity in the period. As she points out, Barbarossa has a very precise referent in the famous pirate Khaired-Din, a renegade who terrorized Europe for decades and took countless captives.[23] The captives in *The Knight of the Burning Pestle* all suffer from syphilis, amplifying the joke that gives the play its title, and the tortures that the barber inflicts are ostensible cures. The foreignness of syphilis, also known as the "French pox," is itself transposed to one of the victims' genealogy:

> 2 Knight: I am a knight, Sir Pockhole is my name,
> And by my birth I am a Londoner,
> Free by my copy; but my ancestors
> Were Frenchmen all; and riding hard this way
> Upon a trotting horse, my bones did ache . . . (III.395–99)

The English victims, ostensibly afflicted by a foreign pox, have all been captured as they depart London, and Rafe sends them back "to the town / where [they] may find relief" (III. 388–89).

Jokes aside, Rafe's confrontation with Barberoso stages a kind of wishful thinking about renegades, as Rafe embodies a fully English identity that is impervious to any seduction. Instead of joining the renegade, as was historically most likely, the heroic Englishman handily defeats him, racing into battle with a cry of "Saint George for me!" (III.339). The scene concludes with an imperfect quarantine, as the barber/pirate promises "henceforth never gentle blood [to] spill" (III.466) and seals his promise with a kiss on Rafe's burning pestle. Yet the bawdy circulation of the pox and the disruption of what was at least in part an establishment for curing the afflicted, suggest how partial and provisional the retrenchment from "foreign" dangers must necessarily be, no matter how loudly Rafe trumpets his English triumph.

The play patriotism continues in Act IV, which begins with Rafe's encounter with Pompiona, Princess of Moldavia. George and Nell insist on this scene, over the pertinent objection of the players' Boy: "Besides, it will show ill-favouredly to have a grocer's prentice to court a king's daughter" (IV. 46–47). The Citizen bristles at the boy's protest, countering with romance models for the lionization of the lowly: "Will it so, sir? You are well read in histories! I pray you, what was Sir Dagonet? Was not he prentice to a grocer in London? Read the play of *The Four Prentices of London*, where they toss their pikes so," (IV.48–51). Sir Dagonet, of course, was the king's fool in Malory's Mort d'Arthur, and nothing in *The Four Prentices* comes close to the exalted union proposed for Rafe, given that the "prentices" in that play are, improbably, the sons of a duke. But, as we soon see, Rafe refuses even so advantageous a union as a marriage to a princess if it means succumbing to foreign seductions.[24]

Rafe introduces himself to Pompiona with, "I am an Englishman / As true as steel, a hearty Englishman / And prentice to a grocer in the Strand." Although the lady speaks positively about England ("Oft I have heard of your brave countrymen," IV.79), amid jokes about ale and salt beef, Rafe will have none of her. He rejects her for her foreignness, and will not even consider converting her, as the Citizen suggests he should do:[25]

> Rafe: I am a knight of a religious order
>   And will not wear the favour of a lady's
>   That trusts in Antichrist and false traditions.
> Citizen: Well said, Rafe; convert her if thou canst.

Rafe: Besides, I have a lady of my own
    In merry England, for whose virtuous sake
    I took these arms; and Susan is her name,
    A cobbler's maid in Milk Street, whom I vow
    Ne'er to forsake whilst life and pestle last.   (IV.92–100)

The domestic and the local are here aligned with the religious difference of a Protestant England, in contradistinction to the "false traditions" of the presumably Catholic princess. Rafe's concerted effort to maintain national distinction trumps both the class advancement that marrying a princess would afford a "Grocer-errant" and the transnational fellowship among aristocrats that characterizes romance. Even though in the play neither of these are serious alternatives, as the lady is clearly one more artifice provided to placate the Citizens, the humor does not undo the scene's privileging of national allegiances over romance fantasy. By upholding a loyalty to England that is more powerful than the illusion that Nell and George orchestrate for him, Rafe replaces his masters' emphasis on class with a fantasy of national belonging. Nell seals the matter with her approval, expressed now in terms of national and local pride: "I commend Rafe that he will not stoop to a Cracovian. There's properer women in London than any are there, iwis" (IV.128–30).[26] Rafe effectively teaches the Citizens to prefer a shared sense of Englishness to the temptations of social advancement through romance.

The act ends with Rafe's obliging performance as May Lord, at the Citizen's request: "I will have Rafe do a very notable matter now, to the eternal honour and glory of all grocers. . . Let Rafe come out on May Day in the morning and speak upon a conduit, with all his scarfs about him, and his feathers, and his rings and his knacks," (Interlude IV.5–11). Historically, urban May Day celebrations had been largely suppressed by this period and effectively replaced with more ordery civic pageantry, as part of the city authorities' efforts to control ribaldry in London.[27] The text instead repurposes the revelry as a national celebration that reaches beyond the city, suturing it to the countryside.

As the revels begin, Rafe forgoes the morris (morisco) dance suggested by the Citizen's wife, with its foreign or Spanish overtones, and launches straight into the celebration of Englishness:

London, to thee I do present the merry month of May.
Let each true subject be content to hear me what I say . . .

Rejoice, O English hearts, rejoice, rejoice, O lovers dear;
Rejoice, O city, town, and country; rejoice, eke every shire. . .
    (Interlude IV.27–37)

With each iteration of rejoicing, Rafe reaches further, convening a centripetal nation around the city as around the maypole. Although the Citizen had requested the celebration "in honour of the City" (Interlude IV.16), when Rafe invites the revelers to "march out. . . to Hogsdon or to Newington" (Interlude IV.54–56) he invokes an Englishness that transcends London. The festival propounds the national as an alternative to the international circulation of both chivalric characters and the texts themselves, reveling in a local pleasure that transcends the satiric thrust of much of the play.

In Act V, the second skit—a muster of soldiers for war—both sends up and recuperates patriotism, as burlesque exchanges about shot-pieces, touch-holes, powder-horns and flint-stones give way to repeated invocations of St. George. Here, too, the individual chivalric ethos gives way to the troop, joined together in a merry company. However performative (and silly) the military might on display here, it evokes for the Citizen actual memories of his soldiering. As he tells his wife, "I was there myself a pikeman once, in the hottest of the day, wench" (V.75–76).

Rafe, for his part, conjures subjects from a wide range of classes in mercantile London:

Gentlemen, countrymen, friends, and my fellow-soldiers, I have brought you this day from the shops of security and the counters of content to measure out in these furious fields honour by the ell and prowess by the pound. Let it not, O, let it not, I say, be told hereafter the noble issue of this city fainted, but bear yourselves in this fair action like men, valiant men and freemen. Fear not the face of the enemy, nor the noise of the guns. For believe me, brethren, the rude rumbling of a brewer's car is far more terrible, of which you have daily experience. Neither let the stink of powder offend you, since a more valiant stink is nightly with you. . . . Remember, then, whose cause you have in hand and, like a sort of true-born scavengers, scour me this famous realm of enemies. I have no more to say but this: stand to your tacklings, lads, and show to the world you can as well brandish a sword as shake an apron. Saint George, and on, my hearts! (IV.140–59)

If these prosaic, though alliterative, measures of honor poke fun at the mercantile version of bravery, they also suggest how theatricality can animate a national spirit for a commercial age, in contradistinction to the exhaustion of chivalry. The humor works from the inside, to confirm Rafe's participation in a knowing, resolutely local, and pragmatic nation that has elaborated its own, anti-heroic brand of patriotism. If this is satire, it embraces rather than ostracizes its targets. Moreover, the muster connects national feeling to the domestic space: these "furious fields" are not in France (well though that might serve Rafe's alliterative bent) but in London itself, and, in the long shadow of the Gunpowder Plot, the soldiers are charged primarily with finding enemies *within* England ("scour me this famous realm of enemies"). Thus patriotism is brought home from the imperial concerns of a play such as *Henry V*, evoked by Rafe's rhetorical flourishes, to a more proximate arena, where heroism might instead animate and bring together the various classes of London.

Perhaps more than any of Rafe's set-pieces, the muster performs a leveling nationalism that sutures class difference, negating not only the historical repression of May-Day festivities in order to control the lower classes, but the suspicion of playgoing by citizens who feared the dissipation of their apprentices and servants. If, as Andrew Gurr has noted, "any apprentice at a playhouse was taking time away from his working day,"[28] in the version offered by Rafe stage-apprentices instead become patriotic exemplars. Merely two years before the 1599 *The Shoemaker's Holiday*, which stages the sanctioned revelry of the apprentices, the Lord Mayor had written to the Privy Council to express the citizens' disapproval of the theater as a place where apprentices and servants might join "in theire designes & mutinus attemptes."[29] Yet Rafe is not involved in mutiny; he has been specifically instructed by his masters to provide them with entertainment. The solidarity of the muster that Rafe recreates, and which leads the Citizen to reminisce about his own time on the battlefield, transcends the class lines that divide masters from servants.[30] Just as when, in an earlier episode, Rafe refuses a foreign princess and brings Nell around to applauding the rejection, Rafe's playacting promotes in his masters a national feeling that transcends class difference and social climbing. In this sense, the entire Rafe plot provides a striking alternative to the swirling plots of *The London Merchant*, the play the Citizens are sabotaging, in which the apprentice's marriage to his master's daughter, after many vicissitudes, is a zero-sum game: for the apprentice to win, the master must lose. Here, by contrast, the apprentice convinces his masters that theirs is a shared enterprise.

Rafe's performances provide a powerful alternative to the more adversarial relations set up between the players' Boy and the audience, on the one hand, and the Citizens on the other. As Zachary Lesser notes, "The Boy of *The Knight* repeatedly refers to the 'Gentlemen' of the audience, urging them to 'rule' George and Nell and prevent them from ruining the play, or excusing the outmoded features George asks for, which 'will not doe so well' with a witty audience whose tastes are au courant."[31] But in fact it is Rafe who manages to rule them, by initially giving them what they want and gradually bringing them around, as in his rejection of Pompiona. Despite the play's privileging of wit and ironic distance, Rafe's rousing defense of the local effects surprising alliances between the classes. Even if, that is, *The Knight of the Burning Pestle* is invested in creating social distinction based on wit, and in censuring the characters on stage,[32] it manages simultaneously to offer a fond version of mercantile heroics, and, more importantly, to bring together apprentices and their masters in a national brotherhood.

These two dimensions do not seem to me incompatible: a more sophisticated audience (including the reading audience sought by Burr upon publication, with which Lesser is primarily concerned) might well have appreciated the satiric thrust of the play as a whole, while a broader audience at the theater might have warmed to the comic, commercial heroics purveyed by Rafe in the muster scene.[33] Ultimately, while *The Knight of the Burning Pestle* both stages and dismantles chivalric romance and popular entertainment, it achieves along the way a performative nationalism that succeeds in eliding the differences between Rafe and his masters.

Rafe's performances also allude to the best known version of Spain on the English stage, Kyd's *The Spanish Tragedy*. Since its initial success in the late 1580s, Kyd's play had been revived multiple times, becoming both a metaphor for theatricality itself and a constant reference. Rafe's introduction of himself as May Lord invokes the famous opening of Kyd's play. "My name is Rafe, by due descent though not ignoble I, / Yet far inferior to the flock of gracious Grocery" (Interlude IV.31–32) reprises the lines spoken by the ghost of the dead Andrea: "My name was Don Andrea; my descent, / though not ignoble, yet inferior far / to gracious fortunes of my tender youth."[34] Yet unlike Andrea, whose death stems from his affair with Bel-Imperia, Rafe seems to have skirted the dangers of foreign princesses and social climbing. Once again, a domestic and domesticated version of mercantile agency replaces heroism.

Instead of tragedy, *The Knight* gives us a mock-death, specifically requested by Rafe's demanding audience. As part of his extraordinarily talkative demise, Rafe reviews his past life, and summons his popular dramatic predecessor with great economy. "When I was mortal, this my costive corpse / Did lap up figs and raisins in the Strand" (V.290–91) closely echoes Andrea's "When this eternal substance of my soul/ Did live imprisoned in my wanton flesh."[35] With its homely and local referents, Beaumont's play domesticates its sources, although in this case what is Englished is not a Spanish text but a dark English fantasy of Spain. The much cited and recirculated faux-Spanish play supplements the extensive material actually taken from Spain, which animates *The Knight of the Burning Pestle* at so many different levels. When Rafe is done playing Quijote, he turns, via Kyd, to a different, and even more improbable, version of Spain.

The Knight is not explicitly about tensions between England and an encroaching Spain; indeed, whatever its exact dating, it is a play of the 1604 peace. Yet it stages via its relation to the Spanish material at its source the self-fashioning of an English commercial subjectivity in contradistinction to the chivalric, and to other threats that—imaginatively, at least—lie beyond England, in the circulation of both pox and pirates. The intrusion of money into the world of romance, which is so discomfiting to Don Quijote, is often the point in *The Knight*, as the Citizen and his wife cough up over and over again to subsidize Rafe or the original players.[36] Rafe the resourceful apprentice—he of the vocal death—does not seem to bear the brunt of the satire that the citizen-grocers or rich merchants suffer.[37] In the person of its most ingenious character, *The Knight* holds out the appeal of the communal and the local despite, or perhaps precisely because of, its own roots in beguiling foreign matter, imperfectly transmuted here into "native" form.

Yet for all its emphasis on local pleasure, *The Knight of the Burning Pestle* itself does not seem to have appealed overmuch to its first audience. From its first printer on, critics have attributed this initial failure on the stage to the lack of sophistication of its audience, unable to make heads or tails of a fragmented plot, or to perceive the irony with which the Citizen and his wife are portrayed. "The wide world," Burre tells us, "for want of judgment, or not understanding the privy mark of irony about it (which showed it was no offspring of any vulgar brain) utterly rejected it" (51). The play nonetheless enjoyed a healthy afterlife, as viewers presumably adjusted to its metadramatic and self-referential exigencies. In the context of the larger theoretical problem of appropriation that concerns me here, *The Knight*'s initial failure suggests just how unstable that process can be. Beaumont starts from a wildly popular text, *Don Quijote*, and effectively transmutes it into a carnivalesque promotion of London and Englishness. Yet the formal discontinuities Beaumont learns from the *Quijote*, no less than its own "privy mark of irony," get in the way, complicating the audience's identification with any character and interrupting the theatrical illusion. Cervantes famously deprives his readers of the pleasure of seamless text, by breaking off after a few chapters, at a crucial moment in Don Quijote's battle with the ornery Vizcayan. He leaves his characters, swords aloft, until the narrator finds some scraps of paper that seem to continue the story in Arabic, and a translator to translate them, in the *Quijote's* own fiction of appropriation. So, too, does Beaumont's imitation constantly interrupt itself, dismantling the fourth wall from the very start and dispensing with any continuity in plot. This appropriated aesthetic of knowing interruption and self-consciousness—perhaps most evident in the Boy's running commentary on the Citizens' follies—suggests that the Spanish source both is and is not trumped in *The Knight of the Burning Pestle*. The play ultimately rejects both chivalric and mock-chivalric content, but not the *Quijote's* form. Yet by impeding identification, that imported and interruptive form in turn undoes the easy pleasures of the local and the familiar that the text otherwise promotes.

Appropriation is an uncertain business. In a moment of early national self-definition, Beaumont's play Englishes its far-ranging sources and foregrounds the local as an alternative. In its eager appropriation of Iberian and mock-Iberian predecessors, from *Palmerín* to *Don Quijote* to *The Spanish Tragedy*, it nonetheless refuses the transnational geography of romance to insist instead on a national frame of reference. Yet the stability of national identity and of national belonging are cast into doubt by the insufficiency of that very process of *translatio*, by the uneasy fit between texts and their new surroundings. As Kathleen Ashley and Véronique Plesch usefully recall, appropriation is a two-way process.[38] While it generates new meanings for a new context, and contributes to the formation of new collective identities around them, those meanings often remain unstable or conflicted, as in the vexed dynamics of identification in Beaumont's play. This is especially the case for the play's Englishing of *Don Quijote*, a text at once wildly popular for its story, but potentially alienating in its reflexivity and self-consciousness. In England, *Don Quijote* becomes a source to be reckoned with, offering in its challenging imported form a treacherous ground for local sympathies.

Chapter 3

Plotting Spaniards, Spanish Plots

Even at the moments of England's closest political rapprochement with Spain and greatest cultural fascination with its literature, taking from Spain was always fraught. The peace of 1604, which I discussed in the last chapter as a key context for *The Knight of the Burning Pestle*, was followed hard upon by the Gunpowder Plot of November 5, 1605, which exacerbated the sense that a militant Catholicism threatened England's very being. Despite James's own commitment to peace and his prolonged efforts to secure a Spanish marriage for his heirs, the memory of Elizabethan resistance to Spain's primacy animated English Protestant nationalism. If the Elizabethans discussed in Chapter 1 trumpeted their open rivalry with Spain and the clear advantages for England in challenging its primacy, Jacobeans seemed more worried about Spain's machinations, despite the peace that had at least momentarily been reached. The fear of Spain's open hostility became a pervasive anxiety about its secret designs on England, as the triumphant vision of stolen intelligence that had animated so many Elizabethan translators gave way to a sustained mistrust, in pamphlets as on the popular stage. Suspicion about why Spain had sought peace at all, and worry about the workings of a "Spanish faction" in James's court, tainted the entire period of the peace.[1] At the same time, the abundant rendering of Spanish materials into English, which had scarcely waned under Elizabeth, reached new heights, as the peace led to the translation of Cervantes's and Alemán's protean fictions, and the frequent use of Spanish sources by a wide range of English dramatists.

Jacobean playwrights found in Spain and Spanish literature abundant settings and source material. While this penchant may surprise readers who expect from such writers as Thomas Middleton or John Fletcher the hispanophobia of good Protestants, it is part of the larger cultural ambivalence about Spain over the course of James's reign, from the initial peace to the increasing anxiety about Spain's continued actions against Protestants on the continent and its secret designs on England, against the backdrop of a possible "Spanish match" for James's children. While popular sentiment had largely turned against Spain by the 1620s, James remained hopeful that an alliance could be secured through the marriage of Charles to a Spanish *infanta*. This ambition was strongly at odds with the crisis developing on the continent, as England sought the restoration of the Protestant Frederick, Elector Palatine, married to James's daughter Elizabeth, in a conflict that would become the Thirty Years' War.

This chapter begins with the heightened moment of the "Spanish match," as the failed dynastic union is generally known, and works backward to consider more broadly the various guises in which Spain made its appearance on the Jacobean stage, from the xenophobic representation of plotting Spaniards to the frequent reliance on an (over)abundance of Spanish plots. Middleton's plays on Spanish sources and themes—*The Lady's Tragedy* (also known as *The Second Maiden's Tragedy*, 1611), *The Changeling* (1622), and *The Spanish Gypsy* (1623)—span this period. Although Middleton's best-known work on Spain, *A Game at Chess* (1624), was also his most direct ideological engagement with Spanish policy, his wider oeuvre shows a sustained attention to Spain. Fletcher, for his part, was perhaps the dramatist who most consistently engaged Spanish sources, especially Cervantes. My focus here on his *Rule a Wife and Have a Wife* (1624), a play largely ignored by modern criticism despite its early success, is an attempt to show the complexity of enlisting *translatio* in nationalist projects.[2]

The multiplicity of representations on the Jacobean stage complicates any simple story about England and Spain: cultural, political, and religious relations were not always perfectly aligned, and even the writers most suspicious of Spanish plots where geopolitics was concerned turned to Spain for literary material. In part, this paradox might be explained by a poetics of piracy that glorifies England's forcible taking from Spain in the cultural arena as the patriotic equivalent of privateering, as I suggest in Chapter 1. Yet the sheer polysemy and range of the Spanish materials appropriated often undoes any simple Englishing of the same. "Spain" is rehearsed in very different keys, from the carnivalesque shenanigans of *The Spanish Gypsy* to the transparent allegory of *A Game at Chess*. Even the most explicitly jingoistic of the plays I discuss here, Fletcher's *Rule a Wife and Have a Wife*, sees its ideological thrust adumbrated by the multiple plots that it attempts to reconcile. Much as the interruptive aesthetic of *Don Quijote* complicates the Englishing of its matter in *The Knight of the Burning Pestle*, as I showed in Chapter 2, the contradictory thrusts of the Spanish plot and subplot in Fletcher's play qualify the ideological force of its *translatio*.

Spaniards, Jesuits, Machiavellians

The possibility of an even closer dynastic rapprochement to Spain in the 1620s made Spanish materials ever more fashionable, even as it fueled anti-Spanish sentiment.[3] The disastrous project to marry James I's heir, the future Charles I, to the *infanta* María of Spain was to founder over the Spanish insistence that Charles convert to Catholicism. The failed match thus marks a moment of desired rapprochement with Spain, as well as a crisis in the construction of an English national identity heavily dependent on religious difference.[4] The protracted negotiations for a possible marriage between Charles and the Spanish princess, the sister of Philip IV, produced a wide range of texts, from plays to anti-Hispanic pamphlets, including John Reynold's fantastic *Vox Coeli*, a heavenly dialogue among past English sovereigns on the advisability of the match.[5] In 1623, in one of the most astounding transgressions of diplomatic protocol in the period, Charles and Buckingham traveled to Madrid to advance the marriage negotiations. Although this was presented as a spontaneous, romantic adventure, Philip IV had known for a year that Charles would undertake such a journey. Philip's powerful *privado*, the count-duke of Olivares, did not favor the match, however, and after months of delays and negotiations Charles finally decided to return to England, sans his Spanish bride. The failure of the match and Charles's safe return from his escapade to Madrid were widely celebrated in England, in an outpouring of anti-Spanish sentiment. Yet a resilient hispanophilia coexisted with the suspicion and prejudice.[6]

The Spanish match produced a wide range of dramatic responses, from Jonson's masque *Neptune's Triumph* to plays as varied as Massinger's *The Renegado*, Middleton's *A Game at Chess*, and Fletcher's *Rule a Wife and Have a Wife*.[7] These monitory (and compensatory) performances offer themselves up for topical readings in which the playwrights subtly or not so subtly veil their ideology in the dramatic conflict, and they must be read for their precise location in the timeline of Anglo-Spanish negotiations. Yet although it is important to reconstruct these precise contexts, it is also crucial to recognize that the English theatrical engagement with Spanish materials extended far beyond the specific moment of the Spanish match, both chronologically and thematically.

The crisis around Charles's possible marriage to a Catholic princess simply serves to underscore how sustained and enduring the fascination with Spain really was, in that it could transcend the potent upwelling of popular sentiment against the union.

Thomas Middleton penned the most scandalous response to Charles's marital adventures, in the wildly successful *A Game at Chess*. Performed in August 1624, the play was unique in the period both for its popularity and for having led to a diplomatic crisis. As Gary Taylor notes in his introduction to the early form of the play, it was "perceived by contemporaries as simultaneously the most subversive and the most commercially successful play of its era."[8] Confronted with the baldly allegorical representation of Spain as the "Black House" (on which more below), the Spanish ambassador, Carlos Coloma, lodged a formal complaint with the Crown, and threatened to leave England if the play continued to be performed. The famous record set by *A Game at Chess*, of nine days of performances, was thus in fact simply the time it took for the authorities to shut it down, as it was still playing to a full house when that occurred. In what may have been a canny choice not to alienate the popular fervor that greeted the play, James gave as the rationale for his censorship the forbidden representation of a sovereign on stage, rather than the play's overwhelming disrespect for Spain.

A Game at Chess is a play of plotting gone mad. Readers are typically befuddled by the multiplication of plots and subplots, including at least one—the gelding of the White Bishop's Pawn—for which no back-story whatsoever is offered. The central plots are the attempt by the Black Bishop's Pawn to seduce the White Queen's Pawn, and the machinations of the Black Knight Gondomar (the former Spanish ambassador to James I, Diego Sarmiento de Acuña) to gain power over the White House, in part by luring the White Knight and his companion, the White Duke, to the Black Court, in a close dramatic echo of Charles and Buckingham's escapade to Madrid. Meanwhile, the Fat Bishop of Spalato (Marco Antonio de Dominis), a former Catholic recently converted to the White House, is lured back to the Black House, while the White King's Pawn secretly works for the Black House. Viewers of the play presumably followed its blatant color-coding ("the houses well distinguished," as the prologue puts it) to track all the plot turns, and enjoyed its more spectacular effects, such as the final "checkmate by discovery" (5.3.174) that sends all the black pieces "into the bag" (5.3.178).[9] As Taylor notes, visually the characters would be quite distinct, even if they are difficult to follow in print.[10] Despite the blatant difference staged by the chess allegory, however, the vulnerability of the White House to seduction and the duplicity of some of its members create considerable suspense, paradoxically reminding viewers of the indeterminacy and illegibility of religious and political allegiance.

The essence of the Black House is its obsessive concern with power and seduction. Although religious difference provides the ostensible rationale for the conflicts, religion per se appears less important than the struggles for power and influence. Middleton stages a potent series of Spanish stereotypes, allegorizing English prejudice into the figures of the chess game. Here, I trace the genealogy of one of those stereotypes, the plotting Jesuit, to show how plottedness itself becomes a key component of Middleton's corpus. To provide the fullest picture of the relation between Spain and English drama in the period, I want to underscore the tension between the fertile plots that Spain contributes to the theater and the English denunciation of plotting as the very heart of Spanish evil. The strong dichotomies of *A Game at Chess* and its repudiation of Spain predispose us to find a similar relation to Spain in Middleton's earlier plays. Yet his corpus instead yields the paradox that the plotting Spaniards (in the political sense) have been providing dramatic plots all along.

Preposterously, I begin here with Middleton's last play, in which the close association between Spaniards and plots makes the Black Knight Gondomar a powerful dramatic figure. Like Barabas in *The Jew of Malta*, the Machiavellian in this text steals the show with his dreams of world domination and unlimited power. But whereas Marlowe invokes the actual "Machiavel" for his Mediterranean fantasy, Middleton instead emphasizes the association of Spaniards and Jesuits with plotting, in a Machiavellian *translatio* that makes Spaniards the new outsized villains.[11] Marlowe's prologue had featured Machiavel himself; Middleton's induction gives us the Spanish founder of the Society of Jesus, "Ignatius Loyola [in his black Jesuit habit] appearing, Error at his foot as asleep," who complains that his children's "monarchy" is "unperfect yet" (Induction, 11–12). The struggle for world domination is the "great game" (Induction, 78) being played on stage, beyond the individual plots. From Gondomar's first appearance, in the wake of Loyola, he is associated with this outsize plotting:

> Black Knight Gondomar (aside):   So, so
>   The business of the universal monarchy
>   Goes forward well now, the great college pot
>   That should be always boiling with the fuel
>   Of all intelligences possible
>   Thorough the Christian kingdoms.   (1.1.243–48)

In this passage as in multiple other instances, the aside serves to portray political duplicity onstage, raising the stakes of this standard dramatic resource. More explicitly, Gondomar gathers intelligence from across Europe ("Look you, there's Anglica, this Gallica," 1.1.301), pulling the strings of his various plots. When his Pawn warns Gondomar, "Sir, your plot's discovered," he counters: "Which of the twenty thousand and nine hundred / Fourscore and five? canst tell?" (3.1.126–28). Thus the fear of endlessly multiplying Spanish plots against England and of a Catholic universal monarchy orchestrated by Jesuits animates Middleton's play.

In England, Jesuits were strongly associated with Spain as well as with Rome, and connected in particular with the Counter-Reformation challenge to Protestantism everywhere. The Anglo-Spanish conflict and the Jesuit missions to England had exacerbated English suspicion of the order, whose members were regarded as both a religious and a political threat. The Jesuits were cast as Machiavellian figures whose political ends trumped any qualms about their means. In particular, they were associated with the doctrine of equivocation or mental reservation—strategies essential for the survival of persecuted Catholics in England but perceived as proof that Jesuits could not be trusted.

Although the order was not responsible for the failed Gunpowder Plot of 1605, the Crown deliberately attempted to implicate it, thus cementing the association between Jesuits and Machiavellian plotting, and scapegoating the "Spanish" order for a plot hatched by English Catholics.[12] As Arthur Marotti has shown, the official account of the Gunpowder Plot trials "kept up a steady attack on the Jesuits as the alleged masterminds of the plot," placing it in a longer continuum of Catholic assaults on England.[13] The connections between Jesuits, Spain, and Machiavellianism soon tarred all Spaniards with the same brush, and by the time of Charles's possible marriage to a Spanish princess, Spanish plotting was loudly invoked against the union.

The demonization of Jesuits in the wake of the Gunpowder Plot increasingly made Catholicism itself appear foreign, aligning England ever more closely with its Protestantism. As Marotti notes, the larger narrative of "recurrent Catholic dangers, plots, and outrages" animated a Protestant English history based on the resistance to a threatening Catholic internationalism.[14] But this focus on supposedly external religious enemies negated the most pressing problem for England in this regard: the internal debate about religion. In the aftermath of the failed Spanish match, animosity against Spain and a Jesuit-mad version of Catholicism could momentarily pave over divisions among Protestants, yet these would be the central religious conflicts in England in the years to follow.

Through his assiduous cultivation of James I, Count Gondomar, the historical Black Knight, who served as Spanish ambassador to England from 1613 to 1618 and 1619 to 1622, was able to repair some of the damage done to English Catholics by the Gunpowder Plot. Yet deep suspicion of Gondomar's own actions expanded the earlier association of Jesuits and plotting to a broader concern with Spanish designs on England. By the 1620s, the association of Spain with plotting and of Gondomar with Machiavelli had become a commonplace of anti-Hispanic pamphlets. Thomas Scott's (1580?–1626) *Second Part of Vox Populi* (1624), on which Middleton appears to have drawn heavily, bears as its alternate title *Gondomar appearing in the likenes of Matchiauell in a Spanish parliament, wherein are discouered his treacherous & subtile practises to the ruine as well of England, as well as the Netherlands*. In the same year, Scott also published *A Second part of Spanish practises, or, A Relation of more particular wicked plots, and cruell, inhumane, perfidious, and vnnaturall practises of the Spaniards with more excellent reasons of greater consequence, deliuered to the Kings Maiesty to dissolue the two treaties both of the match and the Pallatinate, and enter into warre with the Spaniards.* His *Narrative of the wicked plots carried on by Seignior Gondamore for advancing the popish religion and Spanish faction* (London, 1679), though only published much later, sounds the same notes. Protestant paranoia about pro-Spanish sympathizers extended beyond the earthly realm: in Reynold's *Vox Coeli*, Mary Tudor races to write both Gondomar and "the Romane Catholiques of England" with the news that the heavenly debate on the Spanish marriage has come down against it, so that they can compensate on earth with their own corrupt scheming in favor of the match.[15] As this brief catalogue of pamphlets shows, opposition to the marriage solidified a series of anti-Spanish stereotypes that would be rehearsed ever more vividly on Middleton's stage.

The stereotypes of Spanish plotting colored even the more judicious assessments of the match. In a pragmatic reflection on the proposed marriage, English observer James Howell wrote, "For my part, I hold the Spanish match to be better than their Powder, and their Wares better than their Wars, and I shall be ever of that mind, That no Country is able to do England less hurt and more good than Spain, considering the large Trafic and Treasure that is to be got thereby."[16] Even for a sympathetic observer, that is, the alternative to

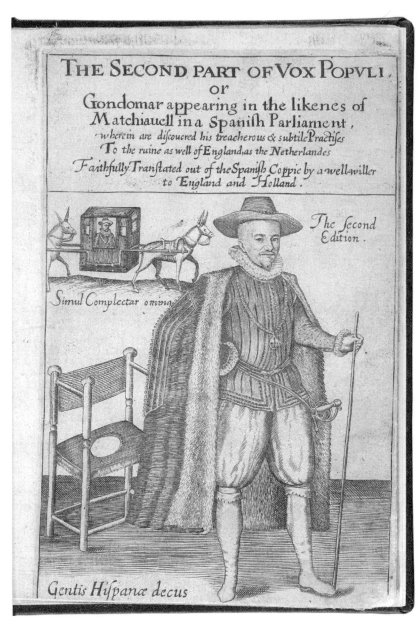

Figure 3. Thomas Scott, *Second Part of Vox Populi*. Huntington Library.

the Spanish match is England's vulnerability to Spain's gunpowder, both in the larger military sense and in powder plots. Yet Howell's assessment underscores the strong connections—commercial and otherwise—that existed despite the demonization of Spain.

In the wake of the Gunpowder Plot, and despite James's peace with Spain, the suspicion of Spanish Machiavellianism transfers to that nation the existing stereotypes of Italy as "a fantasy setting for dramas of passion, Machiavellian politics, and revenge."[17] Spain thus becomes an ancillary Italy, and the pleasure of watching Italians behaving badly is extended to Spain. For popular drama, this is a hugely effective *translatio*, in that Spain, unlike Italy, was a feared rival to England. Although the vision of a corrupt Spain is certainly present in earlier plays such as *The Spanish Tragedy* and *Lust's Dominion*, written during periods of frank emnity, the 1604 peace and the possibility of a dynastic alliance with Spain create an irresistible tension, making Spain newly available while raising the stakes for exposing Spanish duplicity. While the Jacobean peace made the literary traffic between England and Spain more fluid, that is, the concurrent anxiety about a Catholic takeover, whether through violent or dynastic means, found its expression in a series of plays that emphasized the dangers of Spain even as they turned to Spanish sources.

The strong association of Spain and Spaniards with endless plotting culminates in Middleton's *Game at Chess* with its dramatic antithesis: the discovery. As Gondomar triumphantly reveals his dissembling ("What we have done/Has been dissemblance ever," 5.3.158–59), the Black House is unceremoniously swept into the bag, which gapes open "like hell-mouth" (5.3.179). Anagnorisis—that standard moment of revelation in early modern drama—thus becomes politicized, as the play works to confirm the "truths" peddled by the anti-Spanish pamphlets, all of which claimed to warn and protect their readers by bringing to light Spain's shadier dealings. Again, Thomas Scott provides an eloquent example of the anti-conspiratorial, revelatory pitch, with *An Experimentall discoverie of Spanish practises, or, The Counsell of a well-wishing souldier, for the good of his prince and state wherein is manifested from known experience, both the cruelty, and policy of the Spaniard, to effect his own ends* (London, 1623). In a similar vein, the first quarto of *A Game at Chess* highlights the "checkmate by discovery" on the title-page engraving, where the phrase is assigned to the White Knight, as though to promise readers the satisfaction of a revelation that will only confirm their worst expectations.

Middleton's play thus trades in anti-Spanish prejudices, giving literary life to political cliché. Beyond political and religious divides, moreover, Middleton

Figure 4. Thomas Middleton, *A Game at Chess*. Huntington Library.

invokes the frequent racialization of Spain in the period—a facet of the Black Legend that insisted on Spain's miscegenated nature, its Jewish and Moorish blood.[18] Even though the play features its share of double-crossing and duplicity, the blackness of the black characters sets them apart. There are Whites who are secretly Black, such as the White King's Pawn, spectacularly stripped of his white upper garment to reveal a black one beneath (3.1, 262–63). But no Blacks are secretly White, suggesting an essentialist and racialized version of Spanish difference.

Yet while this color-coding would seem to make Spain radically other, the play's allegory also lends itself to more complex understandings of England, the "White House," for its vulnerability and openness to seduction. As Richard Dutton expresses it, "Are [the English figures] virtuous characters who finally turn the tables on the ingenious villainy to which they have been subjected? Or are they weak, easily deluded and perhaps self-important characters, who must bear some responsibility for the danger in which 'the White House' finds itself?"[19] The play's success may be explained by this ambivalence: its surface symbolism offers up a simple xenophobia that would have appealed to most contemporary viewers, while the complexities of its allegory engage more critical readings.

Contrary Plots

The Machiavellian-Jesuitical genealogy of plotting that I trace above finds its literary analog in the hyper-plottedness of a Mediterranean, Italianate group of plays—not quite revenge tragedy, although it overlaps with that genre in important ways—that takes from Cervantes as liberally as from Boccaccio or Cinthio. The very term *plot*, widely used for political conspiracy, is first used to describe a storyline in the aftermath of the Gunpowder Plot. The first literary use is in Beaumont's *The Knight of the Burning Pestle*, itself much concerned with Spanish plots in a comic vein: "The plot of our Plaie lies contrarie, and t'will hazard the spoiling of our Plaie."[20] If we read retrospectively from *A Game at Chess* to Middleton's Spanish plays—*The Lady's Tragedy*, *The Changeling*, and *The Spanish Gypsy*—we find that the stereotypes of plotting Spaniards coexist with an extensive reliance on Spanish sources. Even as Spain is anathemized, Spanish prose fiction furnishes the dramatic materials for English plots.

The Lady's Tragedy (1611), which has usually been known as *The Second Maiden's Tragedy*, is Middleton's first engagement with these Spanish materials. The plot features the Tyrant, "a usurper," who lusts after the Lady, betrothed to the legitimate ruler, Govianus. Her father urges her to improve her lot by giving in to the Tyrant, as his mistress if not his wife. Under assault by the Tyrant's soldiers, the Lady takes her life rather than succumb to his lust. Govianus and the Tyrant then continue their struggle, literally over her dead body. A parallel plot features Anselmus, who, doubting his wife's fidelity, urges his friend Votarius to test her by trying to seduce her. Votarius succeeds only too well, but he and the Wife are betrayed by her servant, Leonella. They die by poison in what was to be only a show-quarrel to placate Anselmus, while Anselmus dies in the aftermath of their struggle.

Closely based on "El curioso impertinente" ("The Curious Impertinent"), an interpolated novella in *Don Quijote* (1605) that tells the story of the doubting Anselmo and his wife Camila, the parallel plot marks *The Lady's Tragedy* as one of the many literary fruits of the peace with Spain in 1604, and of the intense interest in *Don Quijote* in England from the moment of its Spanish publication in 1605. The 1611 dating of *The Lady's Tragedy* suggests that Middleton, who read Spanish, may well have had access to *Don Quijote* in its original language, or have come across Shelton's translation while it was still in manuscript.[21]

The Lady's plot also echoes Cervantes. While these connections do not endorse the fanciful recent claim that *The Lady's Tragedy* is the lost Shakespeare play *Cardenio*, based on the same material, Govianus's position does recall that of Cardenio in *Don Quijote*.[22] Like Cardenio, whose beloved Luscinda is stolen by a duke's son, the impetuous Don Fernando, Govianus finds his betrothal to a lady who reciprocates his love threatened by a more powerful figure. In both cases, might trumps right, and the lady's family encourages her to embrace the usurper. In both cases, too, the rival seems motivated primarily by mimetic desire, although Cervantes makes it much clearer that Cardenio's love for Luscinda inflames Don Fernando in the first place and, of course, his Luscinda remains alive.

Middleton's most interesting innovation to the "Curious Impertinent" plot from *Don Quijote* is his emphasis on the class transgression of the Wife's servant, Leonella. Once the maid discovers the affair between the Wife and Votarius, she repeatedly challenges her mistress, arguing for her own right to a lover: "I know no difference, virtuous madam, / But in love all have privilege alike" (4.1.84–85). The Wife recognizes that her own impropriety has emboldened her servant, yet the dramatic effect is a potent erasure of class.

The Lady's Tragedy features a multiplicity of plots, from the two ladies' stories, which are conceptually related but do not overlap, to the less fully fleshed-out plots of the Tyrant's usurpation of Govianus's throne and of Votarius's quarrel with the dangerous Bellarius. The play presents a world of dissimulation, betrayal, and ruthlessness, where transgression is the standard modus operandi, including in this case the scandalous breach of the Lady's tomb and the Tyrant's necrophiliac passion. With the exception of the court-ier Helvetius—an anchor of "Swiss" Protestant virtue in the play—and the minor figures Memphonius and Sophonirus, the names suggest an Italianate world, as does the Cervantine source. Despite the lack of a specific geographic location, and its Spanish sources notwithstanding, then, the play contributes to the vague association of Mediterraneans with plots and plotting. Although it is not technically a revenge tragedy, it abuts that genre in its violence, its thematic concerns, and its imaginative geography.

No Spanish sources have been identified for Middleton and Rowley's *The Changeling* (1622), although its main plot reprises a story in a collection by the prolific anti-Spanish pamphleteer John Reynolds.[23] Although the play is located in Valencia, the first references to place are more generally Mediter-ranean and maritime. In the opening scene (usually attributed to Rowley) there are mentions of Malta, and of ransoming Greece from the Turk, yet the specific Spanish setting of the source is attenuated.[24] Nonetheless, much as in Fletcher's *Rule a Wife*, the metaphor of privateering legitimates various kinds of forcible taking. As the play opens, Jasperino longs to join his friend Alsemero's wooing, as women become ships and love a conquering venture: "Methinks I should do something too; I meant to be a venturer in this voy-age. Yonder's another vessel; I'll board her: if she be lawful prize, down goes her topsail" (1.1.89–92). The names of the nobles are not particularly Spanish, but participate in a Mediterranean lingua franca of toponymy that under-scores the perceived connections between Italy and Spain. By the end of the scene, however, the Spanish context becomes more insistent, with the inquiry into Alsemero's origins ("Alsemero: A Valencian, sir. / Vermandero: "A Valen-cian?" [1.1.170]), to make sure that no stranger is afforded entry to the "chief strengths" of the city, and a quick reference to the "rebellious Hollanders," whom Alsemero's father died fighting (1.1.186).

In *The Changeling*, transgression and betrayal animate yet another plot-ting play, in which vaguely Spanish aristocrats tragically assume that their own privilege will protect them from moral condemnation, on the one hand, and revenge, on the other. In order to marry Alsemero, the noble Beatrice-Joanna plots to murder the man to whom she is already betrothed, the unsuspecting Alonzo Piracquo. Strikingly, it is a servant, the tellingly named De Flores, who is the most ruthless figure in the play, manipulating his mistress's use of him in her murder plot to his own advantage. A driving, insatiable sexual passion for his mistress animates De Flores, but his sexualization of the "service" he provides Beatrice also introduces a disturbing class dynamic into the play.

While De Flores commits murder for Beatrice, he will not be paid off with money. Instead, as his name anticipates, he demands the right to deflower her, in a scene that comes very close to rape. Given Beatrice's profound distaste for De Flores, and her condescension to him as a servant early in the play, his transgression violates not only her virginity but the class hierarchy of this fictional Spain. As Swapan Chakravorty has noted, "By sexualizing class relations," the play "exposes idealized loyalties of late feudalism as functions of political strength."[25]

Class and sex are similarly at stake in the famous bed-trick scene, in which the desperate Beatrice persuades her servant, Diaphanta, to take her place next to Alsemero in the nuptial bed, in order to disguise her own shame. Beatrice thus restages the violation she herself has suffered, but restores the expected social hierarchy, in which mistresses govern the bodies of their maids. Diaphanta's pleasure in the arrangement, however, further destabilizes the moment, transforming the potential scene of violation into a comic exchange, which leaves the mistress jealous of her servant as pleasure trumps social distinction.

Through the figures of De Flores and Diaphanta, Middleton and Rowley displace anxieties about class onto a rigidly aristocratic Spain of the imagination, where the violation of hierarchies has an outsize effect. In production, it is striking to note how the villain's name, De Flores, which is insistently repeated, is also the one most clearly recognizable as Spanish.[26] Yet both the transgressors come to a bad end, as Diaphanta dies in a fire set by De Flores, and the exposed De Flores chooses to take his own life. Ultimately, both the displaced setting and the obliteration of the upstarts soften the force of these transgressions, which are simultaneously advanced and muted.[27] The play's second plot, usually attributed to Rowley, in which the beleaguered wife of an asylum-keeper resists the overtures of gentlemen disguised as madmen, provides a bourgeois alternative to the aristocratic depravity of the castle, and perhaps yet another echo of *Don Quijote*. Yet the asylum, marked by its own abuses of power, remains an equivocal moral option at best.

While the Spanish setting is only intermittently invoked in *The Changeling*, it locates the play in the Mediterranean and threateningly duplicitous world of revenge tragedy. Margot Heinemann, A. A. Bromham, and Zara Bruzzi, among others, have linked the play more closely with English anxieties about the Spanish marriage, through its possible echo of the Frances Howard case.[28] At thirteen, Frances had been married to the earl of Essex, but she eventually succeeded in having the marriage annulled, claiming that, through no fault of her own, their union had never been consummated. The judicial test of her virginity was widely mocked, and it was suspected that another woman had replaced her. Frances was by then in love with James's favorite, Robert Carr, later earl of Somerset, whom she married as soon as the annulment was granted (Middleton wrote the now lost *Masque of Cupids* for the wedding). In 1615, Frances and Somerset were convicted of the murder in the Tower of Thomas Overbury, a friend of Somerset's who had advised him against the marriage. Although Frances obviously had not killed him herself, she confessed to instigating his poisoning. In 1622, after a few years' imprisonment in the Tower, the Somersets were released by James, which renewed the scandal. As a member of the Howard family, Frances was connected to the Catholic and pro-Spanish faction at court, and James's leniency toward the Somersets was read as an alarming sign of goodwill toward Spain.

The echoes of the Howard case in *The Changeling* are manifold, from the plotting bride who does away with an inconvenient partner to the substitution of that bride by a true virgin in order to feign her purity. In her insightful introduction to the play in the *Complete Works*, Annabel Patterson nonetheless expresses some skepticism about the exhaustive reading offered by Bromham and Bruzzi: "The most that can be argued from this collage of internal signposts and stage historical detail is that *The Changeling* permitted its original audiences to intuit a connection between Spanish/Catholic interests, crimes of violence, and sexuality out of control" (1635). That intuitive connection, I suggest, is fleshed out by the longer genealogy of perceived Spanish plotting I have traced here. Even if the play is not fundamentally about the Howard case, it contributes to the larger association in the English imaginary of Spain and nefarious plotting.

More broadly, one might argue that the play also presents a Spanish marriage as a hopelessly disingenuous move, given the predatory, immoral nature of the bride, as figured in Beatrice-Joanna, and the larger context of venality and betrayal. Just as an Elizabethan would be hard pressed to imagine a dynastic union into the tumultuous world of Kyd's *The Spanish Tragedy*, so Middleton and Rowley's *Changeling* sounds a warning note for Jacobeans about the unreliability of Spanish vows, which the play's setting and dark machinations would have abundantly recalled. It thus anticipates the more blatant notes sounded by *A Game at Chess* in its warning about dangerous seduction by Spain. As Cristina Malcolmson has argued, the sexual vulnerability figured in Beatrice-Joanna, as in the White Queen's Pawn, suggests the political vulnerability of England to Spanish invasion: "the vulnerable female body symbolizes the weakness of the body of the state, disturbingly open to the infiltration of foreign Catholic powers who stand ready to enter England."[29] As depraved instigator of the murder, then, Beatrice-Joanna might remind viewers of Frances Howard or impress on them the danger of a Catholic queen. As victim of De Flores, conversely, she might recall England's vulnerability. All these versions suggest just how powerfully Middleton used sex and class to think through politics.

Perhaps the most fulsome taking from Spain on the Jacobean stage occurs in *The Spanish Gypsy* (1623) the play in which Middleton and his collaborators rely most heavily on Spanish sources, at the very moment when the crisis over the Spanish marriage was at its peak.[30] With Charles newly returned from Madrid, there was tremendous uncertainty over whether the Spanish would agree to a union about which the English themselves felt most ambivalent. Yet the considerable animosity toward Spain that Middleton would fully exploit in *A Game at Chess* is surprisingly muted in this play, which instead turns to Spain for its literary plots.[31] Although the play may have been written under the expectation that there would be a Spanish match, the Spanish materials retained their interest even as the match foundered, and the play proved a great success.[32]

Like Fletcher, Massinger, and other Jacobeans, the authors of *The Spanish Gypsy* find in Cervantes a rich trove of materials. From the *Novelas ejemplares*, the collection of short stories Cervantes published in 1613, they take two of the main storylines for the play: the rape that eventually leads to a restorative marriage, from "La fuerza de la sangre," and the gypsies who are actually aristocrats in disguise, from "La Gitanilla." The sheer multiplication of Spanish plots underscores the fascination with Spanish materials even at a moment of great suspicion of Spain.

Unlike *The Changeling*, whose Spanish setting is not consistently marked, *The Spanish Gypsy* dwells obsessively on its Spanishness from its very title. Its characters have unequivocally Spanish names, and the title assigned to Roderigo's father—Corregidor of Madrid, equivalent to Lord Mayor of London—is both accurate and contemporary. Hence although none of the characters are historical figures, the play is situated in a recognizable Spain, in the very city that Charles and Buckingham had taken by surprise. As Taylor notes, the Madrid setting is insistently referenced, and the authors go out of their way to introduce topical references to the royal escapade.[33] In the opening scene, moreover, characters discuss Spanish traits and mores, reifying national difference in varying attitudes to everything from drink to honor.

The play begins with Roderigo's rape of Clara, closely modeled on

Cervantes's novella, yet in this version the events move much closer to the physical and political center of Spanish authority: Cervantes's Toledo becomes the capital, Madrid, and the unspecified nobleman of the novella, whose lust leads him to violence, is here identified as the son of the Corregidor. Thus *The Spanish Gypsy* presents a profoundly lawless Spain, whose very centers of power are marked by violence and excess. In a play probably penned while Charles was still in Madrid courting his Spanish bride, the vision of Spanish disorder is striking. Yet at the same time the text refigures the tortuous and seemingly impossible dynastic union into an impetuous ravishment. Roderigo brooks no objections, and takes the object of his desire first, leaving any consequences for later. Strikingly even for the period, the rape plot ends happily, with Roderigo recognizing his fault and eventually marrying Clara. Her honorable, patient suitor Luis, meanwhile, is sidelined by Roderigo, whose rape perversely establishes his power over Clara. In Luis's frustrated suit for Clara, despite her parents' repeated promises, Taylor reads allusions to Charles's futile quest.[34] Equally striking, in my view, is the juxtaposition of that failure to a union consummated through violence.

In the text, Spanish aristocrats are generally characterized by their arrogance and violence, in contradistinction to the jovial gypsies. To the rape plot of Roderigo, we may add the complex plot of Luis's revenge for his father's murder. In a dramatically awkward but ideologically striking interlude, the entire episode is related indirectly, as "an old don" reviews past acts of violence and carefully catalogued slights: "I well remember how our streets were frighted / With brawls, whose end was blood" (2.2.83–84). As its awkward introduction suggests, this plot is completely superfluous to the many other strands woven together in the play.[35] While the over-plotting may be due simply to too many cooks for this theatrical broth, it recalls the stereotypes of Spanishness I have charted above, both in its formal excess of plot and its construction of Spanish arrogance and hotheadedness. The shading of the Spanish into the Mediterranean and Machiavellian is strikingly suggested, too, by the completely unmotivated appearance of Roderigo "disguised like an Italian" (s.d. 3.1).

Other stereotypes, however, are handled very differently, as the abundantly plotted play moves from the serious rape and revenge plots to a ludic, carnivalesque scene of gypsies. Reprising Jonson's popular 1621 court masque, *The Gypsies Metamorphosed*, in which the gypsies had actually been played by aristocrats, the play stresses that these gypsies are not dark, not criminal, and not like English gypsies. Thus the world-upside-down of this play actually reverses the stereotypes about gypsies and the commonplaces of the Spanish picaresque into a semblance of order.[36] Moreover, the playwrights radically refigure Cervantes's romance plot, which focuses on a single aristocratic girl, stolen as a baby and brought up by the gypsies, and her disguised noble suitor, into an entire community of "Spanish Gypsies, noble Gypsies!" (2.1.11), whose actual relation to Spain is much discussed.

The Spanishness of these irresistible entertainers is both insistently noted and occasionally qualified. The leader of the gypsies offers that if one Spanish city cannot sustain them, another will: "Does Madrid yield no money? Seville shall. Is Seville close-fisted? Valladolid is open; so Cordova, so Toledo" (2.1.54–56). Yet his imaginative geography soon moves beyond Spain: "Do not our Spanish wines please us? Italian can then, French can" (2.1.56–57). In a similarly ambivalent moment, the "foolish gentleman" Sancho (a name made famous by *Don Quijote*), who also passes for a gypsy, refers to them as "Egyptian Spaniards," "jugglers, tumblers, anything, anywhere, everywhere" (3.1.51–53). In their self-consciousness about their own artifice, these gypsies both represent a stereotypical Spain and transcend it.

Sancho's self-referential moment is just one among many. For *The Spanish Gypsy* refers constantly to its characters as entertainers and to itself as entertainment, showing a remarkable awareness of the conventionality and artificiality of "Spain" on the English stage, even at this early date. Strikingly, in this register Spain is viewed favorably, whatever its moral failings. The improbably unmarked gypsies of this play thus represent a consumable "Spanishness" on the English stage (and, in the picaresque or Cervantine sources, on the printed page) that provides pleasure to viewers and readers, transcending the immediate political crisis. In the Spanish source text for these scenes, the gypsy entertainers also provide immense pleasure: Preciosa, the titular "gitanilla" of Cervantes's novella, is famous in Madrid for her grace, and she is showered with both money and poems by her admirers. Yet when the novella is Englished, Spain itself becomes the source of literary pleasure, packaged for easy, no-strings-attached consumption by London audiences. Just as the prodigal Sancho dismisses land in favor of gold—"Hang lands! It's nothing but trees, stones and dirt. Old father, I have gold to keep up our stock" (3.1.85–86), the gypsy plot on stage refuses the territoriality and referentiality of politics, replacing it with the free circulation of carnivalesque pleasure.

The Spanish Gypsy thus appears as a play at odds with itself: insistently Spanish, it supplies both ample stereotypes of Spanish identity and a highly self-conscious version of "Spanishness" as theatrical property. It even reflects on the dynamics of imitation and translation, by making the sometime villain Roderigo into a faux-Italian comedian who will join Sancho in writing plays for the gypsies. Sancho welcomes him warily: "A magpie of Parnassus! Welcome again! I am a fire-brand of Phoebus myself; we'll invoke together—so you will not steal my plot" (3.1.68–70). When the play ends with a series of anagnorises, as the various gypsies are revealed to be missing aristocrats, the artifice of this "Spain" is further underscored. Nothing is what it seems to be, but the equivocation makes for good theater. Unlike the morally and ideologically loaded "discovery" of *A Game at Chess*, which marks the ultimate division of White House and Black House, the revelations here offer a vision of national difference as a valuable theatrical commodity, mobile and profitable.

Middleton's Spanish plays thus mark the enormous distance between popular jingoism and official policy, on the one hand, and between political rivalry and literary allegiance, on the other. Despite James's attempts to cement a dynastic allegiance with Spain, the popular theater was never more successful than when Spain was reviled, as in *A Game at Chess*. Because the differences between Spain and England were never as pronounced as black versus white, however, the power of Middleton's allegory lay in oversimplifying the complexities of national and religious identity and disavowing the inevitable points of contact between the two polities. At the same time, even as Spain became increasingly associated in the popular imagination with a Machiavellian excess of plotting—from Jesuit plans for world domination to the Gunpowder Plot to the machinations of Gondomar—English plays turned to Spain both as a fertile source of literary plots and a rich, all-purpose Mediterranean setting for stories of intrigue and betrayal. The tension between reviled plotting Spaniards and desired Spanish plots animates a corpus that relies on Spain more often than we might imagine.

The Taming of the Shpanish

The Spanish plays of Middleton and his collaborators frame Spain in a variety of ways, alternately invoking and confuting stereotypes, deterritorializing Spanishness into a kind of all-purpose Mediterranean Machiavellianism, fixing it via allegory, or, as in *The Spanish Gypsy*, reveling in the contradictions that made the play appealing in a confusing political moment. In what follows, I turn to a different vector of the Spanish connection, focusing on the Jacobean playwright who made the most frequent use of Spanish sources, and

particularly of Cervantes's prose oeuvre. From the novella "La señora Cornelia" to the Byzantine romance *Los trabajos de Persiles y Sigismunda*, Cervantes
provides the source for a number of Fletcher's plays.[37] Yet as Gordon Mc-
Mullan perceptively notes, Fletcher's prefatory poems to *The Rogue*, Mabbe's
translation of Alemán's *Guzmán de Alfarache*, which I discussed in Chapter 1,
attempt to "separate literary appreciation from political implication."[38] Ven-
triloquizing the Spanish rogue, Fletcher challenges the view of the Spaniard as
plotting Machiavellian:

> I come no Spy, nor take
> A Factious part; No sound of Warre I make,
> But against sinne; I land no forraine mates;
> For Vertues Schooles should Free be in all states.[39]

Instead, Fletcher announces a common literary concern with exposing vice.
As McMullen suggests, Fletcher's praise of the rogue Guzmán for his "strange
bifronted posture," which "can better teach by worse meanes," expresses an
aesthetic based on irony, a central tenet of Fletcher's own production.[40] As
I will argue below, the ironies attendant upon the use of Spanish sources are
multiple, and only partially contained by the author's own nationalist sympathies, or even his "politics of unease," as McMullen fruitfully terms it.

Fletcher's Cervantine penchant, perceptively discussed by McMullen, has
been addressed in recent criticism, most thoroughly in Alexander Samson's
overview, "'Last Thought upon a Windmill'?: Cervantes and Fletcher." Yet the
1624 *Rule a Wife and Have a Wife* has been largely ignored, despite its popularity in its day.[41] The play combines two Spanish sources: the lively *comedia
El sagaz Estacio, marido examinado*, by Salas Barbadillo (apparently never published before 1620, although authorized for publication in 1613), and the better
known Cervantes novella, "El casamiento engañoso" ("The Deceitful Marriage," published as one of the *Novelas ejemplares* in 1613).[42] Like *The Spanish
Gypsy* and *A Game at Chess*, *Rule a Wife* was first staged during the public up-
roar at the ever-postponed "Spanish match," a mere three months after Middleton's *succès de scandale*. Yet unlike Middleton, who resorts to color-coded
allegory to address the disappointments of the failed match, Fletcher weaves a
jingoistic thread into his very *translatio*, evoking English triumphs over Spain
at a particularly fraught point in the relations between the two nations.

The context for *Rule a Wife* includes both the geopolitcal events and
their unsubtle dramatic rendition in Middleton's allegory. Fletcher's Prologue

pointedly reminds the audience of both the earlier play and the dynastic debacle:

> doe not your looks let fall,
> Nor to remembrance our late errors call,
> Because this day w'are Spaniards all againe,
> The story of our Play, and our Sceane Spaine:
> The errors too, doe not for this cause hate,
> Now we present their wit and not their state.
>
> (Prologue, 3–8)

The distinction between "wit" and "state" nicely renders the English fascination with Spanish culture despite political and religious differences. Even as it recalls the success of *A Game at Chess*, *Rule a Wife* distances itself from its predecessor's more blatant allegories of state, presumably to avoid a similar repression. Tongue firmly in cheek, the Prologue also reassures the ladies in the audience that the "grosse errors" they will see on stage, of a wanton beauty seeking "to abuse her husband," would never occur in their own kingdom (9–12). From the start, then, the play foregrounds the comparison between the two nations, and the delicate business of representing for the sake of pleasure a reviled popular enemy, who nonetheless provides abundant material for the English stage.

Fletcher resolves this tension by staging the comeuppance of the rich Spanish intended. As its title suggests, *Rule a Wife and Have a Wife* revolves around marriage. In the main plot, a lascivious wealthy lady of loose morals, Margarita, seeks a compliant husband as cover for her erotic adventures. She is tricked into marrying the foolish soldier Leon, only to find him transformed into an exacting husband (echoes of Shakespeare's Petrucchio) when it is too late. Subdued, Margarita recognizes Leon's dominion over her, accepts her fate, and agrees to become a properly subservient wife. Leon triumphantly tames his wife and takes possession of her person and property, reasserting his masculine privilege while enriching himself in the process. If the Stuart "Spanish marriage" founders because of Spain's insistence that it has the right to dictate the terms of the union, Fletcher rewrites the dynamic in his play as the triumph of a wily husband over a dominating, over-assured Spanish wife. In the picaresque subplot, meanwhile, a soldier and a disreputable serving-woman trick each other into marriage, only to discover that they have been conned in return by their victim—there is no taming here, only a sustained connection between marriage, wealth, and misrepresentation.

In its main plot, *Rule a Wife* distinctly renders the proposed dynastic union between England and Spain as an act of pillage. Margarita's riches are much more important in Fletcher's version than in the Spanish source; even the heroine's name (Marcela in the original) has been changed to emphasize the wealth of the Spanish bride, referred to by one of her suitors as "the pearle of Spaine, the orient faire one, the rich one too" (3.3.33–34).[43] Leon, the husband who tricks her and gains possession of all her riches, recalls the lions of English royal heraldry, in what is perhaps a more subtle reference to the prince's proposed marriage. But the most explicit connection of this farcical domestic comedy to the fraught stage of international relations comes through a minor character, the usurer Cacafogo, who is entirely Fletcher's invention. While the name is partly a scatological joke, it is most pointedly a reference to Elizabethan attacks on Spain, recalling for readers a highly romanticized moment of English privateering and plunder. In compensation for the humiliations of the Jacobean rapprochements, Fletcher evokes Elizabethan heroics against Spain. For the *Cacafuego* was, famously, the spectacular Spanish prize that Francis Drake captured on his circumnavigation (1577–80), an event described in the narrative of that voyage:

> It fortuned that John Drake going up into the top, descried her about three of the clocke, and about sixe of the clocke we came to her and boorded her, and shotte at her three peeces of ordnance, and strake downe her Misen, and being entered, we found in her great riches, as jewels and precious stones, thirteene chests full of royals of plate, foure score pound weight of golde, and six and twentie tunne of silver.[44]

The routine personification of the Spanish ship as female (tellingly, here, a penetrated female) in the narrative of Drake's voyage anticipates the metaphorics of nuptial pillage in Fletcher's play, in which both Margarita, the Spanish pearl, and the hapless Cacafogo will serve to enrich Leon.

The playwright makes a point of foregrounding the reference to Drake, lest his audience miss it. Cacafogo is a bit of the roaring boy, emboldened by his recent inheritance. When he first comes on stage, he announces: "My Fathers dead: I am a *man of warre* too, / Moynes, demeanes; I have ships at sea too, captaines" (1.5.33–34). He is first warned about Dutch pirates: "Take heed o'the Hollanders, your ship may leake else" (1.5.36), but the text soon gets to the real piracy in question. After Cacafogo bullies Leon, the usurer's companion tells him: "You have scap'd by miracle, there is not in all Spaine,

/ A spirit of more fury then [sic] this *fire drake*" (1.5.51–52).[45] These not-so-subtle nudges from the author suggest that there is more at work here than mere onomastic coincidence. Elizabethan heroics haunt the play; while they may appear simply as faint echoes in a farcical context, they signal *Rule a Wife*'s investment in Anglo-Spanish rivalry as popular dramatic and political currency. The comical Cacafogo serves to remind the audience of the time before the proposed "Spanish marriage," and of their most antagonistic feelings toward Spain. As Cacafogo evolves from Leon's rival for Margarita's hand to rich victim of the newlyweds' subterfuge, pillage becomes also a means to reconciliation, providing the embattled couple with a shared sense of purpose. The arrogant Spaniard—a familiar caricature—is brought low through trickery and becomes the play's scapegoat.

The humbling of Cacafogo is actually preceded by a striking scene of Spanish disarmament. When Leon first puts an end to Margarita's escapades, his wife's former lover, the Duke, assigns him a false command to fight in Flanders. Leon calls the lovers' bluff, however, by ordering that his untrustworthy wife, and all the household goods, accompany him. The Duke confidently taunts Leon, "I saw your mind was wedded to the warre, / And knew you would prove some good man for your country" (4.3.95–96), but once his plot is revealed no-one goes to war. Instead, Leon decides to visits Margarita's "Land ith Indies" (4.3.199), later amended to her peaceful "country house" (5.3.1). Although the Duke presents Leon with a captaincy—a "true comission" (5.5.160)—to make amends at the end of the play, any warring is projected far off into the future, when Margarita will "deliver [Leon] to the blew Neptune" (5.5.175). For the space of the play, the domestic conflict suffices to contain Spanish military expeditions; alternatively, the fighting in Flanders is never more than a pretext for domestic misrule.[46]

Yet if the main plot seems audacious in its use of a Spanish source to stage the triumph over a Spanish wife and the neutralization of Spain, the Cervantine subplot somewhat complicates matters. The redoubled intertextuality produces a text that is far more ambiguous in its message, as the deceitful marriage of soldier and serving-woman, so closely copied from Cervantes, casts a skeptical, even ironic shadow on the main plot. Both marriages, after all, depend on misrepresentations, but in the subplot no-one wins, and there is no patriarchal or national triumph to redeem the trickery. Here the problem of translation and adaptation from the Spanish becomes truly interesting: while Fletcher's text undoubtedly references the Spanish marriage, the rather simplistic jingoism of its allusion is undone precisely by the breadth of his borrowing, and by the multiple intersections of plot and subplot with each other and with their redoubled sources. In producing an intertextual Spanish match—one that refers to Spain, takes from Spain, yet draws on Spain—the text reveals itself as far more hybrid a product than its strident nationalism would suggest.

The overriding irony of such a text lies in plundering Spanish materials to stage an allegorical victory over Spain. Yet this tension would be obvious only to bilingual, sophisticated readers or viewers of *Rule a Wife*, and would not impede the general audience's enjoyment of the dramatic put-down. Fletcher's appropriation thus participates in the poetics of piracy that I chart throughout this study, which recasts English co-optation of foreign texts to England's advantage.[47] A key example of this pirated corpus, *Rule a Wife and Have a Wife* provides invaluable evidence of the vexed dynamics of cultural indebtedness and national distinction that characterize Anglo-Spanish drama. Yet it also reminds us that despite the proliferation of stereotypes and appropriations that I have charted throughout this chapter, *translatio* remains fundamentally unstable, and cannot necessarily be placed at the service of a particular ideology, particularly once plays are published and read instead of simply performed. Literary history might thus be charged with reconstructing not only the rhetorical valence of a performance in its own time, but also how that valence shifts in subsequent, retrospective rereadings or restagings.[48] While this is a fraught operation when the original text is lost, as in the case of the Shakespeare and Fletcher *Cardenio* that I discuss in Chapters 4 and 5, redactions and recreations provide abundant evidence of the text's inherent interest.

Chapter 4

Cardenio Lost and Found

A drama cannot be national and take during its formative period any elements which are not born out of the spirit of the people themselves.
—Rudolf Schevill

With the 400th anniversary of *Don Quijote* in 2005 and of the 1612 Shelton translation in 2012, Shakespeare and Fletcher's lost *Cardenio*, based on the unhinged lover-turned-wild-man in the first part of Cervantes's novel, has moved center stage, in a series of academic, dramatic, and popular reconstructions. In this chapter and the next, I explore how the field of early modern English has negotiated *Cardenio*'s absent presence, and the role its disappearance has played in how we read Anglo-Spanish relations in early modern drama. I turn in this chapter to the textual history of the early *Cardenio* and to the theoretical assumptions underlying the search for the lost text; Chapter 5 explores how contemporary scholars, playwrights, and directors have attempted to supply its loss with a burgeoning collection of *Cardenios* for our time. While the critical and creative interventions I chart in these chapters all trade in Shakespeare's cultural capital, their very multiplicity challenges notions of Shakespearean singularity. The Cervantine sources of *Cardenio*, moreover, allow us to rethink the national parameters of a literary history in which Shakespeare takes center stage and recognize instead the transnational context out of which national canons are wrought.

"None but himself can be his parallel"

Cardenio may or may not be entirely lost to us, and this ambiguity in part explains the enduring critical and popular fascination with the play. As is by now well established, we know of the play's existence from two seventeenth-century references. In 1612–13, Shakespeare's company, the King's Men, was paid for two performances of *Cardenno* or *Cardenna* at court.[1] On September 9, 1653, publisher and bookseller Humphrey Moseley entered *The History of Cardenio* on the Stationer's Register, as a play written "by Mr. Fletcher. & Shakespeare" (with the telling extra end-stop before the second name), although there is no extant trace of subsequent publication. Yet that is not the end of the story. In 1727, Shakespearean editor and adapter Lewis Theobald produced *Double Falshood, or The Distrest Lovers*, a play based on the erotic misadventures of the interpolated narratives in *Don Quijote*. When the play was published in 1728, the title page helpfully explained: "Written Originally by W. Shakespeare; And now Revised and Adapted to the Stage by Mr. Theobald, the Author of *Shakespeare Restor'd*."[2] While foregrounding his authority as a Shakespearean editor, Theobald claimed that this text was his version of a Shakespeare play "built upon a Novel in *Don Quixot*," and based on several manuscripts in his possession.[3]

While we cannot know what the plot of the missing *Cardenio* might have been, the appeal of the Cervantes source material is evident. In part I of *Don Quijote*, Cervantes narrates the unfortunate loves of Cardenio, Luscinda, Fernando, and Dorotea, mismatched couples struggling to transcend class differences and avoid the tragic consequences of erotic competition. Don Quijote barely participates in the action. His role is primarily to serve as an audience for the complex reconstructed narration of the lovers' adventures, which he, and the reader, must piece together from papers found in an abandoned suitcase, the story intermittently told by the mad Cardenio in rare moments of lucidity, the partial account of her own seduction by a ruined maid dressed as a shepherd, and the almost magical coincidences that bring all parties to the same inn. Reordered, the plot reads as follows. The noble Fernando, Cardenio's so-called friend, plans to steals Cardenio's beloved Luscinda after being moved by his glowing description of her, and sends Cardenio to the court on a fool's errand. Luscinda manages to send him a message warning that she is to be forced to marry Fernando, and Cardenio rushes back. Hidden behind a curtain, Cardenio is unable to stop the wedding, at which Luscinda whispers her assent before falling into a dead faint. Cardenio goes mad at the perceived double betrayal by his friend and his beloved, and seeks refuge in the mountains, where he is fed by kindly shepherds despite his occasional violent attacks on them. Fernando's new adventure leads him, in turn, to abandon Dorotea, the rich farmer's daughter he had earlier seduced with a promise of marriage. Dorotea cross-dresses to pursue her faithless lover and restore her honor, as she, too, flees to the mountains. Meanwhile, Luscinda takes refuge in a convent from which Fernando forcibly removes her. In a suspenseful sequence, the four characters all arrive by chance at the same fateful inn. There virtue triumphs over rank as the noble seducer Fernando is forced to recognize the excellence of his supposedly inferior victim Dorotea. Through her irrefutable arguments, all are reunited with their rightful partners.

The intersections of this plot with the preoccupations of early modern English drama are patent: while these lovers' primary antagonists are not their elders, they must nonetheless validate their love-matches against convention and class-bound expectations. This is achieved largely through the transition into the liminal space of the Sierra Morena, akin to Shakespeare's "green world." Cross-dressing provides the injured heroine Dorotea with mobility and agency, and the moment of her anagnorisis is highly charged. Most important, perhaps, the striving of that upwardly mobile, most recognizably modern character is rewarded with her marriage to Fernando, who is of much higher social standing than she.

Theobald's *Double Falshood* renames Cervantes's characters: instead of Cardenio, Luscinda, Fernando, and Dorotea, we have Julio, Leonora, Henriquez, and Violante. Leonora, Julio, and Henriquez's fathers all play larger roles, and, rather than relying on fate or coincidence, the resolution is orchestrated by Roderick, the villainous Henriquez's virtuous elder brother. The plot is also reordered into a chronological sequence, as dramatic immediacy replaces the suspense of Cervantes's partial and interrupted narration, and Don Quijote, whose presence in these stories is marginal in the source, disappears entirely.

Theobald's 1727 production was a great success, playing for ten nights at the Drury Lane Theater and creating, as Michael Dobson puts it, a "minor sensation."[4] Despite *Double Falshood's* popularity, however, Theobald's claim of a Shakespearean original was received with considerable skepticism, especially because he never produced the manuscripts in question.[5] Supporters pointed to the play's success as proof of Shakespearean greatness: "By the unanimous Applause, with which this Play was receiv'd by considerable Audiences, for *ten* nights, the true Friends of the *Drama* had the satisfaction of seeing that *Author* restor'd to his rightful Possession of the stage," claimed one "Dramaticus" in *The Weekly Journal or the British Gazetteer*,[6] deliberately recalling Theobald's earlier edition of "that *Author*," entitled *Shakespeare Restor'd*. Detractors also emphasized issues of "rightful possession," accusing the attorney's apprentice Theobald of stealing Shakespeare's name:

> See T——— leaves the Lawyer's gainful train,
> To wrack with poetry his tortur'd brain:
> Fir'd, or not fir'd, to write resolves with rage,
> And constant pores o'er SHAKESPEAR'S sacred page
> ————————Then starting cries, I something will be thought:
> I'll write—then—boldly swear 'twas SHAKESPEAR wrote.
>   Strange! He in Poetry no forgery fears,
>   That knows so well in Law he'd lose his ears.[7]

For this outraged critic, any similarity between the texts was no longer a matter of Renaissance *imitatio*, but a much more modern forgery trading on Shakespeare's name. If *Cardenio* first saw the light under the former regime, that is, by the time Theobald attempted to capitalize on the Shakespearean provenance of *Double Falshood* the notion of authorial property had evolved so that his claim registered as a crime against intellectual property.

The larger quarrel was over the intellectual ownership of Shakespeare himself, into which Theobald had charged with his *Shakespeare Restor'd*, sharply correcting Alexander Pope's edition of *Hamlet*.[8] Situating the *Cardenio* debates in this broader contest over Shakespearean authority, Howard Marchitello argues that the very notion of proprietary authorship depends on proprietary editorship, placing Theobald at the crux of these developments:

> Theobald's Shakespearean work represents a critical moment in the development of the modern idea of authorship—in the figure of the author made available, that is, by the consolidation of those cultural forces encrypted within the discourse of the monument. Moreover, the emergence of proprietary authorship was enabled by the prior development of proprietary editorship—an accomplishment that was achieved, it is worth stressing, primarily by people such as Theobald (and also Rowe and Pope before him, and Edmond Malone and Edward Dowden after, to name only a few of the major figures in this history), specifically through their efforts in the editing of Shakespeare and in the production of an approximately stable Shakespeare canon.[9]

Although Marchitello himself privileges the kind of editorial practice that emerges in the early eighteenth century over much earlier editorial projects, such as Ben Jonson's publication of his own works, or the First Folio, he usefully reminds us of the role of the modern editor in constructing an author and a canon.

The tension between Theobald's editorial work and his argument for a Shakespearean *Double Falshood* can be traced in the published—and unpublished—versions of the play. Theobald's initial claims are striking in their bald desire to connect Shakespeare to the excellence of the play. In the preface to the first published version of *Double Falshood* he argues that, despite the text's marked resemblance to Fletcher, its quality marks it as Shakespearean:

> Others again, to depreciate the Affair, as they thought, have been pleased to urge, that tho' the Play may have some Resemblances of Shakespeare, yet the Colouring, Diction,and Characters, come nearer to the Style and Manner of Fletcher. This, I think, is far from deserving any Answer; I submit it to the Determination of better Judgments; tho' my Partiality for Shakespeare makes me wish, that Every Thing which is good, or pleasing, in our Tongue had been owing to his Pen.[10]

Yet the second edition, published scarcely two months later, registers Theobald's increasing recognition of Fletcher's role, as he changes his desideratum above to read: "my partiality for Shakespeare makes me wish, that Every Thing which is good, or pleasing, *in that other great poet,* had been owing to his Pen."[11] This bespeaks the more pragmatic desire, rather than to arrogate to Shakespeare every felicitous line written in English, merely to transfer to him whatever worthy lines his collaborator may have penned. As Brean Hammond notes, Theobald's reluctant recognition of Fletcher's role may explain why he neglected to include his discovery in his subsequent edition of Shakespeare, given his doubts "about its status as an unaided and unaltered work by Shakespeare."[12]

Theobald's neat identification of Shakespeare with "Every Thing which is good, or pleasing, in our Tongue" long served as the guiding principle in studies of *Cardenio/Double Falshood*, so that any doubts about their authorship and attribution stemmed from a priori notions of Shakespeare's unalienable excellence. As John Freehafer noted years ago, "The internal evidence for Shakespeare's authorship is persuasive, but not compelling enough to convince those who can see his hand in nothing but work of supreme literary excellence."[13] Or, as Kenneth Muir put it even earlier, "one can understand the desire to relieve Shakespeare of all responsibility for a play which, at least in its present form, can add nothing to his reputation."[14] For critics convinced of Shakespeare's greatness, any falling away from such excellence signaled instead the hand of Theobald, or, for those more willing to believe in Theobald's "Shakespearean" manuscripts, of the inferior collaborator, Fletcher. More recent studies have focused on the role of Fletcher, although even these assess the play for its distance from the impossible benchmark of indisputably Shakespearean language: "Thus we see that echoes of Shakespeare, if they are not evidence of Shakespeare's authorship, might as easily be the work of Fletcher as of Theobald."[15] Ironically, it is the presence of Fletcher that ultimately suggests the hand of Shakespeare, since there would be no reason for Theobald to write like Fletcher if he were attempting a forgery of a Shakespearean original.[16] As Marchitello eloquently puts it, "We are always in the process of finding *Cardenio*, and when we do we are made to confront a set of related issues that together serve as the ground for the invention of Shakespeare—not only in the early decades of the eighteenth century, and the emergence during that important moment of what I will call proprietary editorship, but even in our own time, which witnesses still the endless process of the invention and reinvention of Shakespeare."[17]

Studies of *Double Falshood* are symptomatic of a certain cult of Shakespeare that fetishizes the original Bard, the hand of the master, the inimitable creation. Questions of intellectual property, authenticity, and origins are of paramount importance, but the inquiry itself is carefully charted so that all philological roads lead to Shakespeare. Even a highly sophisticated recent study, Tiffany Stern's widely noted article in *Shakespeare Quarterly*, is laden with the language of value where Shakespearean authenticity is concerned, and far less interested in Fletcher's possible role in the text. Regardless whether the end result is to proclaim Shakespeare's role in the text or deny it, the Shakespearean imprimatur remains the marker of authenticity and excellence.

The burgeoning field of textual studies has convincingly exposed the "romantic aesthetic obsessions with unity and individuality" that underlie such critical desiderata for the one, privileged Author.[18] As Leah Marcus cogently puts it,

> What if, rather than flowing effortlessly and magically from Shakespeare's mind onto the unalterable fixity of paper, the plays were from

the beginning provisional, amenable to alterations by the playwright or others, coming to exist over time in a number of versions, all related, but none of them an original in the pristine sense promised by Heminge and Condell? Nothing we know about conditions of production in the Renaissance playhouse allows us to hope for single authoritative versions of the plays.[19]

Yet despite these vigorous challenges, the dubious text continues to live or die by its relationship to an idealized Shakespeare; its only claim to fame its evanescent link to the Bard. No-one is interested in discredited apocrypha, also-rans in the contest for canonicity, however fascinating these may prove in their own right; what sustains critical attention to these texts is the hope of catching a glimpse, a whiff, a ghost of Shakespeare. The line I take as my title for this section—"None but himself can be his parallel"—and which Pope singled out as a particularly infelicitous imposture by Theobald,[20] encapsulates the reflexive nature of these philological inquiries.

Discussions of *Cardenio* or *Double Falshood* have largely limited themselves to the problem of authorship, with only a few exceptions that venture to imagine its missing content. In an ambitious historicist attempt by Richard Wilson to place *Cardenio* in its 1612 context, using the text of *Double Falshood*, he reads *Cardenio/Double Falshood* as a thinly veiled allegory of the Frances Howard case, thus explaining the odd performance at court of a play full of hearses and interrupted nuptials precisely at the time of Prince Henry's death and the betrothal of Princess Elizabeth to the Elector Palatine.[21] While I find Wilson's reading highly provocative, I am not ultimately convinced that we can relate to Jacobean politics an eighteenth-century text that may share only a story-line with its predecessor, and, in the best case, presents Shakespeare and Fletcher's text with a heavy overlay of eighteenth-century concerns. Thus in what follows I limit my own reading of the *Cardenio/Double Falshood* dyad to the curious erasures in the latter's paratexts, which enact Shakespearean greatness at the expense of his sources.

Simply to limn other possible lines of inquiry, one might mention the striking use of transvestism in the text. Whereas Cervantes returns the cross-dressed Dorotea to feminine dress long before she challenges her seducer, in *Double Falshood* the equivalent character, Violante, is presented to Henriquez still dressed as a boy. As the "page" insists that Henriquez has "won my Youth, and Duty, from my Father"[22] a set of rich double entendres ensues, which Wilson reads in terms of the relations between James and his minions. The reliance on cross-dressing for spectacular anagnorisis suggests a direct connection to Elizabethan and Jacobean theatrical practice. Beyond the intense interest in the equivocation of gender that marks so much early modern drama in both England and Spain, is there anything specifically English about this substitution? Do the early modern prohibition against actresses on the English commercial stage and the gender trouble it enables leave their traces on the much later redaction? Without any certainties about the text, these questions must remain speculative where *Cardenio* is concerned. In more general terms, one could certainly conjecture about the appeal of Cervantes to the Jacobean playwrights—his ironic yet probing investigation of familial and social identity, class mobility, and the inalienability of the individual's choice in marriage all translated well to an English setting. Yet this attraction, so evident elsewhere in the English dramatic canon, cannot actually be documented for an absent text.

The absence of *Cardenio* has not impeded its notional place in the Shakespearean canon. The second edition of both the *Oxford Shakespeare* and the *Norton Shakespeare* based on it include "*Cardenio*: A Brief Account," in their lists of plays, as a placeholder for the lost text.[23] (As I note in Chapter 5, Gary Taylor and Stephen Greenblatt, two of the scholars involved in these major editions, have each produced a recreation of *Cardenio*.) The 2010 publication of *Double Falshood* in the Arden Shakespeare, in Hammond's edition, significantly advances that play's claims to some kind of Shakespearean genealogy, both because of Hammond's detailed if somewhat speculative reconstruction of the possible transmission of a Jacobean text through a Restoration adaptation and into the hands of Theobald, and, crucially, by conferring on it the Arden imprimatur. The benefit is mutual: Arden sells a "new" "Shakespeare" play, while *Double Falshood* is adopted into the canon. Yet it is possible to consider this transaction in a more generous light: surely one of the effects of this addition to the Arden Shakespeare, however unintended, is to chip away at the sterling, single-author Shakespeare canon that has held critical sway for so long. In this sense, the canonization of *Double Falshood* corresponds to new and more nuanced critical understandings of the role of collaboration and transmission in the construction of what we know as a "Shakespeare play." It updates the canon not, as the popular press would have it, through a miraculous discovery, but through the recognition of different modes of being Shakespearean. Jonathan Gil Harris reaches a similar conclusion when he states, "The edition's inclusion in the Arden Shakespeare series may just have the edifying effect of making us realize how *all* 'authentic' Shakespeare is spectral, riddled with the traces of other absent presences—including our desire for authentic Shakespeare."[24]

Hammond's exhaustive introduction reviews the critical literature, evaluating the evidence for possible modes of transmission, on the one hand, and traces of Shakespearean and Fletcherian language, on the other. His central discovery is that of a Bodleian manuscript catalogue listing "*The History of Cardeino* [sic] by Fletcher & Shakespear" among the Moseley copyrights assigned to Jacob Tonson the Younger in 1718. Tonson commissioned Pope's edition of Shakespeare and was one of the publishers of Theobald's, and so may have been the source for his knowledge of the play and perhaps even the manuscript(s) of the same.[25]

None of this solves the fundamental problem that a play with some traces of Shakespeare and Fletcher is still quite far from being a Shakespeare/Fletcher play, or the impossibility of reconstructing that play retrospectively. Hence the carefully delimited claims, both in the "General Editor's Preface": "This edition makes its own cautious case for Shakespeare's participation in the genesis of the play,"[26] and frequently in Hammond's own introduction. The latter announces at the start, "This introduction posits some relationship between the lost play performed in 1613 and the play printed in 1728,"[27] and then, only slightly less cautiously, states: "This edition complicates the story by suggesting that Theobald could have known and probably did know, that there was a Cardenio play and that in 1718 it may have been acquired by the publishing firm claiming to own the sole rights to publish the works of Shakespeare, that of Jacob Tonson."[28]

It is hard to argue with the most careful version of these claims, even if their modesty often seems at odd with their confident publication in the Arden Shakespeare, which has the effect of completely erasing Theobald from the book's cover or title page. Bernard Richards, in a review of Hammond's edition, beautifully sums up the problem with the philological hunt for Shakespearean "DNA": "Shakespeare" that sounds most like Shakespeare is itself suspicious, as the evidence for authenticity—"it sounds just like Hamlet/ Antony and Cleopatra/Much Ado/etc."—collapses into the evidence for deliberate falsification.[29] My point here is not to weigh Hammond's claims, which remain in the salutary realm of conjecture, by engaging in my own philological excursus, but to show what gets left out of his exhaustive inquiry.

What are the costs of circumscribing our inquiry into *Cardenio* to the enduring trace of Shakespeare? The disappearance of *Cardenio*, and the protracted discussions of Shakespeare and Fletcher's possible hand in *Double Falshood*, obscure what I see as the central issue. For the obsession with a Shakespearean *Cardenio* masks what otherwise should be no surprise: the widespread reliance by English dramatists of the early modern era on contemporary Spanish prose, and particularly on Cervantes, which I have charted in earlier chapters. While recent essays on Fletcher, Cervantes, and the Jacobean stage by Alexander Samson and Trudi Darby attempt to correct this elision, few critics extrapolate from Fletcher to the general availability and seductiveness of Spanish source material.[30] Hammond dwells briefly on the context that would have produced the Shakespeare/Fletcher *Cardenio*, yet emphasizes personal Hispanophile networks and incidental connections. Stern expands on this context for the eighteenth century, charting Theobald's own fascination with Cervantes and his possible role in a contemporary novella, *The Adventures on the Black Mountains*, which relates the Cardenio plot in language that very closely follows Shelton's 1612 translation of *Don Quijote*.[31] Yet her elucidation of the eighteenth-century connections does not address the earlier history: as I have shown in this volume, there is widespread engagement with Spanish materials in this period, even at moments when relations with Spain are most strained, as in the aftermath of the failed Spanish match, and by playwrights least likely to have political or religious sympathy for Spain, such as Middleton or Fletcher himself.

The emphasis on Cervantes's early reception in England in recent years is a salutary corrective to the obsessive search for *Cardenio*. Yet the fascination with Spanish materials was not limited to *Don Quijote*, and the focus on this exceptional source, often treated as an honorary English novel, leaves the larger story of the substantial connection with Spain untold. Even to dwell on Cervantes for a moment, however, and consider his larger influence on English literary production, as two recent collections do, is to recognize how relatively unimportant *Cardenio* appears in the larger context of the English reception of Cervantes.[32] That is, however compelling *Cardenio* proves in Shakespeare studies as a tantalizing marker and endless philological detective game, it is insignificant in comparison to the abundant corpus of extant plays that take from Spain, and to the wider currency of Spanish literature in England. Although both Ardila's *The Cervantean Heritage* and Randall and Boswell's *Cervantes in Seventeenth-Century England* largely fail to theorize the implications of the Cervantine *translatio* that they identify, the sheer number of texts they cite, not only on the stage but across the disciplines, provide an important corrective to the neglect of Anglo-Spanish borrowings in the field. The multitude of instances confirms the two powerful, intertwined stories I have attempted to trace in this book: first, of the insistent turn to Spain for material even by strongly anti-Spanish writers in England, even at the times of greatest tensions with Spain, and, second, of English writers' awareness of developments in Spanish prose from an early date, long before the supposedly proprietary English birth of the novel.

Why do these stories nonetheless have so little purchase on the field, especially in comparison with the *Cardenio*-mania of recent years? My contention is that it is difficult to reconstruct a transnational literary history when literary history has organized itself along national lines. The situation is exacerbated for the case of Spain and England, given the *longue durée* of the "Armada paradigm" I have charted over the course of this book. Taking from Spain thus either goes unacknowledged or is subsumed into a history of violent appropriation and made analogous to the triumphal English supplanting of Spain as the world's most powerful empire. It is instructive in this sense to consider how the Elizabethan dyad of Shakespeare and the Armada has been rehearsed at later moments to signal English preeminence, in arms as in letters.

Poets and Privateers

Literary history has erected Elizabethan and Jacobean drama as great national monuments, with the playwright ensconced in the pantheon of plucky Englishness somewhere between Elizabeth and her dashing privateers. Beyond the facile myth, the early modern national theater clearly accompanies the consolidation of the nation-state. Shakespeare, in particular, has long occupied a central role in the construction of an exclusively national literary canon. Already in Ben Jonson's elegiac "To the Memory of my Beloved, the Author Mr. William Shakespeare, and What He Hath Left Us," which prefaced the 1623 folio, the playwright disports himself for the English monarchs:

> Sweet Swan of Avon! what a sight it were
> To see thee in our water yet appear,
> And make those flights upon the banks of Thames
> That so did take Eliza, and our James!

While Jonson's Shakespeare rises above Chaucer, Spenser, Beaumont, "our Lyly," Kyd, and Marlowe, his greatness simultaneously summons forth the canon of English writers.[33] Just as crucially, Jonson places Shakespeare over "all that insolent Greece or haughty Rome / Sent forth; or since did from their ashes come," exclaiming, "Triumph, my Britain! Thou hast one to show / To whom all scenes of Europe homage owe." What he hath left us, it seems, is a well-defined national canon that places Shakespeare at the apex not only of English but of European cultural productions.

As I observed in Chapter 1, while it might be tempting to dismiss the "puffery" of elegies or commendatory poetry as so much conventional flattery, the terms of praise invoked can tell us much about historical standards for literary value and cultural capital. Strikingly, the terms of Jonson's early praise of Shakespeare as constituent of the nation's greatness recur in the pedestrian poetry that frames *Double Falshood*. Although Dobson does not discuss these texts, they seem like signal examples of "the extensive cultural work that went into the installation of Shakespeare as England's National Poet."[34]

The prologue to *Double Falshood*, by poet and dramatist Philip Frowde, plants Shakespeare's native genius firmly in a fertile English landscape:

> As in some Region, where indulgent Skies
> Enrich the Soil, a thousand Plants arise
> Frequent and bold; a thousand Landskips meet
> Our ravisht View, irregularly sweet:
> We gaze, divided, now on These, now Those;
> While All one beauteous Wilderness compose.
>
> Such Shakespeare's Genius was:—Let Britons boast
> The glorious Birth, and, eager, strive who most
> Shall celebrate his Verse; for while we raise
> Trophies of Fame to him, ourselves we praise:
> Display the Talents of a British mind,
> Where All is great, free, open, unconfin'd.
> Be it our Pride, to reach his daring Flight;
>   And relish Beauties, he alone could write.

By comparing Shakespeare's genius not simply to the landscape but to the ocular possession thereof, the prologue conflates literary excellence and sovereignty and makes of the literary terrain a national property.[35] In an illuminating paradox, Shakespeare is at once unique and representative of "a British mind," a source of pride for patriotic Britons.

Originality is for Frowde the defining quality of the Bard's genius:

Most modern Authors, fearful to aspire,
With Imitation cramp their genial Fire;
The well-schemed Plan keep strict before their Eyes,
Dwell on Proportions, trifling Decencies;
While noble Nature all neglected lies.
Nature, that claims Precedency of Place,
Perfection's Basis, and essential Grace!
Nature so intimately Shakespeare knew,
From her first Springs his Sentiments he drew;
Most greatly wild they flow; and, when most wild, yet true.[36]

Frowde is so intent on contrasting Shakespeare to the neoclassical follies of his age that he completely elides the basis of *Double Falshood* not in the "first Springs" of "noble Nature" but in an earlier Spanish text. [37] While Shakespeare was persistently associated with "Nature" from the publication of the First Folio, as Margreta de Grazia has noted, the claim here occludes not just any predecessors, but specifically the Spanish original on which the play is based.[38] Despite Theobald's own acknowledgment that the play is based on "Don Quixot," Frowde keeps Shakespeare pure and wild like the originary springs. Here, truly, is the "effortless and magical" Shakespeare that Marcus challenges.

The epilogue (printed, for some reason, before the play itself), "Written by a Friend," pokes fun at the earnest "Gothick" morals of the characters, comparing them unfavorably with the sophistication of the modern, "reforming" age. Yet it ends with a sincere paean to Shakespearean patriots:

In Shakespeare's Age the English Youth inspir'd,
Lov'd, as they fought, by him and Beauty fir'd.
'Tis yours to crown the Bard, whose Magick Strain
Cou'd charm the Heroes of that glorious Reign,
Which humbled to the Dust the Pride of Spain.

While the prologue simply sweeps all predecessors under the green rug of natural Shakespearean inspiration, the epilogue pointedly avoids the fact that Spain—dusty though her pride might be—provided the source material for the play the audience is encouraged to applaud. Together, the paratexts erase the play's source in Cervantes to enshrine Shakespeare as origin and bathe the text in nostalgia for Elizabethan exploits both poetic and pugnacious.

In his recent edition of *Double Falshood*, Hammond contextualizes the jingoism of the paratexts by noting how by the 1720s Shakespeare himself had become a powerful brand of Englishness, to be sought after and fought over by different political factions. Hammond notes "a general sense that Shakespeare, rapidly coming to be seen as the greatest voice of his country's Elizabethan golden age, was himself worth co-opting as a spokesman of supposedly timeless and national virtues."[39] Crucially, Shakespeare serves to effect restoration and restitution—operations analogous to those of the editor of mangled texts (*Shakespeare Restor'd*) or the redactor of lost plays (*Double Falshood*). In this sense, the framing of *Double Falshood* aligns itself perfectly with Theobald's earlier project, the *Memoirs of Sir Walter Raleigh*, which he published in 1719.

In this strongly jingoistic text, which Hammond describes as "hagiographic," Theobald mounts a defense of Raleigh the privateer against Spanish intrigues, restoring the reputation tarnished by his execution under James. Christine Gerrard identifies Raleigh as the most useful figure for channeling what she calls "political Elizabethanism" in the era: whereas it was somewhat challenging to claim Elizabeth herself as a promoter of the British empire, given her "personal reluctance to initiate colonial expansion," Raleigh, "As a naval hero, poet, historian, and Renaissance man of letters who incurred the disfavour of the monarchy. . . became a potent symbol for patriotic values held in contempt by the administration." So strong was this identification of Raleigh with British greatness, Gerrard argues, that "The Elizabethan naval cult might in one sense more properly be called a Ralegh cult."[40]

In restoring Raleigh, Theobald revives the notorious figure of the Spanish ambassador Gondomar, who figures so prominently in seventeenth-century accounts of Machiavellian Spanish plotting (including, as I note in Chapter 3, Middleton's *A Game at Chess*) as the central antagonist to the brave and patriotic privateer. The subtitle announces: "In which are Inserted, The Private Intrigues between the Count of Gondamore, the Spanish Ambassador, and the Lord Salisbury, then Secretary of State."[41] Raleigh, Theobald notes, "had the Advantage of a stirring Age to second his Ambition," and proceeded to "humble the insolence of Spain"[42] at Cadiz and in the Azores. In Theobald's version, Raleigh fell from favor under James primarily because he resisted the peace with Spain. He thus becomes a synecdoche for an Elizabethan antagonism to Spain far preferable to Jacobean amity, and the unjust persecution of that earlier, glorious age by a latter and diminished one. Of the court context that leads to Raleigh's fall, Theobald observes:

Besides, the Spaniard was so powerful at that time at Court, as That
Faction could command the Life of any Man who might prove
dangerous to their Designs: And it was thought one of the greatest
Master-pieces of *Gondamore* to purchase *Raleigh*'s Head, who had done
their State such singular Mischiefs and with whom (as *Cato* of old us'd
to say, *Delenda est Carthago*;) it was a constant Maxim, *That* Spain *was to
be humbled.*[43]

The dastardly Gondomar is here revived as the perfect antagonist to the heroic Elizabethan privateer, brought low by court intrigue. The parenthetical
reference to Rome's war on Carthage succinctly invokes the larger project of
translatio imperii studiique that Raleigh espoused and Theobald revives.

The Machiavellian Gondomar's condemnation of Raleigh, which Theobald vividly ventriloquizes, is the strongest proof of his hero's excellence:

Gondamore, that look'd upon him as a Man that had not only high
Abilities, but Animosity enough to do his Master mischief, (being one of
those Scourges, which that *old Virago*, (Queen *Elizabeth*) as he call'd her,
used to afflict the *Spaniards* with) having gotten him into his Trap, laid
now his Baits about the King.[44]

In Theobald's heightened account, Raleigh becomes a martyr to the cause of
anti-Spanish sentiment and a conduit for Elizabethan nostalgia.

The *Memoirs*' evocation of a heroic, strongly anti-Spanish Elizabethan
era recurs repeatedly in the paratexts to *Double Falshood*, illuminating the
latter's seemingly incongruous turn to patriotism to introduce a romantic
comedy based on Spanish materials. The *Memoirs* evince a different order
of transmission from that which concerns Hammond: whether or not a
manuscript of *Cardenio* survived from the Jacobean to the Augustan age,
the suspicion of Spain and glorification of Elizabethan "humblings" thereof
certainly did.

Theobald's 1719 *Memoirs of Sir Walter Raleigh* and the various paratexts of *Double Falshood* both suggest the need to antedate the "political
Elizabethanism" that has been associated with the 1730s.[45] One might even
argue that the invocations of Elizabeth exert their ideological force more
widely over the course of the early modern period, even if they peak at
times such as the 1730s. For example, Dobson notes the continued association of Shakespeare with the "manlier, Spain-bashing days of 1588," citing

a slightly later anti-Gallican poem by Mark Akenside, "The Remonstrance of Shakespeare" (1749), in which the ghost of Shakespeare looks back on earlier glories:

> I saw this England break the shameful bands
> Forg'd for the souls of men by sacred hands,
> I saw each groaning realm her aid implore,
> Her sons the heroes of each warlike shore,
> Her naval standard (the dire Spaniards bane)
> Obeyed thro' all the circuit of the main;
> Then too great Commerce for a late-found world
> Around your coast her eager sails unfurl'd;
> New hopes new passions thence the bosom fir'd.
> New plans new arts the genius thence inspir'd,
> Thence ev'ry science which private fortune knows
> In stronger life with bolder spirit rose.[46]

Although the principal antagonist in this ode is not Spain but France, the poem shows how readily Shakespeare was yoked to an idealized, warlike version of Elizabeth's reign, in which military and literary glories fully coincided. When such Elizabethan fervor frames *Double Falshood*, however, one must assume either a willed blindness to its Spanish origins, or, more likely, a desire to treasure it as part of the loot poetic piracy yields.

Modern criticism has inherited some of the assumptions of these eighteenth-century enthusiasts. The quarrels over Shakespearean authorship, Shakespeare versus Fletcher, or even a Shakespeare-Fletcher collaboration versus a Theobaldian forgery, continue to erase Cervantes and the Spanish influence, as though that powerful fiction of Elizabethan supremacy had laid them to rest. The dispute thus remains a domestic one, concerned primarily with policing the internal borders of the Shakespearean or early modern dramatic canon, as the absence of *Cardenio* becomes the absence of Spain. As I have attempted to show throughout this book, however, in order to reconstruct fully the extent of England's turn to Spain, we need to read *extant* plays that draw on Spanish materials, albeit ones not graced by a connection to Shakespeare.

Parallels Versus Intersections

Would the discovery of an unassailable edition or manuscript of *Cardenio* change what we make of the Anglo-Spanish connection? It is hard to say. The play is most useful, as I have tried to suggest, for reminding us of what goes unexplored in early modern English drama. Yet surely, one might argue, scholars have compared the English and Spanish national theaters? Walter Cohen's groundbreaking Marxist study, *Drama of a Nation: Public Theater in Renaissance England and Spain* (1985), led to a surge of interest in the topic. Yet subsequent comparisons are constrained by a number of unspoken limitations. First, with very few exceptions, there is a strict regard for generic categories: most studies focus solely on the theater and discount the larger role of Spanish prose fiction in England. John Loftis (whose work on the topic actually predates Cohen's study), for example, seems much more interested in noting the paucity of influences from one theater to another than in analyzing how Spanish prose fiction was appropriated in English plays.[47] Yet if, as Barbara Mowat has argued, the obvious intertexts for drama range far beyond stage genres to a literary culture of much wider scope, surely this more capacious intertextuality should be considered when examining the transnational movement of texts.[48] Second, much of the recent work on England and Spain is a criticism of coincidence, with a tendency simply to juxtapose texts rather than exploring possible ideological complexities.[49] The comparative approach in this case has meant essentially placing artifacts side by side—recent collections have titles such as *Parallel Lives*, or *Comedias del Siglo de Oro and Shakespeare*—instead of finding more intricate, historically determined connections between the national literatures, or even interrogating their development as such.[50]

Most troubling, perhaps, is the fact that most of the scholars embarked on this comparative Anglo-Spanish enterprise work primarily on Spanish literature, the less esteemed and vocal of the two disciplines in our own academy. This contemporary institutional imbalance makes it difficult to recover the very different situation in the early modern period, with England as the latecomer to any sense of cultural authority. Early modern English writers looked to Spain for inspiration, and relied heavily on Spanish originals, yet our own academy, marked by the Black Legend and sustained anti-Spanish prejudice, is unable to recognize those early debts. When English specialists encounter England's abundant use of Spain, their first question is often, "What about the reverse?"—what did Spain take from England? The answer—that this exchange was largely one-sided, because Spain had the cultural capital England sought—rarely satisfies, as it fails to align with the entrenched relative standing of the disciplines in our own time.

The recent explosion of interest in *Cardenio* may finally yield a new wave of studies, less constrained by the often unwitting nationalism that has colored literary history, and Shakespeare studies in particular. Gregory Doran's "reimagined" *Cardenio* at the Royal Shakespeare Company, which I discuss in detail in Chapter 5, turns to *Don Quijote* to supply the scenes deemed missing from Theobald's *Double Falshood.* Valerie Wayne, in an essay, a short version of which appeared in the RSC *Cardenio* program, considers the intriguing possibility that *Don Quijote* may have influenced the turn to romance by Shakespeare and his collaborators.[51] The increased recognition of the importance of collaboration for the late Shakespeare has opened the door to studies of his partners, along with other contemporary playwrights for whom collaboration and the turn to Spain were habitual: Fletcher, of course, but also Beaumont, Middleton, Massinger, Rowley. Change might also come from the renewed interest in Golden Age theater in England, which may lead to a consideration by theater practitioners of how English plays rework Spanish materials.[52] Catherine Boyle, discussing the RSC's 2004 Spanish Golden Age season, endorses the decentering of Shakespeare, but reverts to the same language of rivalry I have identified in English literary history: "Accompanying the sense, shared by a number of critics, of the importance of the RSC fulfilling one of its core objectives—'to peer around the great bulk of Shakespeare at his contemporaries and examine to what extent he really was a stand-out genius'—was a thirst for a type of revelatory moment, when the audience and critics would recognize that they were in the presence of a masterpiece and faced with a tradition to rival the Elizabethans."[53] My own goal is neither revanchist philology nor the compensatory staging of Spanish materials, but instead to probe how we get the very idea of the Golden Age and English Renaissance drama as rivals, and to expose the far reach of what I have called the poetics of piracy.

Canon-formation, the apotheosis of the national playwright (or poet, or novelist), and the dissemination of a national tradition are operations that occur in a transnational as well as a national context. Restoring the multivalent and transhistorical Anglo-Spanish connection, I propose, quickly moves us beyond source studies, rivalries, and even the effort to demonstrate how English dramatists drew on Spanish texts of all sort, to a more sustained consideration of how national canons are made. The larger point of this work is not to redress the marginalization of early modern Spanish culture within

English studies, though this is an important first step. Instead, I hope to have demonstrated the ideological force of what is Englished, whether by authors, editors, critics, or readers, and how the erasures and transformations that they effect participate in the larger development of an insular national canon. Only by restoring their wider context can we transcend the powerful and long-standing fictions of native genius and exclusive national properties.

Chapter 5

Cardenios for Our Time

La España de charanga y pandereta,
cerrado y sacristía,
devota de Frascuelo y de María,
de espíritu burlón y de alma quieta,
ha de tener su mármol y su día,
su infalible mañana y su poeta.
—Antonio Machado

As the reception of *Double Falshood* both in the eighteenth century and in our own time demonstrates, the critical anxiety about finding the hand of "the Bard" in the play has largely occluded the important question of the early modern dramatic use of Spanish sources in England. I turn now to how the Spanish question recurs in contemporary recreations of the lost *Cardenio*, by the noted Shakespearean scholar Stephen Greenblatt and the playwright Charles Mee, on the one hand, and by the director Gregory Doran for the Royal Shakespare Company, on the other.[1] Their texts and productions suggest that matters of intellectual property and national belonging remain central to our own negotiation of an Anglo-Spanish heritage, in an ongoing and vibrant tussle over representation. Because of the tremendous stakes where the Shakespeare canon is concerned, the play continues to serve as a lightning rod for questions of attribution and originality. Moreover, as a marvelously efficient synecdoche for Cervantes and Shakespeare, the two most canonical figures in their respective national traditions, *Cardenio* remains a privileged site for exploring the complexities of literary transmission from Spain to England. In what follows, I explore how *translatio* changes in our own time, for practitioners faced with the exigencies of making classical theater viable and relevant in the modern world, even as transnational collaboration offers the occasion for redoubled *Cardenios*.

Disavowal

As the recipient of a Distinguished Humanist Award from the Mellon Foundation in 2002, Greenblatt decided to turn to playwriting in order to explore the "theatrical mobility" of texts, as he put it in the essay he later wrote about the experience.[2] Greenblatt's explicit interest lay in "what happens with materials being recycled, what happens when things are moved from one place to another, one culture to another, one mind to another."[3] Hence his affinity for the work of Charles Mee, whose plays rework classical sources, and whom Greenblatt admiringly describes as a "cunning recycler."[4] On Mee's website, *The (Re)Making Project*, which details his creative process, the playwright provocatively describes his work on his sources as pillaging, and invites others to repeat this operation on his own plays:

> Please feel free to take the plays from this website and use them freely as a resource for your own work: that is to say, don't just make some cuts or rewrite a few passages or re-arrange them or put in a few texts that you like better, but pillage the plays as I have pillaged the structures and contents of the plays of Euripides and Brecht and stuff out of Soap Opera Digest and the evening news and the internet, and build your own, entirely new, piece—and then, please, put your own name to the work that results.[5]

Yet there are limits to the use of the plays; certain kinds of taking clearly constitute piracy, less fancifully construed, in the playwright's eyes. He adds: "But, if you would like to perform the plays essentially or substantially as I have composed them, they are protected by copyright in the versions you read here, and you need to clear performance rights," and concludes with the contact information for his agents. For Mee, then, dismantling the Romantic cult of the author by no means implies forgoing the right to ownership of intellectual property.

Greenblatt and Mee joined forces to update *Cardenio* as a romantic comedy of Americans in Tuscany, a play subsequently advertised and discussed primarily with reference to Shakespeare. Although Burt Sun's poster for the

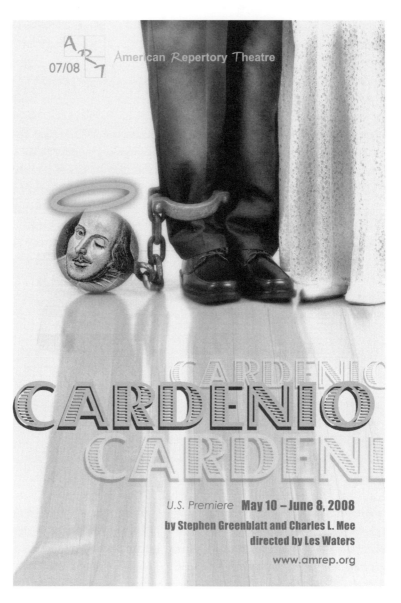

Figure 5. Burt Sun, poster for Stephen Greenblatt and Charles Mee's *Cardenio* at the American Repertory Theater, Cambridge, Massachusetts.

play shows the Bard emblazoned on the unhappy groom's ball-and-chain, Shakespeare was clearly supposed to provide the weighty ballast for a frothy comedy of contemporary manners, which received its first U.S. production at the American Repertory Theater in Cambridge in May 2008. On the theater's website, an interview with the co-authors further illuminated Mee and Greenblatt's breezy approach to appropriation. Mee volunteers, "And then one of us said that there must be a lost play by Shakespeare we could work on. So we decided we'd do what Shakespeare himself did—steal somebody else's idea and write our own play," and then specifies his method:

> For years people have said to me that the Western world's greatest playwrights are the Greeks and Shakespeare. So I've tried to do what they did, which was to never ever, not once in their entire lives, ever write an original play. They stole somebody else's play or story and made their own play out of it. It's not really adaptation—or else you'd have to call all of Shakespeare's plays adaptations. It's really stealing from a common treasury and running it through your own psyche, feeling no particular obligation to being faithful to the person you ripped off. And feeling free to steal not only the idea or the theme or the story or the characters, but also the guy's best dramaturgical tricks.[6]

Mee's exuberant account suggests a dashing privateer rather than a pirate: this act of pillage is an admirable creative endeavor, taking only from a "common treasury" that belongs to the world (with echoes here of Ben Jonson's poem on Mabbe's translation). Who could argue with such a process? Individual expression, Mee suggests, makes new texts out of preexisting materials, with little regard for proprietary rights. Mee's emphasis on the forceful appropriation of unmatched Shakespearean ore reanimates the glorification of the Bard and the privateers as twin pillars of Elizabethan triumph. Moreover, it makes Shakespeare himself into just such a privateering figure, a second-order creator who always worked with "stolen" materials. While this account may in fact conform to our notions of Renaissance imitation and of Shakespeare's relation to his sources, it makes appropriation newly transgressive and heroic. The almost reflexive turn to metaphors of treasure and piracy, which I first charted in sixteenth-century accounts of Anglo-Spanish translation, thus continues to haunt contemporary accounts of "Shakespearean" creation.

Despite Mee's lionization of transgressive appropriation, the actual play he and Greenblatt produced brings up important questions of attribution.[7]

For in fact their play is minimally based on *Double Falshood*, or the putative Shakespearean *Cardenio*, and instead follows quite closely Cervantes's "El curioso impertinente" ("The Curious Impertinent"), a novella found and read at the pivotal inn to which Don Quijote and the various characters from the interpolated stories gravitate. In the novella, Anselmo begs his great friend Lotario to help him test the fidelity of his wife, Camila, by attempting to seduce her, with disastrous consequences for all. The protagonists of the Mee/ Greenblatt play are also named Anselmo and Camila, as in the novella, with a Will added in for good measure. The sole acknowledgment of this debt in the program for the Greenblatt/Mee collaboration glosses over it rather quickly:

> We have taken the traces of the lost Shakespeare play and used them as the inspiration for our Cardenio. The parts of *The Double Falsehood* likeliest to bear Shakespeare's own imprint appear in the play-within-the-play that the characters perform, and the main plot is based on the story of the "Curious Impertinent" recounted in the Cardenio section of *Don Quixote*, Shakespeare's source. In fact Shakespeare's fingerprints are all over our play. But, as with one of Shakespeare's own comedies, the audience does not need to know anything about the sources to enjoy the play.

Although the main plot of the new play comes from Cervantes and not from Shakespeare, the authors nonetheless claim to find the Bard's fingerprints all over their play, presumably, one must conjecture, in its expression. And yet if expression is what Mee and Greenblatt do to the source material, it seems counter-intuitive to locate the play's "Shakespearean" qualities there.

In addressing their resort to "El curioso impertinente" in his subsequent essay, Greenblatt terms it an "ontological switch," by which the text embedded in the Cardenio narrative within *Don Quijote* became the main plot for their recreation, while the story of Cardenio became a play-within-the-play, a performance held to celebrate the wedding of their Anselmo and Camila:

> To set Cervantes, Shakespeare and Fletcher, and Theobald in motion and to bring their linked stories into the present, what we needed to do first was to switch the ontology. The fictional story-within-the-story— the tale the priest finds in a book and reads aloud to the company at the inn—became our real story, while the story of the trials of Cardenio became a fictional story or rather, in keeping with the medium, a play-within-the-play.[8]

There are two problems with this chiasmic account, however. First, and most important, *Double Falshood* contains no reference whatsoever to "El curioso impertinente," and it seems highly unlikely that Shakespeare and Fletcher's *Cardenio* would have, either. The recreation, pillaging, or reimagining in the new play is thus of *Don Quijote*, and not of a lost Shakespearean play. Second, "El curioso impertinente" is not contained in the Cardenio story in the novel, but woven through episodes that deal also with Sancho, Don Quijote, and other characters, as Greenblatt himself recognizes elsewhere in his essay. It is thus actually part of the novel rather than of the interpolated novella, although of course it echoes that novella in important ways.[9] While it is therefore certainly possible to read "El curioso impertinente" as the "distorted mirror image" of the Cardenio story, as Greenblatt suggests,[10] it is fundamentally not part of that story, or interchangeable with it, but an entirely different Cervantes source-story, and one which itself proved quite popular on the Renaissance stage, making its appearance in the Anselmus and Votarius plot in Middleton's *The Lady's Tragedy* (1609/10) (as I discuss in Chapter 3), Nathaniel Field's *Amends for Ladies* (1618), and possibly also Beaumont and Fletcher's *The Coxcomb* (1609). Establishing the separate presence of a "Curioso" tradition is not my point here, however, as it was well documented by philologists in the early and mid-twentieth century.[11] Instead, I want to challenge the privileging of the Shakespearean provenance for Greenblatt and Mee's work, which has completely occluded its Cervantine roots.

Yet why harp on these distinctions, which do not fundamentally change the light comedy of Americans abroad that is the Greenblatt and Mee *Cardenio*? I dwell on them because the mystique of the lost Shakespearean play reimagined has been foregrounded again and again in almost all the reviews and responses to their work. Theater historian and critic Martin Puchner, to give one example, praises Mee and Greenblatt for their originality, without really grappling with their use of Cervantes's interpolated tale:

> The new *Cardenio* pays homage to Shakespeare without trying to imitate him. It uses sources as if they were left-over pieces from a puzzle that no longer add up but that can be assembled to form a new picture. Tom Stoppard, in *Rosencrantz and Guildenstern are Dead*, had created a modern Hamlet from the perspective of Hamlet's two college friends. Mee and Greenblatt have done something similar, only without the benefit of the original play. Perhaps their *Cardenio* is what Shakespeare, himself famously irreverent with models and sources, might have written had he been confronted today with the challenge of writing a lost play by Shakespeare.[12]

Puchner's response suggests a tension between the frankness of Mee's magpie aesthetic, which proudly acknowledges taking from everywhere, and a critical establishment accustomed to privileging originality. However Mee and Greenblatt acknowledge Cervantes, the audience and the critical tendency to attribute to Shakespeare what is essentially a second Cervantes plot erase their most important debt, emphasizing instead the supposed re-creation of a lost Shakespearean source, in a gesture reminiscent of the erasure of Cervantes in readings of *The Knight of the Burning Pestle* that I traced earlier.

This negotiation of originality versus debt is symptomatic of a long critical tradition of arguing for Shakespearean exceptionality. Despite the widespread recognition that Shakespeare found his own sources in a variety of texts, his vaunted originality was central to his canonization.[13] Recall that the first mention in print of Shakespeare as dramatist is the famous attack by Robert Greene, whose *Pandosto* Shakespeare would later use as a basis for *The Winter's Tale*. Greene denounces Shakespeare as "an upstart Crow, beautified with our feathers, that with his Tygers hart wrapt in a Players hyde, supposes he is as well able to bombast out a blanke verse as the best of you . . . in his owne conceit the onely Shake-scene in a countrey."[14] Yet by the rule-bound eighteenth century it had become a commonplace to speak of Shakespeare's native genius, and his spontaneous inspiration in nature, as in the paratexts to *Double Falshood* that I analyzed in Chapter 4. This is the Shakespeare that we have largely inherited and that the critics long to find in Greenblatt and Mee, however often the authors themselves note that Shakespeare's peculiar genius lay in reworking the plots of others. The critical insistence that Shakespeare's fingerprints are all over a plot borrowed from Cervantes—and which Shakespeare most likely never used—bespeaks the persistence of an almost fetishistic investment in an intangible, elusive trace of genius.

More important, Mee and Greenblatt's sleight-of-hand vis-à-vis Cervantes reflects a larger disavowal of Spanish literature and Hispanic influence in the Anglo-American world, underscored here by the substitution of a Tuscany of vacationing Americans for the presumably Spanish setting of the *Cardenio* source-texts. In the fairly extensive media coverage of the Greenblatt and Mee *Cardenio*, the specific debt to Cervantes via "El curioso impertinente" largely disappears. When mentioned at all, the second story is subsumed under the first, under the erroneous impression that in the Cardenio source-story the protagonist "tests the chastity of his wife by asking a friend to seduce her," as the *Boston Globe* puts it, when, in truth, this happens only in "El curioso impertinente," and is a wholly inaccurate description of Cervantes's (and, presumably, Shakespeare's) Cardenio plot.[15] The reviews endlessly ponder the traces of Shakespeare in the text, while ignoring the much more direct debt to Cervantes.

Mee and Greenblatt's use of "El curioso impertinente" has another, unfortunate effect, surely unintended. It indirectly supports Hamilton's highly improbable theory, which I address in Chapter 3, that Middleton's *The Lady's Tragedy* is in fact Shakespeare and Fletcher's *Cardenio*, the "Golden Fleece of literature."[16] Arguably the most powerful argument against Hamilton is the fact that his candidate connects to *Don Quijote* primarily through a subplot based on "El curioso impertinente," rather than through the story of Cardenio, to which it bears only a certain structural resemblance, but Mee and Greenblatt's text has now muddied the lines. Hamilton, who has seen strong sales of his own supposed *Cardenio*, promotes a jingoistic and agonistic model of literary history, one unfortunately aided by the erasure of Cervantes in the Greenblatt/Mee play.[17]

Cardenios the World Over

Addressing the occlusion of Spanish sources is especially important given that writing the play was only the first part of Greenblatt's project: its larger component, an experiment in "cultural mobility," involves engaging theater companies around the world in writing their own versions of *Cardenio* according to Greenblatt's specifications, and with his funding. As Greenblatt himself explains it, "Making contact with theater companies in different parts of the world, I invited them to take the same materials, now including the play Mee and I had written, and rework them into a form that was appropriate for their particular culture."[18] As a result, new plays have now been written and performed in Yokohama, Calcutta, Zagreb, and elsewhere, and are now available on Greenblatt's Cardenio Project website, http://www.fas.harvard.edu/~cardenio. Yet it is difficult to tell how much detail was conveyed to the individual companies that participated in this project about the sources made available to them, or whether they would have recognized the "Curioso impertinente" plot in the Greenblatt/Mee *Cardenio*.

Although patronage that increases the sum total of new plays in the world is obviously a positive development, the Cardenio Project is complicated by certain easy assumptions about the homogeneity of cultures along national lines, and by the privileged position of the U.S. spectator (and patron). What does it mean to have a play represent a national culture? How are the assumptions about Shakespeare's own status as a synecdoche of sorts for "culture" in an Anglo-American context here globalized, with partial and imperfect results? Greenblatt's idea seems to be to offer an English or Anglo-American theatrical tradition as "the basic source material" for others to work with, to set "Shakespeare's fingerprints" on their way across the globe. Yet however self-conscious its latest practitioners are about the constructedness of that tradition, the project nonetheless purports to disseminate Shakespeare and his cultural capital, when in fact Cervantes is the source-material in question.[19] As in the response to the Greenblatt/Mee *Cardenio* in Boston, the reviews of the new plays often conflate the Cardenio story and "El curioso impertinente," repeatedly claiming for the former the latter's plot, and in the process erasing the actual debt to Cervantes.[20]

The various theater companies' negotiations with the redoubled sources in individual cases provide the most interesting elaborations of my argument here, and the new Cardenio Project website makes it possible to assess their responses. Several of the versions seem to hear *appropriation* where Greenblatt announces *mobility*, and the corpus as a whole would make a fascinating case study in the politics of the transnational culture industry. I will focus here on the Spanish version by Jesús Eguía Armenteros, itself entitled *The Cardenio Project* in the original, since it is the most pertinent to the larger concerns of this book.

Eguía's company, which existed before the commission from Greenblatt, is significantly named "Yelmo de Mambrino," with reference to Don Quijote's fanciful construction of a barber's basin as the helmet of a romance knight. The company's emphasis on the liberating power of the imagination seems to have coexisted rather uneasily with the constraints of a commission. The negotiations between Eguía and his Harvard patron address the problems of transmission and representativity, as well as the particular challenges of "returning" the text to Spain. Greenblatt's commission was more explicit in projecting a national culture for his collaborators abroad than his own subsequent version of the project implies: whereas in his essay cited above Greenblatt only mentions "particular cultures," his initial letter to Eguía emphasized the national: "You are invited to do something entirely new and interesting with these materials, appropriate for your company, theatrical interests, literary tradition, national culture."[21]

The focus on the national becomes even more emphatic in subsequent correspondence: "If the whole enterprise is to work, you would have to make the whole thing yours, that is, to return it to Spain, both the Spain of the

Golden Age and the Spain of the present,"[22] and in the letter Greenblatt wrote
to help the company promote the play, and which was originally included in
the program: "The adaptation will take the basic source material, the story in
Cervantes, and our version of *Cardenio* and transform it to fit the concerns
and the theatrical conventions of Spanish culture and society."[23] Thus what
begins as an open-ended exercise in cultural mobility gradually reifies cultural
difference along national lines, as communications become less nuanced in an
effort to transcend the linguistic distance between the patron, his collaborators, and their audiences. Strikingly, Eguía's suggestion that his play also be
performed in English, using bilingual actors, falls flat, as it presumably does
not conform to expectations of linguistic and cultural difference.[24] Moreover,
although this never emerges in the text or in Eguía's negotiations with Greenblatt, Spain is a particularly vexed entity of which to demand a "national" play,
given the struggles over regional identity and the uncomfortable fit of Catalan,
Valencian, Basque, or Galician identities in any notion of Spanish culture.[25]
Leaving aside the particular political and cultural fault-lines of contemporary
Spain, Greenblatt recognizes the particularly strong resonance of "returning
the story to Spain," which leads to an offer of generous funding for the production.[26] The same recognition makes for very interesting decisions by the
Spanish playwright.

Eguía's play addresses the problems of provenance and intellectual property head-on from its very title, which claims for itself the name of Greenblatt's larger endeavor. The author describes his decision to name his own play
The Cardenio Project as a gesture of resistance, an attempt to claim his own,
and Cervantes's, territory.[27] A highly self-conscious and metatheatrical piece,
Eguía's *Cardenio Project* centers on an "Autor" who has been commissioned
to write a version of *Cardenio*, as part of Greenblatt's Cardenio Project. The
second scene, which I reproduce below from Greenblatt's eponymous website,
rehearses the terms of "El Autor"'s arrangement with "Greenblatt":

ESCENA 2
*OSCURO. En el Cerebro de EL AUTOR resuenan los ecos de una
conversación con el profesor Stephen GREENBLATT de Harvard
University, coordinador de* The Cardenio Project. *Las palabras de uno y
otro se simultanean y confunden.*
EL AUTOR
¿Qué es real? No sé que es real. Sólo quiero no engañarme a mí
mismo. Ser feliz. No quiero sufrir. Tener una vida digna de ser vivida,

eso es. ¿Ser un ingenuo, un hipócrita, un loco? A estas alturas ya no me importan los demás. No puedo seguir viviendo con ella y me acaban de pedir que escriba una historia de amor. No me gusta su olor. ¿Lo tienes claro? Debes tenerlo claro porque no podrás echarte atrás. Soy un cobarde. No quiero hacerle daño.

GREENBLATT

I think that it could help you to understand the Cardenio Project. Shakespeare and Fletcher evidently took their plot from the story of Cardenio as it is episodically recounted in Part One of *Don Quixote* of Cervantes.

EL AUTOR

Me acaban de pedir que escriba una historia sobre Cardenio porque Shakespeare leyó a Cervantes y escribió *Cardenio*, sobre una parte del Quijote pero se perdió o se quemó—no me he enterado muy bien—y alguien afirma que la ha encontrado. ¿La Royal Shakespeare Company? No lo sé. No me he enterado muy bien qué quieren que escriba. La Universidad de Harvard. ¿Lo que yo quiera? Eso ha dicho. No me he enterado muy bien. No hablo muy bien inglés. Hace diez años hablaba mejor inglés. I don't know exactly what I must do. I would write a piece inspirited in it, an adaptation of Shakespeare, of Cervantes, of the both at the same time?

GREENBLATT

I have special interest in to observe something I call "cultural mobility."

EL AUTOR

¿Estará publicada en español? No lo sé. Joder, no me he enterado muy bien. Pagan bastante. No puedo decir que no: es la Universidad de Harvard.

GREENBLATT

. . . that is, the transmission and transformation of cultural materials across time and space. The adaptation will take the basic source material, the story in Cervantes, and our version of Cardenio and transform it to fit the concerns and the theatrical conventions of Spanish culture and society.

EL AUTOR

Cardenio es un personaje que lucha por el amor. No sé como hacer para dejarla. No quiero hacerle daño. Soy un cabrón. ¿Qué es lo que realmente quieren que haga? No me he enterado muy bien. I don't know what are "the theatrical conventions of Spanish culture and society". No quiero sentirme culpable.

GREENBLATT

Your play will be the answer. I don't know what are in your mind. You are free to do with it as your imagination sees fit.

EL AUTOR

Tu obra será la respuesta. No sé qué hay en tu mente. Eres libre de hacer lo que tu imaginación te dicte.[28]

[SCENE 2]

Dark. The Author's conversation with Harvard Professor Stephen GREENBLAT [sic], coordinator of The Cardenio Project, echoes in his brain. The words resound simultaneously and become obscured.

THE AUTHOR

What is real? I don't know what is real. I don't want to fool myself. I want to be happy. I don't want to suffer. I want a life worth living, that's it. Be naive, a hypocrite, a lunatic? I don't care about the others any more. I cannot go on living with her. I don't like her smell. Is that clear to you? It should be, because you won't be able to step back. I don't want to live with her any longer and they just asked me to write a love story. Being with her is an absolute waste of time. How do you tell someone that being with them is an absolute waste of time? I'm a coward. I don't want to hurt her.

GREENBLATT

I think it could help you understand the Cardenio Project. Shakespeare and Fletcher's plots were obviously inspired by Cardenio's story as told in Cervantes's *Don Quixote*.

THE AUTHOR

I've just been asked to write a story about Cardenio. Apparently Shakespeare read Cervantes' masterpiece and wrote about it. However, it was lost or burned, I'm not too sure, but now someone claims to have it. The Royal Shakespare Company? I don't know. I didn't really understand what they wanted me to write. Harvard University. Whatever I want? That's what he said. I haven't found out much. My English isn't very good. It used to be, but not anymore. I forgot a lot. I should take some lessons. Ten years ago I could speak much better. There you go, that's a good goal to set for the New Year: improve my English. I don't exactly know what I have to do: write a piece inspired on [sic] Shakespeare's version of Cervantes, Cervantes's story, or both?

GREENBLATT

I'm especially interested in an idea I call "cultural mobility."

THE AUTHOR

Is it published in Spanish? Who knows? Shit, I really don't know about this. It's good money. I can't say no. It's Harvard. Greenblatt, Stephen Greenblatt or Greenbalt? I don't know. I didn't get it right. I have to look him up.

GREENBLATT

. . . That is, the transmission and transformation of cultural material through time and space. The text should derive its material from its basic source, Cervantes' story, and from our version of Cardenio, to then adapt it to the concerns and theatrical conventions of Spanish culture and society.

THE AUTHOR

Cardenio is a character who fights for love. I can't figure out how to break up with her. I don't want to hurt her. I'm an asshole. What do they actually want me to do? I don't get it. I have to take English lessons. Yes. . . But I don't know what the "theatrical conventions of Spanish culture and society" are. She's paying the rent. I don't want to feel guilty.

GREENBLATT

Your play will be the answer. I don't know what you have in mind. You are free to do with it whatever your imagination tells you.

THE AUTHOR

Your play will be the answer. I don't know what you have in mind. You are free to do with it whatever your imagination tells you.[29]

Eguía Armenteros's response to his commission attempts to grapple with the artificiality of the exercise, in part by engaging in his own ontological switch, by which the patron becomes one more character, called upon to explain time and again how exactly the play of which he is part came into being. Graciously participating in his own transformation, Greenblatt himself was recorded for the production, and his image projected on a screen. Strikingly, as Eguía recalls, in a non-U.S. context, where Greenblatt was hardly a household name, most audiences assumed that both he and the entire pretext for the play were fictional.[30] "El Autor," for his part, challenges the notion of the complete creative freedom offered him, noting his inability either to refuse the money or prestige conferred by the U.S. university, on the one hand, or to deliver a pat version of "Spanish culture and society," on the other. The individual imagination is offered as a solution that would allow the author to transcend his misgivings about cultural representativity, yet, as quickly becomes apparent, the individual is already heavily colonized by tradition.

Moreover, as the translation of the passage above by Greenblatt's collaborators at Harvard (also included on the Cardenio Project website) shows, there is no such thing as the individual imagination in a project fundamentally concerned with transmission. The translation into English takes certain liberties with the original that render the project a virtual hall of mirrors: material is added (there are no New Year's resolutions to learn English in the original), "Greenblatt"'s English is cleaned up, and the "Autor"'s English ripostes to "Greenblatt" in the original go unmarked, so that he becomes much more fully isolated in the language translated. While these inconsistencies may in some cases stem from different versions of a new and presumably shifting text (reminding us, in the process of the artificiality of any notion of a stable Shakespearean original even for extant plays), they also evince how transmission challenges any notion of the proprietary—or proper—text, and how quickly it becomes enmeshed in such complex ideological matters as the relative value of Spanish and English in the text or of the native versus the foreign tongue, amid linguistic and literary expertises that may be difficult to ventriloquize.

What follows the solipsistic scene cited above is a play of sexual and psychological violence, of friends and lovers betrayed. Perhaps most interesting is the text's constant thematization of control: how much authority does anybody have over anyone else, except if those others become mere characters in the story that we write? Yet the considerable privilege of "El Autor" as creator of the entire fantasia is qualified by his obligation to his patron, in this case "Greenblatt," and the need to somehow deliver a hypercanonical Spanish text into an English context that, as he claims over and over, he understands only imperfectly. "El Autor" repeatedly invokes his obligation to "The Cardenio Project" as his excuse for his neglect of his girlfriend, Luscinda, whom he has seemingly stopped loving. While he toils away, she consoles herself with his best friend (and her past lover), Fernando, whom "El Autor" has actually asked to seduce her as a way to break up the cumbersome relationship, thus commingling the stories of Cardenio and "El curioso impertinente." Fittingly, "El Autor"'s name is Anselmo, although by the play's end he proclaims, about himself:

> No es ni Cardenio ni Anselmo, es los dos a la vez. El Autor es los dos
> personajes, tanto Cardenio como Anselmo. El uno explica al otro, el
> otro explica al uno. Son un espejo.[31]

> He's not Cardenio or Anselmo, he is both simultaneously. The Author is
> both characters, Anselmo as well as Cardenio. Each explains the other.
> They are a mirror.[32]

In his self-pity, "El Autor" even names himself Quijote, dazzling us with his ability to reimagine himself as virtually any of the characters in the entire section of *Don Quijote* that includes the Cardenio material.

While Eguía's updating of the Cervantine love triangles fulfills the mandate of Greenblatt's Cardenio Project, the author does not stop there: he augments his text with long passages of *Don Quijote*, quoted verbatim and minimally altered in some cases. There is no effort to hide this debt, clearly announced on the title-page and typographically as well as linguistically set off from Eguía's own text. *The Cardenio Project*'s title page claims that parts of the text have been "extraídas, fragmentadas y descontextualizadas de la infinita novela del manco de Lepanto" ["excerpted, fragmented, and decontextualized from the infinite novel of the one-armed man of Lepanto"], yet there is actually very little alteration of Cervantes's text. Under the circumstances of its creation, of which the text constantly reminds us, the unreconstructed *Quijote* excerpts become an anchor dragging against cultural mobility, as well as a rejoinder to the foreign patron, with his foreign tongue, as they insist with every iteration that the central text in the entire exercise is actually the one that Eguía Armenteros can access most directly, and which does not require of him English lessons or New Year's resolutions. This direct connection is made explicit in the poster for the show (which Greenblatt's website erroneously describes as "scrapped because it was thought to wrongly represent the production as comic"[33]), and which shows "El Autor" wearing the "yelmo de Mambrino" and embraced by a Sancho figure, as he furiously writes on his laptop in an effort to beat the preposterously large alarm clock on his desk, a reminder of his time-sensitive obligation to compose, on a Mac whose own proprietary symbol—apple of temptation and knowledge—has been replaced by a brain. The commission and the obligation are reemphasized in the brochure for this production, which reads, in my translation:

> In 1612, Shakespeare reads the first translation of *Don Quijote de la
> Mancha*, and, with a young padawan, adapts the story of Cardenio, a

THE CARDENIO PROJECT
Yelmo de Mambrino Teatro
Juan Díaz
Ernesto Gil
María Felices
Rafael Navarro
Ramón Moreno
Alba Alonso Bayona
Stephen Greenblatt
sala AZARTE
C/ SAN MARCOS 19
A partir del 16 de febrero
Jueves a Sábado a las 21h.

Figure 6. Poster for Jesús Eguía Armentero's *The Cardenio Project*, Sala Azarte.

work from which we only have an eighteenth-century adaptation by one Lewis Theobald, supposedly based on another copy, also lost, of William's own manuscript. Now Greenblatt (Harvard), who knows most about the Bard in the U.S.A., asks me to adapt what they adapted; he'll pick up the tab. He talks to me about Spanish culture. I have no idea what he's talking about. The time is almost up. My girlfriend just moved in with me and I can't stand her. At last Greenblatt lays this on me: "You are free to do with it as your imagination sees fit."

Given such free, albeit commissioned, rein, Eguía ranges widely over the entire text of *Don Quijote*, refusing a central tenet of the adaptations by Shakespeare, Fletcher, Theobald, Greenblatt, and Mee: the excision of Don Quijote and Sancho themselves from the stage versions of the Cardenio story. In a rejoinder to previous adaptations, Eguía's own "Cardenio project" involves the reinsertion of the dramatic material into the larger context of *Don Quijote* and the reiteration of its connections with the broader concerns of the novel, such as the force of the imagination, the tension between idealism and materialism, and the dangerous potential for violence in erotic fascination, all of which are updated here. The heavy use of Cervantes also returns us to central questions of intellectual property and its creative reuse, except that here they have been even more explicitly monetized. How much *Don Quijote* can Eguía include, and still fulfill his contractual obligation to provide a "new" version, or one that rewrites Greenblatt and Mee, however preposterously? Conversely, what could be more Spanish, more authentic than *Don Quijote*? In its extensive rewriting of *Don Quijote* as it was written, Eguía Armenteros's play recalls the games of Borges's supremely ironic meditation on authorship and intellectual property, "Pierre Menard, escritor del Quijote": Eguía's text is different because of its recontextualization, even when it repeats.

Although I focus here on the particular complications of "returning" *Cardenio* to Spain, the project of globalizing *Cardenio* proves quite fraught even in settings that do not, prima facie, participate in the tensions of Anglo-Spanish appropriation. The Japanese version, *Motorcycle Don Quijote*, by Akio Miyazawa, provides a wry counterpart to any notion that cultural mobility might proceed along predictable or even fully comprehensible lines. As Greenblatt notes in "Theatrical Mobility":

> Conditioned perhaps by Gilbert and Sullivan as well as Roland Barthes, I expected lacquered fans, folding screens, and the delicate sound of the koto harp. What I saw instead was a play called *Motorcycle Don Quixote*, set in a grimy motorcycle repair shop in which the sounds of revving engines mingled with loud American rock music. Cultural projection is not a one-way street.[34]

Greenblatt's self-awareness is refreshing, and the Cardenio Project website on which the plays have now been posted goes out of its way not to ascribe national circumstances or national character to the different versions, emphasizing instead Greenblatt's request to "theater companies in different parts of the world" that they produce a Cardenio "for their own cultural circumstances."[35] Clearly such delicacy is a vast improvement over assigning each national culture its expected dramatic product, and yet, conversely, it tends to occlude the powerful neo-colonial and political dynamics of the project, which I have traced most clearly for the case of Spain. The website's map of the world makes these dynamics more obvious: Spain is the only Western European nation to host the Cardenio Project, perhaps because the financial incentives were less irresistible to other first-world companies or because their cultural difference was not perceived as pronounced enough. In any case, Spain keeps company in this project with African, Asian, South American, and Eastern European nations.

My critique here is not *contra* cultural mobility, which is inevitable, or even transnational patronage, which makes available resources in parts of the world where they might otherwise be scarce. It is simply intended to reiterate that the vectors of cultural transmission are ideological vectors, in our time as in the early seventeenth century. Cultural mobility is necessarily enmeshed in cultural, political, and economic realities, and no transaction, however generous or well intended, can transcend those.

Return to Sender

I turn now to a very different version of Spanish materials in the hugely successful 2011 Royal Shakespeare Company version of *Cardenio*, "reimagined" by chief associate director Gregory Doran. Because of the RSC's significant cultural authority and resources, this production carried enormous weight, in contrast with the minor productions of *Double Falshood* in London and New York earlier the same year.[36] Much like the different versions of Spain on the English stage that I analyzed in Chapter 3, the RSC *Cardenio* makes it clear that transnational appropriation involves not only questions of intellectual property but the reification and even fetishization of cultural difference. On the one hand, the marketing for the production has prominently featured Shakespeare, playing on the notion of the missing play restored to the fold. Under the headline "*Cardenio*: Shakespeare's Lost Play Reimagined," the RSC website taunts the potential viewer and Shakespeare aficionado: "Think you've seen every Shakespeare play?

Think again. Join us on a journey to 16th century Spain as RSC Chief Associate Director Gregory Doran re-imagines Shakespeare's 'lost play' *Cardenio*."[37] Yet, on the other hand, Doran and the RSC have been playful and even exaggeratedly transparent about their sources, making much of the play's complex genealogy and emphasizing their return of the play to Spain.

The published *Cardenio* playscript problematizes the question of authorship from cover to cover. The spine shows no author and the cover reads *Cardenio: Shakespeare's "Lost Play" Reimagined*, information repeated on the primary title page. A few pages later, however, there is a second title page, which amply makes up for the first's lack of an author by supplying multitudes:

Cardenio

Shakespeare's "Lost Play" Re-imagined

After
Double Falshood; or The Distrest Lovers
by Lewis Theobald (1727)

Apparently revised
from a manuscript in the handwriting of John Downes
and conceivably adapted by William Davenant for
Thomas Betterton from
The History of Cardenio
by Mr. Fletcher and Shakespeare (1612)
performed at Court in 1612/13

Which may have been based on an episode in
Don Quixote
by Miguel de Cervantes
which was translated into English
by Thomas Shelton
First published in 1612

And here adapted and directed by Gregory Doran
for the Royal Shakespeare Company
With additional Spanish material supplied by Antonio Álamo
via a literal translation by Duncan Wheeler
and developed in rehearsal by the original cast[38]

This playful, even performative version of authorship is genially inclusive—everyone from the translator Shelton to the "conceivable adapter" Davenant gets a nod. The second title page recognizes quite openly not only the complex mechanisms of textual transmission for early modern theatrical texts but also the fact of collective authorship in the context of production. The tongue-in-cheek emphasis on possibility and probability, eschewing the proper authority of a title page, bespeaks a sophisticated recognition, in the light of the most up-to-date criticism, that what we call a "Shakespeare play" is a highly artificial and constructed product. At the same time, the repeated inverted commas around "lost play" suggest a further instability: is the lost play only purportedly "lost" because there is no such thing, or because it has been abundantly found, by the long laundry list of contributors to *Cardenio* cited above?

But even this is not the last word on authorship: before the back cover, a copyright page duly notes "Gregory Doran with Antonio Álamo" to be the copyright holders for "this adaptation of *Cardenio*."[39] Yet what exactly is held in copyright, given that no text of *Cardenio* exists? The text before us most closely approximates Theobald's *Double Falshood*. The well-populated second title page for the RSC *Cardenio* now appears in an entirely different light, as the generous multiplication of author-figures contextualizes the appropriation by Doran and his Spanish collaborator of Theobald's fully extant text.

The process, though not its scope, is duly noted in Doran's introduction, where he stresses the collaborative nature of *Cardenio*:

> Theater is the most collaborative of the arts; and collaboration has been the key note of *Cardenio* since William Shakespeare and his younger colleague John Fletcher decided to write a play together, based on an episode in the Spanish best-seller *Don Quixote* by Miguel de Cervantes Saavedra, first published in England in 1612, in a translation by Thomas Shelton.[40]

As Doran explains, he had long been interested in the "potential" of *Double Falshood* but had found "that the plotting (particularly at the beginning) was convoluted and it was missing several scenes."[41] The breakthrough comes when Doran realizes "that those missing scenes "might be reimagined from the very same source material that Shakespeare and Fletcher must have used," and takes on a Spanish collaborator in the playwright and novelist Antonio Álamo. As Doran puts it in the RSC promotional materials:

> It has been a really interesting process of putting together the best telling
> of the story of *Cardenio* that I can, with a stable of writers that would
> make the credits on any Hollywood blockbuster look paltry. I have in
> my team of writers: Cervantes, Shakespeare, Fletcher, Shelton, Lewis
> Theobald and a bit of help from here and there. And that is pretty good
> collaborative list—my job was to bring the whole piece together.[42]

The new adaptations consist mainly of astute additions of material from Cervantes's *Don Quijote* to explain what seems obscure or insufficiently developed in Theobald's version. Doran adds a scene between Cardenio and Fernando at court, which fleshes out the friendship between the two men (1.5). He also gives us Fernando's seduction of Dorotea at far greater length, including their secret marriage (1.6), and stages Fernando's spectacular abduction of Luscinda from the convent where she had attempted to take refuge from him (4.3), both of which are retrospectively narrated in *Double Falshood* but never shown. This last provides one of the most theatrically effective moments in the production, as Fernando leaps out of the coffin where he had concealed himself in order to enter the convent, in a marvelous detail that Theobald repurposes from a different episode in *Don Quijote*. Doran also adds a few lines to other existing scenes, and transposes lines to make scenes more effective. Although these interventions provide useful background and insight into the characters' motivations, they leave the text of *Double Falshood* largely unchanged. In fact, the most significant departure from Theobald's version is arguably the return to Cervantes's nomenclature: *Cardenio* rather than *Double Falshood*; Fernando, Dorotea, Cardenio and Luscinda rather than Henriquez, Violante, Julio, and Leonora. As I discuss below, this strategic foregrounding of the Cervantine and Spanish sources, in a move to "reinvest the play with a sense of its Spanish past,"[43] as Doran puts it, gives it an aura of immediacy and authenticity that *Double Falshood* never achieves.

The RSC's "reimagined" *Cardenio* works in two directions. On the one hand, it makes strategic, surgical additions to Theobald's text, driven by the dramatic exigencies of staging and production. On the other, it restores an earlier nomenclature as part of an effort at authenticity, in Doran's own return *ad fontes*. Together, the two moves tend to obscure Theobald's text as the material that is actually being played in these performances. Given the many layers to Theobald's own confection, and the enduring critical debates over *his* authorship, any appropriation or marginalization of *Double Falshood* would seem par for the course, and yet it seems difficult to take this as a separate text, which is what the copyright page attempts to establish. Different regimes are at work here: "copyright" is too blunt an instrument to discern the scale and import of the authorial contributions by Doran and Álamo, yet the very authors who on their second title page recognize and showcase the limits to individual authorship cannot afford to relinquish the rights to their version, however slightly it adapts their immediate source.[44] The exigencies of intellectual property become particularly pressing when the property in question so ably harnesses the cultural capital of both Shakespeare and Cervantes to become a valuable commodity, as the success of the production confirms.

In contrast to both the Greenblatt/Mee *Cardenio* and the recent attempts to revive *Double Falshood*, Doran's production foregrounds Cervantes and Spain. But if the Greenblatt/Mee version, with its "ontological switch," has the effect of erasing Cervantes to foreground a Shakespearean genealogy, Doran's turn to Spain risks a different form of cultural appropriation, fetishizing Spanish difference and exoticizing the setting of the play. Beyond the re-Hispanicization of the text itself via the return to Cervantes, the intense theatricality and sensuality of Doran's production stems in part from its effective use of guitar music, Spanish voices, and flamenco; a fiesta complete with peasants tossed in blankets; religious processions and Catholic paraphernalia; and the ornate baroque gates that are the centerpiece of the scenery. To top off all this Spanishness, the play concludes with a flamenco-inflected dance number and the entire company coming together in a lusty shout of "Olé!"

The public account of the production's development on Doran's RSC *Cardenio* blog shows how central the foregrounding of Spain was to the entire enterprise. Doran had initially envisioned a far more collaborative project: Brean Hammond, in his edition of *Double Falshood*, cites him as planning a different route to "Spanishness," in association with the Almagro Festival of classical theater: "It will be worked up with Spanish as well as British actors, in an attempt to re-Spanishize the feel of Shelton and Theobald."[45] Yet the financial crisis that engulfed both Spain and the UK in 2008 dashed such hopes of collaboration, which would have made the production far more expensive, so Doran resorted to working with Álamo and employing Spanish musicians.[46] "Reinvesting the play with a sense of its Spanish past" thus became mainly a question of careful research, detailed by Doran in his extensive blog. Yet even this most Hispanophilic and responsible of productions finds its available repertoire of Spanishness constrained by a long tradition of Spanish stereotypes. As Doran's entries reveal, his version of Spain is constructed not just out of

Figure 7. Fernando before the gates, with musicians in the background. Gregory Doran's *Cardenio*. Ellie Kurtz ©RSC.

his own repeated visits and the research trip on which he embarks with the production designer, Niki Turner, but also out of a long tradition of exoticizing Spain from a North European and Protestant perspective. In this sense, Doran's Spain is the Spain of the many travelers whose fascinated gaze exoticized the westernmost part of continental Europe. Their vision constructed Spain as hardly European: "Africa begins at the Pyrenees," as the famous line-in-the-sand attributed to Dumas puts it.[47]

Doran's Spain owes much not only to the *longue durée* of simultaneous English fascination with and suspicion of Spain that I have traced throughout this book, but specifically to the nineteenth-century French Romanticist construction of Spain, which found in Spain a proximate primitivism of gypsies, flamenco, and "duende." Hence the notion of "Spanishness" as just the thing to infuse Theobald's production with feeling and local color:

> I visited Antonio [Álamo] in Seville in February 2008. We spent a
> concentrated couple of days trying to understand what the Cardenio
> episode meant in the context of *Don Quixote*; what the impact of the
> story might have been in seventeenth century Spain and how the central

Figure 8. Company rehearsing the fiesta. On Doran's "Re-Imagining *Cardenio*" blog, the caption reads, "The Cardenio company in fiesta mood." Ellie Kurttz ©RSC.

characters were regarded in that country today. All very illuminating. It made me realise that the plot in the *Double Falshood* had become rather thinned out. Frankly, by adapting the story for the sensibilities and tastes of his eighteenth century audience, Theobald had emasculated the play, and we needed to put the Iberian 'cojones' ["balls"] back into it!

To see just what a bit of Spanish flare and passion could produce, last week, Antonio recommended a visit to the Flamenco Festival at Sadlers' Wells. . . . Gerard Brenan, in his book *South from Granada*, writes about the singing of cante jondo, of music that has 'black sounds' in it, and of dancers whose feet can summon up the spirit of 'duende' (a hard to define concept in Spanish arts, a kind of heightened state of emotion in response to music, in particular). . . .

The entire acting company have been taking flamenco classes . . . so they are learning about how to concentrate and focus a passion that seems to rise from the ground. It is up to Mike Ashcroft, our choreographer, to translate that into a language that the actors can comprehend and master in the time we have. But even after one session last week, the company all seem taller. Perhaps, they are beginning to understand something about the Spanish people that Jan Morris describes beautifully in her book *Spain* when she says that the Spanish are more "perpendicular" than any other nation.[48]

The Spain of perpendicular people invoked here is timeless, frozen into spectacle and local color.[49] Flamenco, which is first recorded in the late eighteenth century and reaches its apogee in the late nineteenth, is pressed into service for representing early modern Spain, and retrospectively projected as relevant to a seventeenth-century story. A similar oversimplification is at work in Doran's account of his collaboration with New York's LABrynth Theater Company in the development of *Cardenio*: "So, for example, Cardenio was played by a Mexican, and Don Bernardo by an actor from Los Angeles, which certainly revealed and rooted the play's Spanish temperament."[50] In a gesture of geographical and ethnic leveling, "Spanishness" is extended to these nameless actors from Mexico and California, whose Hispanicity brings out the occluded true temperament of *Double Falshood*.

Doran's research into all things Spanish leads him to the abundant travel literature on Spain, some of it from the early modern period. An entry on the "fiesta" reveals how the production's very effective design comes together, and simultaneously underscores how vexed are the available sources for an English version of Spain:

> We had a good session on the fiesta last week. Cervantes says that in order to win Dorotea's affection Fernando bribed the servants, and paid for music and dancing in the village every night, so we are staging this in the production. We scanned all the research material we had collected for inspiration: the amazing photographs by Christina Rodero of Spanish Festivals and rituals, Goya's dark carnival painting *The Burial of the Sardine*, and read a lively diatribe against the festivities enjoyed at Shrovetide in "popish countries" in the sixteenth century by Thomas Kirchmaier, "englyshed" by Barnabe Googe in 1570. We note how certain factors are common to all: the dressing up, the presence of devils, and masks, and a love of drag!

> > "But some again the dreadful shape of devils on them take,
> > And chase such as they meet, and make poor boys to fear and quake.
> > Some naked run about the streets, their faces hid alone,
> > With visors close, that so disguised, they might be known of none.
> > Both men and women change their weed, the men in maid's array,

And wanton wenches dressed like men, do travel by the way,

Some like wild beasts do run abroad in skins that divers be
Arrayed and eke with loathsome shapes, that dreadful are to see:
They counterfeit both bears and wolves, and lions fierce to fight,
And raging bulls. Some play the cranes with wings and stilts upright.
Some like the filthy form of apes, and some like fools dressed,
Which best beseem these papists all, that thus keep Bacchus feast."

I like the idea of cranes or storks, like the ones we saw on the roof tops
of Alacala [sic] de Henares. And stilts could be effective.[51]

Doran recognizes the 1570 Googe translation as an anti-Catholic diatribe, yet his own extravagant staging of the fiesta—a passing detail in the Cervantes source—conjures a folkloric Spain of grotesquerie and excess. What makes the Googe passage so powerful is precisely its visuality and exaggeration, its images of animality and carnivalesque havoc. The theatrical potential of the fiesta is irresistible and to some extent predetermined: stereotypes appeal because they confirm what we think we already know. Moreover, if, as performance criticism has argued, the function of drama is to serve as a form of cultural memory, re-telling stories "that bear a particular religious, social, or political significance for their public," then this production serves that goal magnificently, as it rehearses English notions of Spain.[52] To judge from the audience's gasps of delight at the performance I attended, Doran's staging of the fiesta proves wildly successful in theatrical terms, however problematic some of its early sources.

Much of what Doran focuses on in his research for the production is of much later provenance than the Cervantes source-text. In an entry entitled "Serenatas in Spain," Doran charts his fascination with Gustave Doré's illustrations for *Don Quijote* and for Jean-Charles D'Avillier's enormously popular account of their travels through Spain in the 1860s:

I have been looking at Gustave Dore's [sic] illustrations for *Don Quixote.*

I have always been fascinated by Dore's engravings. My Auntie Mary and Uncle Bob in Slaithwaite had a huge old Victorian tome of Dante's Inferno with illustrations by Dore. Whenever we went over to Huddersfield for Christmas or Easter, I would ask to see it, and sit absorbed for hours staring at Dore's terrifying illustrations of the circles of Hell and their tortured inhabitants.

Dore's illustrations for Don Quixote hold a similar fascination for me now, and the scene where the mad Don tilts at the windmills and he and his horse Rozinate [sic] are swept high into the air is surely a definitive depiction of that episode.

Dore traveled throughout Spain in the 1860s with the Baron Jean-Charles Davillier, who wrote a book about their travels, which Dore illustrated. He sketches bull fights in Seville, gypsies dancing Flamenco in the grottoes of Sacro-Monte. Here is the mournful magnificence of the Escorial, the great Alcazar of Toledo, the horseshoe arches of the Mezquite mosque in Cordoba, and shifty looking tourists in Granada, chipping out azulejos tiles in the Alhambra. He draws everything from a shepherd in Estremadura, to a procession of penitents in their white pointed hoods.

As I read Davillier's account of their journey through Andalucia, several interesting descriptions leap out, which might be very useful in trying to deepen our understanding of the story of Cardenio.[53]

The director's Spain is thus constructed not just out of his and his designer's own impressions when they travel to Spain, but of a much longer tradition of representing a colorful, folkloric, and timeless Spain for audiences elsewhere in Europe. Their citational vision rehearses recognizable versions of Spain that have solidified into the stereotype of an "España de pandereta," or tambourine Spain, in the European imagination.

Already in the nineteenth century, D'Avillier was conscious that he wrote as the latest installment in a well established tradition of travel literature, and he cites frequently from his predecessors, even when he candidly confesses to not finding what he expected of picturesque Spain, as in the furiously modernizing city of Barcelona: "The *mantilla* is rarely seen, and it is in vain we have tried to discover the least trace of the 'Andalouse au teint bruni' of Alfred de Musset. Even in Andalusia they become rarer every day, and Doré never lost an opportunity of studying those we came across, for a day will come when railways, forming a network over Spain, will cause them to disappear."[54] Granada, for its part, recalls Washington Irving: "Of the governor Monchot, *el Gobernador Manco*, Washington Irving has given an amusing portrait."[55] This iterative citationality produces a familiar Spain, always already known from some earlier text, which Doré lavishly illustrates.

The stereotypical counterpoint to the vivacious and stubbornly enduring Spain of Doré and D'Avillier is its political and economic decline since the reign of Philip II, or, more precisely, since the defeat of the Armada. Inevitably, Doran's visit to Philip II's sober palace of El Escorial leads him to just such a consideration of decay and English primacy:

> As we wander round this humourless mausoleum of a palace, I get a profound sense of death as a central theme in Spanish life. This persistent flavour of mortality gives me a strong sense of the opening of *Cardenio* where the Duke Ricardo, contemplating his imminent death with a steady gaze, tells his son not to grieve . . .
>
> We leave the pantheons of the dead infantas, and head back into the cloisters. The vast spectacular mural painted by Luca Giordano on the vault of the Main Staircase of the Escorial depicts the then King, Carlos II, at the end of the next century, pointing to the apotheosis of King Philip II as he is welcomed into heaven, surrounded by vast hordes of saints and angels in a vortex of pink and golden clouds. Carlos looks for all the world as if he is commenting blithely on a particularly charming sunset, and indeed in a way he is, for the sun had set by then upon *The Glory of Spanish Monarchy* as this baroque masterpiece is known. For with Philip II, the Spanish Empire died also, the empire he had ruled over for so long, slipping into decadence and losing its influence and grip, as the Inca and Aztec gold from its South American empires was frittered away.
>
> The high point of Don John's glorious victory over the Ottoman Empire at the Battle of Lepanto should have been matched by trouncing the upstart English with a magnificent Spanish Armada in 1588, but instead, their defeat at the hands of the Queen Elizabeth's ships marked the start of a slow decline.[56]

This funereal entry confirms that Spain's glory is past, and dates its decline from the moment of the Spanish encounter with an "upstart" England. Once again, the connection between Cervantes and Shakespeare (the "upstart crow") is mapped onto the political and religious rivalry between Spain and England. The larger historical framework that I have limned throughout this book—the

Armada paradigm—thus conditions even the most sympathetic observer as he seeks the connections between the two hypercanonical writers.

To judge from the reviews, Doran's production has been inordinately successful at restoring *Cardenio*'s Spanishness in English eyes. Yet these responses demonstrate also how the careful research that went into the production is received at a much more basic level, as a catalog of Spanish stereotypes. Michael Billington's glowing review in *The Guardian* describes a play "adorned with an abundance of Catholic ritual, dance-filled fiestas, and the blend of sex and death that marks the Spanish temper,"[57] while Charles Spenser, in the *Daily Telegraph*, notes, "Doran's production sweeps along with terrific brio, combining humour with moments of deeper feeling and a strong atmosphere of Catholicism, heat and lust."[58] Paul Taylor's review in *The Independent*, entitled, "Shakespeare with a Stylish Spanish Twist," ends in a note of distaste: "How one wishes one could push Falstaff and his anti-honour speech on to the stage. In shame-cultures such as this women, as here, wind up having to woo the men who have raped them. Not exactly edifying."[59] The reviews reduce Spain to a fantasy of Catholic and Mediterranean excess, a lusty, dusty Andalusía that is wildly enjoyable but also emphatically *not us*.

Yet what over-sensitive, politically correct viewer could find fault with what is actually—as the reviews all emphasize—a marvelously effective piece of theater? My point is not to criticize Doran, whose involvement with Spanish materials is devoutly to be desired, but simply to recall the long history of appropriations of Spain into which this new Anglo-Spanish fantasia falls, and to complicate the assumptions about a Spanish "temperament" that animate it. In a sense, Doran's dilemma is that posed by the totalizing Foucauldian model of *Orientalism*: given the existence of a powerful discourse that conditions our vision of another culture, how are we to step outside it, especially in the case of the theater, which arguably depends on recognition and on larger-than-life gestures that viewers can comprehend? The solutions to such a bind may well come from companies and contexts that have made the representation of other voices and other places their explicit political and ideological goal, or from an even closer collaboration between English and Spanish practitioners, such as Doran had initially hoped for. The more frequent staging of Spanish Golden Age plays in England or the United States could also offer solutions, by loosening the hold of a stereotypical version of Spain. As Jonathan Thacker notes in his discussion of Golden Age drama in England:

One consequence of the British audience's ignorance of the tradition of Spanish classical drama is that many directors have felt the urge in their productions to provide a comforting notion of Spain to cling to. Thus, in costume, music and dance a clichéd Spanishness has tended to hold sway, to provide a familiar background. The publicity for productions also often borrows from the limited imagery of the holiday advertisement, stressing the presence of Spanish passion and mystery and the notion of Spanish difference.[60]

Although *Cardenio*, as an English play based on Golden Age material, necessarily presents a vision of Spain from elsewhere, in Doran's production that vision, too, seems constrained by the paucity of a Spanish tradition that Thacker identifies.

Contemporary Spain—a cultural composite of the very different Comunidades Autónomas—strains at the stereotypical depictions that, in the absence of a stage tradition, seem so hard to dislodge from the Anglo-American imaginary. To give just two, highly impressionistic, recent examples: in a land of supposedly timeless Catholic religiosity, the August 2011 visit to Madrid by the Pope led to indignant protests by the already *indignados* of the Plaza del Sol and a multitude of lay organizations. These coexisted with respectful coverage, displays of fervor, and the odd sight of portable confessionals in the Parque del Retiro (duly satirized by cartoonists).[61] On another front, while Spain's own Tourism Office has often relied on the most folkloric version of Spain to attract visitors (as Thacker notes above), their latest campaign strikes a new note. The 2010 "I need Spain" campaign eschews the folkloric and instead abstracts the appeal of Spain into a highly personal need for immediacy, connection, and naturalness. In this sophisticated vision, directed by Basque film director Julio Medem for the multinational agency McCann Erikson, Spain is what the viewer makes of it, but without resorting to stereotype.

On the stage, what alternatives might there be to the folkloric Spain that proves so effective in Doran's RSC *Cardenio*? One is the Greenblatt and Mee decision to set their *Cardenio* in a Tuscany populated almost exclusively by visiting Americans, yet their play's reflexive gaze does not ultimately address the ideological questions that concern me here, except by bypassing them. Another might be Eguía Armenteros's *The Cardenio Project*, set in a cosmopolitan, modern, European Spain whose immediate connection to Cervantes's text does not seem to depend on folkloric timelessness. Yet Eguía's play carries much less cultural capital than the RSC *Cardenio*; its self-conscious connection to Cervantes is profoundly ironic and, with no sponsorship thus far

Figure 9. Raúl Salazar, "Madrid, plagada de confesionarios portátiles," from "Un respeto a las canas, www.unrespetealascanes.com."

from national cultural institutions, it plays in festivals to reduced audiences. In Eguía's own understanding, the play's edgy conjoining of new and old has complicated its acceptance at festivals geared exclusively to classical or to contemporary theater, suggesting that in Spain as in England it is easier to produce safely recognizable versions of the past.[62]

Yet could a production of the extant texts of *Cardenio/Double Falshood* harness some of the self-consciousness and Brechtian distancing of Eguía's *Cardenio Project*? Is there a way to recover the Spanish origins of these texts that neither stereotypes Spain nor leaves the company whistling in the dark? The remarkable explosion of interest in *Cardenio* in the last few years suggests that we may have the chance to assess the possibilities in future productions. Moreover, the recent wave of interest in Golden Age theater in England could provide valuable contexts for such productions, reinserting *Cardenio* into a literary and theatrical culture from which its Shakespearean exceptionality has tended to divorce it. Certainly, broader interest in Spanish materials does not prevent the ready recycling of Elizabethan hallmarks: the Royal Shakespeare Company chose to advertise its 2004 Golden Age season by promising "the last great unopened treasure chest of world drama,"[63] presumably leading to an attack on the theater by an audience of dashing privateers. Yet director Laurence Boswell, whose groundbreaking Golden Age seasons at the Gate theater and the RSC led to an RSC production of Lope in Madrid, and to his own directorial work in Spain, strikes a very different note, emphasizing the need for Anglo-Spanish collaboration.[64] In his own vision for future productions, Boswell muses:

> I'm sure there will be another Golden Age season, and I'm sure it'll be a development from the last RSC season. And I think the way it will develop will be through an enhanced collaboration between Spanish and English practitioners. I would like to have Spanish and English actors working together, Spanish directors working with English directors, Spanish designers with English designers, etc. I want to develop the momentum of cultural fusion. And to do that we'd have to look more broadly at the repertoire—dig up hidden masterpieces, certainly, but not be afraid either to take on some of the great plays we already know, perhaps taking translation into different forms as well. I also think I would like to combine a contemporary Spanish play in the season.[65]

Fusion and collaboration are key to Boswell's project as they were to Doran's. Yet in the freeing absence of a Shakespearean connection Boswell here seems less bound by a "timeless," folkloric version of Spain. In her doctoral thesis on the 2004 RSC Golden Age season, Kathleen Jeffs argues that a collaboration that "balances the interrelating needs of 'equivalence' in translation and the practicalities of theatre that 'works' . . . requires a representative from the fields of academic study of the play in the original, a translator writing for the stage, and a director charged with realizing the production."[66] Although Jeffs is not primarily concerned with the representation of Spanishness, her work as a dramaturg for the RSC suggests how the Anglo-American stage might move beyond the stereotypical.

In California, there has been some attempt in recent years to make Shakespeare legible to multicultural and largely Hispanic audiences, in such initiatives as Hugh Macrae Richmond's popularizing video *Shakespeare and the Spanish Connection* (2007), which focuses on parallels between the theatrical traditions and general "cultural affinities," or Jill Holden's bilingual *Shakespeare Unbound* for Los Angeles high-school students. Although *Cardenio* has not yet figured in these efforts, it would offer fascinating possibilities for complicating the "Englishness" of Shakespeare as it is presented to broader audiences.

My own excursus into the proliferation of new *Cardenios* is an attempt to bring the problems of appropriation and translation somewhat closer to our own, arguably post-national sphere. However postmodern and global our own productions, the disavowal of Spain colors the Anglo-American literary and dramatic heritage, and the traces of a pugnacious early modern competition among national literatures haunts even the most generous projects of cultural mobility or theatrical reconstruction. Our challenge is to imagine alternatives, whether via collaboration, transnational exchanges, or simply a more engaged and self-aware dialogue between contemporary practitioners and the historical traditions that shape us.

Notes

INTRODUCTION

1. On Sidney's poetic project and its relation to Spanish imperialism, see Roland Greene, *Unrequited Conquests: Love and Empire in the Colonial Americas* (Chicago: University of Chicago Press, 1999). For a recent account of the Sidney circle and his use of *La Celestina*, see Elizabeth Bearden, "Sidney's 'Mongrell Tragicomedy' and Anglo-Spanish Exchange in the *New Arcadia*," in *The Spanish Connection*, ed. Barbara Fuchs and Brian Lockey, special issue, *Journal of Early Modern Cultural Studies* (Spring/Summer 2010): 29–51.

2. Diana de Armas Wilson takes issue with Ian Watt's Anglocentric account in her *Cervantes, the Novel and the New World* (Oxford: Oxford University Press, 2000).

3. Antonio de Corro, *The Spanish Grammar*, trans. John Thorius (London: J. Wolfe, 1590). Harvey's copy is at the Huntington Library (ref. no. 53880). For an account of Anglo-Spanish trade, see Jason Eldred, "'The Just Will Pay for the Sinners': English Merchants, the Trade with Spain, and Elizabethan Foreign Policy, 1563–1585," in Fuchs and Lockey, eds., 5–28.

4. John Minsheu's 1599 *Spanish Grammar*, based on the work of Richard Perceval, incorporates excerpts from such Spanish best-sellers as *Celestina, Lazarillo,* and *Diana,* as well as Alonso de Ercilla's epic *La Araucana,* among others. While Minsheu's extensive title provides the rationale for including these texts, they also suggest a Spanish canon fully established in England. Richard Perceval and John Minsheu, *A Spanish grammar, first collected and published by Richard Perciuale Gent. Now augmented and increased with the declining of all the irregular and hard verbes in that toong, with diuers other especiall rules and necessarie notes for all such as shall be desirous to attaine the perfection of the Spanish tongue. Done by Iohn Minsheu professor of languages in London. Hereunto for the yoong beginners learning and ease, are annexed speeches, phrases, and prouerbes, expounded out of diuers authors, setting downe the line and the leafe where in the same bookes they shall finde them, whereby they may not onely vnderstand them, but by them vnderstand others, and the rest as they shall meete with them* (London: Bollifant, 1599), 75–82.

5. *Lazarillo,* as noted above, had been translated by Rowland before 1586 and published in multiple editions; the earliest surviving one is the second: *The Pleasaunt*

Historie of Lazarillo de Tormes a Spaniarde wherein is Conteined His Marueilous Deedes and Life. With the Straunge Aduentures Happened to Him in the Seruice of Sundrie Masters. Drawen out of Spanish by Dauid Rouland of Anglesey (London: Jeffs, 1586); *Examen de ingenios para las ciencias* was translated by Richard Carew from the Italian version by Camilo Camilli in 1594, and published as *Examen de ingenios: The examination of mens wits: in which by discouering the varietie of natures, is shewed for what profession each one is apt, and how far he shall profit therein* (London: Adam Islip, for Richard Watkins, 1594). Carew's translation was published again in 1596, 1604, and 1616. The *Diana* saw only one edition, *Diana of George of Montemayor: translated out of Spanish into English by Bartholomew Yong of the Middle Temple Gentleman* (London: Bollifant, 1598), yet, Dale Randall notes, "the single printing of Yong's rendition is no accurate gauge of England's reception of the Spanish romance" (*The Golden Tapestry: A Critical Survey of Non-Chivalric Spanish Fiction in English Translation [1543–1657]* [Durham, N.C.: Duke University Press, 1963], 80), as Barnabe Googe had included partial translations in his own published poetry as early as 1563, and the book had also circulated widely in the original. Tracing the broader echoes of the *Diana* across a variety of texts, Randall concludes that the subject of the book's reception is virtually inseparable from that of its influence (81).

6. The inscription is on the penultimate leaf of Harvey's copy of *The Spanish Grammar*.

7. As Randall's subtitle makes clear, a full account of Spanish chivalric fiction in English translation (which he briefly considers) would easily take another volume. On chivalric fiction, see Donna Hamilton, *Anthony Munday and the Catholics, 1560–1633* (Burlington, Vt.: Ashgate, 2005), and Deborah Uman and Belén Bistué, "Translation as Collaborative Authorship: Margaret Tyler's *The Mirrour of Princely Deedes and Knighthood*," *Comparative Literature Studies* 44, 3 (2007): 298–323.

8. Richard Helgerson, *Forms of Nationhood: The Elizabethan Writing of England* (Chicago: University of Chicago Press, 1992), and "Language Lessons: Linguistic Colonialism, Linguistic Postcolonialism, and the Early Modern English Nation," *Yale Journal of Criticism* 11, 1 (1998): 289–99.

9. For a related project, see Eric Griffin, *English Renaissance Drama and the Specter of Spain: Ethnopoetics and Empire* (Philadelphia: University of Pennsylvania Press, 2009), in which he explores the role played by drama in the increasingly racialized and hostile representation of Spain in England and, conversely, the role of the Black Legend of Spanish cruelty on the drama and English culture more broadly.

10. See *Intricate Alliances: Early Modern Spain and England*, ed. Marina Brownlee, special issue *JMEMS* 39, 1 (2009), and Fuchs and Lockey, eds., *The Spanish Connection*.

11. The term appropriation is useful for reminding us of the agency and the various relations of power that underlie literary "transmission." See Kathleen Ashley and Véronique Plesch, introduction to *The Cultural Processes of "Appropriation"*, special issue, *JMEMS* 32, 1 (2002): 3.

12. Johann Wolfgang von Goethe, *Conversations with Eckermann, 1823–1832*, trans. John Oxenford (San Francisco: North Point, 1984), 133.

13. Ben Jonson, "On the Author, Work, and Translator," in *The Rogue, or the Life of*

Guzmán de Alfarache, Written in Spanish by Mateo Alemán and Done into English by James Mabbe, 1623, ed. James Fitzmaurice-Kelly (London: Constable, 1924), 31.

14. I take the term from Christine Gerrard, *The Patriot Opposition to Walpole: Politics, Poetry, and National Myth, 1725–1742* (Oxford: Oxford University Press, 1994), and analyze this moment further in Chapter 4.

15. See my *Mimesis and Empire*, Chapter 5 and Claire Jowitt, *The Culture of Piracy, 1580–1630: English Literature and Seaborne Crime* (Burlington, Vt.: Ashgate, 2010).

16. Adrian Johns, *Piracy: The Intellectual Property Wars from Gutenberg to Gates* (Chicago: University of Chicago Press, 2009), 13.

17. Ibid., 23.

18. Joseph Loewenstein, *Ben Jonson and Possessive Authorship* (Cambridge: Cambridge University Press, 2002), 85.

19. See Richard L. Kagan, "Prescott's Paradigm: American Historical Scholarship and the Decline of Spain," *American Historical Review* 101 (1996): 423–46, and *Spain in America: The Origins of Hispanism in the United States* (Urbana: University of Illinois Press, 2002).

20. T. G. Tucker, *The Foreign Debt of English Literature* (London: Bell and Sons, 1907), 225.

21. Tucker, 229.

22. Rudolf Schevill, "On the Influence of Spanish Literature upon English in the Early 17th Century," *Romanische Forschugen* 20 (1907): 604–34, 627.

23. Ibid., 633.

CHAPTER 1. FORCIBLE TRANSLATION

Epigraphs: *Timber, or Discoveries*, in *Ben Jonson's Literary Criticism*, ed. James D. Redwine, Jr. (Lincoln: University of Nebraska Press, 1970), 31; Charles Whibley, *Literary Studies* (London: Macmillan, 1919), 60.

1. ". . . siempre la lengua fue compañera del imperio," in the Prologue to Queen Isabel, Antonio de Nebrija, *Gramática castellana*, ed. Miguel Ángel Esparza and Ramón Sarmiento (Madrid: Fundación Antonio de Nebrija, 1992).

2. On early modern translation as cultural negotiation, see Peter Burke, "The Renaissance Translator as Go-Between," in *Renaissance Go-Betweens: Cultural Exchange in Early Modern Europe*, ed. Andreas Höfele and Werner von Koppenfels (Berlin: Gruyter, 2005), 17–31, and Peter Burke and Ronnie Po-Chia Hsia, eds., *Cultural Translation in Early Modern Europe* (Cambridge: Cambridge University Press, 2007). See also Massimiliano Morini, *Tudor Translation in Theory and Practice* (Burlington, Vt.: Ashgate, 2006).

3. Morini, 28.

4. See *Renaissance Go-Betweens*, 11. Even Morini, who dedicates part of his chapter on "Practice" to the two early modern English translations of *La Celestina*, largely leaves Spanish out of his discussion of theories of translation, as when he notes: "English, as compared with Greek and Latin, but also with more prestigious contemporary languages (Italian and

French), is seen as poor, rude, plain, barren, barbarous" (39). And yet at least some of the translators who theorized their practice, such as George Pettie, included Spain in their list of source languages to contend with:

> There are some others yet who wyll set lyght by my labours, because I write in Englysh: and those are some nice Travaylours, who returne home with such quaesie stomackes, that nothyng will downe with them but French, Italian, or Spanishe, and though a woorke be but meanely written in one of those tongues, and finely translated into our Language, yet they wyll not sticke farre to preferre the Originall before the Translation. . . , but they consider not the profit which commeth by reading thynges in their owne Tongue.

(Stefano Guazzo, *The Civile Conversation*, trans. George Pettie [London: Richard Watkins, 1581], iir, v). On Pettie as a translator, see Carmela Nocera, "George Pettie and his *Preface* to *The Civile Conversation* (1581)," in *Thou Sittest at Another Boke . . . : English Studies in Honour of Domenico Pezzini*, ed. Giovanna Iamartino, Maria Luisa Maggioni, and Roberta Facchinetti (Monza, Italy: Polimetrica, 2008), 75–84.

5. Following Yehudi Lindeman and Theo Hermans, Morini recognizes the significance of the metaphorics of translation:

> Attempts at defining and systematizing translation always call for figurative language, for the nature of the process seems too fleeting to be described through the naked syntax of denotation. But the figures, if they serve the purpose of apt description and reader-persuasion, are also liable to betray their wielders. If closely read, they reveal deep-seated notions on the nature and process of translation which may either illustrate or give the lie to the translators' explicit statements on their art and principles. (35)

Yet because Morini examines primarily literary texts, he misses the strong current of pugnacious metaphors that appear in translations of a broad range of texts from the Spanish in the later sixteenth century. Peter Burke, for his part, notes that early modern translation involves emulation—competition between the translators and the original authors—but he does not consider this in a political or transnational context ("Renaissance Translator," 28).

6. Terence Cave, *The Cornucopian Text: Problems of Writing in the French Renaissance*, (Oxford: Oxford University Press, 1979), 3.

7. Cave, 3, 6.

8. Richard Foster Jones, *The Triumph of the English Language* (Stanford, Calif.: Stanford University Press 1953); Richard Helgerson, *Forms of Nationhood: The Elizabethan Writing of England* (Chicago: University of Chicago Press, 1992), Paula Blank, *Broken English: Dialects and the Politics of Language in Renaissance Writings* (London: Routledge, 1996), especially Chapter 2, "The Thieves of Language" (33–68).

9. Pettie, "Preface" to *The Civile Conversation*, iii.

10. Blank, *Broken English*, 33. Blank cites from Carew's short treatise on *The Excellency of the English Tongue* (c. 1595), first published in William Camden, *Remaines Concerning Britain* (1614), 41. As Blank recalls, "the period 1500–1659 saw the introduction of between

10,000 and 25,000 new words into the language, with the practice of neologizing culminating in the Elizabethan period" (40).

11. Carew, 40.

12. Carew, 43, 40.

13. Samuel Daniel, *Musophilus* (1599), in *Samuel Daniel: The Complete Works in Verse and Prose*, ed. Alexander Grosart, 5 vols. (New York: Russell and Russell, 1963), 1:957–62.

14. Stephen Greenblatt discusses Daniel's "linguistic colonialism" in "Learning to Curse: Aspects of Linguistic Colonialism in the Sixteenth Century," in his *Learning to Curse: Essays in Early Modern Culture* (New York: Routledge, 1990), 16–39.

15. On the English rivalry with Spain, and its implications for England's construction of its national identity, see Richard Helgerson, "The Voyages of a Nation," in his *Forms of Nationhood*, and "Language Lessons."

16. For a survey of how translation functioned within the larger context of English competition with Spain, see Jonathan Hart, *Representing the New World: The English and French Uses of the Example of Spain* (New York: Palgrave, 2000).

17. Philemon Holland, *The Historie of the World, Commonly called, The Naturall Historie of C. Plinius Secundus. Translated into English by Philemon Holland, Doctor in Physycke, The First Tome* (London: Adam Islip, 1601), "The Preface to the Reader," unpaginated.

18. All citations from Luis Gutiérrez de la Vega, *A Compendious Treatise entitled De Re Militari*, trans. Nicholas Lichfield (London: Thomas East, 1582), "The Epistle Dedicatorie to the right Worshipful Maister Philip Sidney, Esquire," Aii. Lichfield also translated Lopes de Castanheda's *The first booke of the historie of the discouerie and conquest of the East Indias, enterprised by the Portingales, in their daungerous nauigations, in the time of King Don Iohn, the second of that name* (1582) from the Portuguese, and dedicated it to Francis Drake.

19. For the legal context for the Smerwick massacre, see Brian Lockey, *Law and Empire in English Renaissance Literature* (Cambridge: Cambridge University Press, 2008), 1–4.

20. Philip Sidney, *The Defence of Poesie* (London: William Ponsonby, 1595), I3.

21. Ibid., C2.

22. Greene argues that Sidney's own poetic project "produces lyrics that treat geopolitics more directly than most poems of the preceding generations ever do," giving voice to "the English impulse to rule abroad" (*Unrequited Conquests*, 178, 180).

23. Francisco de Valdés, *Dialogue of the Office of a Sergeant Major*, trans. John Thorius (London, 1590), A2.

24. *Theorique and Practise of Warre, Written to Don Philip Prince of Castil, by Don Bernardino de Mendoza. Translated out of the Castilian tonge into Englishe, by Sr. Edwarde Hoby, Knight. Directed to Sr. George Carew* (London, 1597). The above citations are all from the dedication, "Al muy Illtre. y discreto Cavallero Don Jorge Carew, Lugarteniente general de la Artillería, por su Sacra Cesárea Católica, Real Magd Donna Elizabeth nuestra Señora, en todos sus reinos, provincias y estados."

25. Clark Hulse, *Elizabeth I: Ruler and Legend* (Urbana: Illinois University Press, 2003), 55.

26. The normal clarification in these cases, "all translations mine unless otherwise noted," hardly seems adequate here. It is ironic that a chapter on English translations from the Spanish should require my translations of those very same texts from Spanish into English, but it does. Therefore: all translations of English translators writing in Spanish are mine; actual translations of Spanish texts into English are for the most part theirs.

27. Hoby, 9–10.

28. Richard Perceval, *Bibliotheca Hispanica* (London, 1591), unpaginated dedication.

29. Ibid.

30. George Carew, *The Historie of Aravcana written in verse by Don Alonso de Ercilla translated out of the spanishe into Englishe prose allmost to the Ende of the 16 Canto*, transcribed with an introduction and notes by Frank Pierce (Manchester: Manchester University Press, 1964), 2. Here is the original passage in Ercilla:

> Hacen su campo, y muéstranse en formados
> escuadrones distintos muy enteros,
> cada hila de más de cien soldados;
> entre una pica y otra los flecheros
> que de lejos ofenden desmandados
> bajo la protección de los piqueros,
> que van hombro con hombro, como digo,
> hasta medir a pica al enemigo.
>
> Si el escuadrón primero que acomete
> por fuerza viene a ser desbaratado,
> tan presto a socorrerle otro se mete,
> que casi no da tiempo a ser notado.
> Si aquél se desbarata, otro arremete,
> y estando ya el primero reformado,
> moverse de su término no puede
> hasta ver lo que al otro le sucede.
>
> De pantanos procuran guarnecerse
> por el daño y temor de los caballos,
> donde suelen a veces acogerse
> si viene a suceder desbaratallos;
> allí pueden seguros rehacerse,
> ofenden sin que puedan enojallos,
> que el falso sitio y gran inconveniente
> impide la llegada a nuestra gente.
>
> Del escuadrón se van adelantando
> los bárbaros que son sobresalientes,
> soberbios cielo y tierra despreciando,

ganosos de estremarse por valientes.
Los picas por los cuentos arrastrando,
poniéndose en posturas diferentes,
diciendo: "Si hay valiente algún cristiano,
salga luego adelante mano a mano."

Hasta treinta o cuarenta en compañía,
ambiciosos de crédito y loores,
vienen con grande orgullo y bizarría
al son de presurosos atambores;
las armas matizadas a porfía
con varias y finísimas colores,
de poblados penachos adornados,
saltando acá y allá por todos lados.

Hacen fuerzas o fuertes cuando entienden
ser el lugar y sitio en su provecho,
o si ocupar un término pretenden,
o por algún aprieto y grande estrecho;
de do más a su salvo se defienden
y salen de rebato a caso hecho,
recogiéndose a tiempo al sitio fuerte,
que su forma y hechura es desta suerte:

señalado el lugar, hecha la traza,
de poderosos árboles labrados
cercan una cuadrada y ancha plaza
en valientes estacas afirmados,
que a los de fuera impide y embaraza
la entrada y combatir, porque, guardados,
del muro los de adentro, fácilmente
de mucha se defiende poca gente.

Solían antiguamente de tablones
hacer dentro del fuerte otro apartado,
puestos de trecho a trecho unos troncones
en los cuales el muro iba fijado
con cuatro levantados torreones
a caballero del primer cercado,
de pequeñas troneras lleno el muro
para jugar sin miedo y más seguro.

En torno de esta plaza poco trecho
cercan de espesos hoyos por defuera:
cuál es largo, cuál ancho, y cuál estrecho,
y así van sin faltar desta manera,
para el incauto mozo que de hecho
apresura el caballo en la carrera
tras el astuto bárbaro engañoso
que le mete en el cerco peligroso.

También suelen hacer hoyos mayores
con estacas agudas en el suelo,
cubiertos de carrizo; yerba y flores,
porque puedan picar más sin recelo;
allí los indiscretos corredores
teniendo sólo por remedio el cielo,
se sumen dentro, y quedan enterrados
en las agudas puntas estacados.

(Alonso de Ercilla, *La Araucana*, ed. Isaías Lerner [Madrid: Cátedra, 1993],
1: 23–32.)

31. For a full reading of *La Araucana* as a traveling text, see my "Traveling Epic: Translating Ercilla's *La Araucana* in the Old World," *Journal of Medieval and Early Modern Studies* 36, 2 (Spring 2006): 379–95.

32. Richard Hakluyt, *The Principal Navigations, Voyages, Traffiques and Discoveries of
the English Nation* [1589/1600], 12 vols. (Glasgow: Maclehose and Sons, 1903), "The Epistle
Dedicatory to Sir Robert Cecil" [1599], 1: lxvi. For Hakluyt's role in promoting England's
early imperial expansion and recuperating failures, see Mary Fuller, *Voyages in Print: English Travel to America, 1576–1624* (Cambridge: Cambridge University Press, 1995). On the
emulation of Spain, see Hart, *Representing the New World.*

33. Donald Beecher, "The Legacy of John Frampton: Elizabethan Trader and Translator," *Renaissance Studie*s 20, 3 (2006): 320–39, citation on 321.

34. Beecher, 322.

35. Frampton entitled his translation *Joyfull Newes out of the Newe Founde Worlde
wherein is declared the rare and singular vertues of diverse and sundrie hearbes, trees, oyles,
plants and stones, with their applications, as well for phisicke as chirurgerie* (London: William
Norton, 1577).

36. Beecher, 329.

37. All citations from the Dedication to Gilbert, Frampton, trans., *A Brief Description
of the Ports, Creeks, Bays, and Havens of the West India* (London: 1578).

38. Beecher, 332.

39. Joseph Loewenstein, *The Author's Due: Printing and the Prehistory of Copyright*
(Chicago: University of Chicago Press, 2002).

40. Franklin Williams's *Index of Dedications and Commendatory Verses in English Books*

Before 1641 (London: Bibliographical Society, 1962) is one exception to the general critical neglect of the genre. Even Williams, however, dismisses commendatory verses as "metrical puffs" (xi). See also his "Commendatory Verses: The Rise of the Art of Puffing," in *Studies in Bibliography: Papers of the Bibliographical Society of the University of Virginia*, 19, ed. Fredson Bowers (Charlottesville: University Press of Virginia: 1966).

41. Jonson leads the way, by Franklin's count, with 30 commendatory poems to his name ("Commendatory Verses," 6). Jonson's habitual participation is obliquely recognized in William Cartwright's defense of John Fletcher in his own verses for the Beaumont and Fletcher folio, which Franklin cites:

> Nor hadst thou the sly trick, thy selfe to praise
> Under thy friends names, or to purchase Bayes
> Didst write stale commendations to thy Booke,
> Which we for *Beaumonts* or *Ben. Johnsons* tooke.

42. In this respect, Jonson's canonization of Shakespeare is more intriguing for its concern with an international stage—"Triumph, my Britain, though hast one to show, / to whom all scenes of Europe homage owe"—than for the English literary history it puts forth. As Heather James points out in her *Shakespeare's Troy: Drama, Politics, and the Translation of Empire* (Cambridge: Cambridge University Press, 1997), "When Shakespeare bests the great dramatists of Greece and Rome, not to mention Elizabethan England, his credit wondrously affects England as an emergent nation," 7.

43. For Jonson's denunciation of the would-be poet who "makes each man's wit his own," see *Epigrams* LVI, "On Poet-Ape," LXXIII, "To Fine Grand," LXXXI, "To Prowl the Plagiary," C, "On Playwright," and CXII, "To a Weak Gamester in Poetry."

44. Jonson's poem, generally grouped with the "Miscellaneous Poems" in modern editions, follows Drayton's in the 1618 *Georgicks of Hesiod* (London: H. Lounes for Miles Partrich). Subsequent citations are from this edition.

45. Chapman's translation of the *Iliad* was completed in 1611; the first half of the *Odyssey* appeared in 1614 and the second in 1615. *The Georgicks of Hesiod* followed in 1618.

46. As Millar MacLure underscores in his *George Chapman: A Critical Study* (Toronto: University of Toronto Press, 1966), "however [Chapman] might inveigh against detractors who claimed that he turned his Greek 'out of the Latine onely,' he always availed himself of the ease of a bilingual edition" (212).

47. In his *Imitation and Praise in the Poems of Ben Jonson* (New Haven, Conn.: Yale University Press, 1981), Richard S. Peterson notes that "even the name '*Chapman*,' or peddler, contributes to the mercantile metaphor here." Peterson reads the imagery of discovery as one of Jonson's "central, classically inspired metaphors for the process of imitation in writing," stressing Chapman's individual "monopoly excluding competition with potential rivals" rather than imperial rivalries between emerging powers (14). It is precisely the imbrication of the discourses of imperial discovery and of cultural value that interests me here. While other poets—including Chapman himself, in his own earlier commendatory poem to Jonson—use the imagery of the voyage and

discovery of classical culture, Jonson seems particularly intent on the enrichment of England through such excursions.

48. See Foster Jones's chapter "The Eloquent Language," in his *The Triumph of the English Language*.

49. *A Worlde of Wordes, Or Most copious and exact Dictionarie in Italian and English*, 1598, "To the Reader," cited in Jones.

50. Cf. Drayton's commendatory poem, published alongside Jonson's:

> *Chapman*; We finde by thy past-prized fraught,
> What wealth thou dost upon this land conferre;
> Th'olde Grecian Prophets hither that hast brought,
> Of their full words the true Interpreter:
> And by thy travell, strongly hast exprest
> The large dimensions of the English tongue;
> Delivering them so well, the first and best,
> That to the world in Numbers ever sung.
> Thou hast unlock'd the Treasury, wherein
> All Art, all Knowledge have so long been hidden:
> Which, till the gracefull Muses did begin
> Here to inhabite, was to us forbidden . . .

Like Jonson, Drayton describes Greek culture as treasure and celebrates the expansive possibilities of an English language of "large dimensions." Yet Drayton emphasizes the artless past of England, a land where the Muses have only recently alighted.

51. For the English voyages "Made to the North and North-east quarters of the World, with the directions, letters, privileges, discourses, and observations incident to the same," see Hakluyt's *Principal Navigations*, vols. II, III. The OED cites Richard Eden on the fabled Northeast passage in its nautical definition of the term: "Into the frosen sea . . . and so forth to Cathay (yf any suche passage may be found)." The parenthetical conditional is highly revealing.

52. See, for example, the ambivalent, hypothetical "Certain arguments to prove a passage by the Northwest " (1580), or the "Second voyage of John Davis for the Northwest Passage" (1586), collected in Hakluyt's *Principal Navigations*, VII, 191–203, 393–407. For the history of exploration "North and Northwest," see the chapter of that title in Kenneth Andrews, *Trade, Plunder and Settlement: Maritime Enterprise and the Genesis of the British Empire: 1480–1630*, (Cambridge: Cambridge University Press, 1984).

53. Hakluyt, VII, 191.

54. *The Voyages of William Baffin, 1612–1622*, ed. Clements. R. Markham (London: Hakluyt Society, 1881), 150, cited in Andrews.

55. Hakluyt himself contributed to the textual inflation of English accomplishments. As T.E. Armstrong has pointed out, many of the Arctic sea-routes for which Hakluyt claimed English primacy were well established in Russian and German sources ("The Arctic," in *The Hakluyt Handbook*, ed. D. B. Quinn, 2 vols. [London, 1974], 1: 254–60).

56. See, for example, the account of the "Second voyage made by Sir John Hawkins

to the Coast of Guinie" in Hakluyt's collection, which describes how the English force the Spaniards to trade with them in the West Indies (*Principal Navigations* X, 9–63).

57. The trope of translation as glorious imperial achievement, which Jonson applies to *The Works and Days*, is central to a far more famous poem on Chapman's translations, John Keats's "On First Looking into Chapman's Homer" (1816). Keats's sonnet figures literary exploration as a voyage of discovery:

> Much have I travell'd in the realms of gold,
> And many goodly states and kingdoms seen;
> Round many western islands have I been
> Which bards in fealty to Apollo hold.
> Oft of one wide expanse had I been told
> That deep-brow'd Homer ruled as his demesne;
> Yet did I never breathe its pure serene
> Till I heard Chapman speak out loud and bold:
> Then felt I like some watcher of the skies
> When a new planet swims into his ken;
> Or like stout Cortez when with eagle eyes
> He star'd at the Pacific—and all his men
> Look'd at each other with a wild surmise—
> Silent, upon a peak in Darien.

The English version of Homer domesticates the "wide expanse" of Greek letters, subjecting the newly discovered realm to the proprietary glance of the adventurer. Strikingly, the sonnet's last lines link the English translation of a Greek original to a glorious moment of *Spanish* discovery, and feature Hernán Cortés—the leader of the Spanish conquest of Mexico, perhaps the ultimate "realm of gold"—instead of the historically correct but less prestigious figure of Vasco Núñez de Balboa. While Keats does mention the English discovery of the planet Uranus, the metaphoric voyage out culminates in a return home from "western Islands"— the West Indies of the Spanish Main—to an English translation, with a pirating of Spanish discovery along the way, replacing the lackluster early history of British discoveries with a more prestigious narrative of Spanish imperial exploits. Moreover, by reprising Jonson's poem to Chapman, the sonnet inscribes itself within a preexisting tradition of such appropriations, which prospectively authorize its imperial vagaries.

58. For Fletcher's own relation to Spanish materials, see Chapter 3.

59. Jonson's own satirical response to the fashion for all things Spanish pervades *The Alchemist* (1610), a play in which even pretending to be a Spaniard guarantees success.

60. There is a similar operation at work in Jonson's "To Mr. Joshua Sylvester" (Epigram CXXXII), in which Jonson praises Sylvester's translation of Du Bartas by commending the translation over the original:

> Bartas doth wish his English were now his.
> So well in that are his inventions wrought,
> As his will now be the translation thought,

Thine the original; and France shall boast.
No more, those maiden glories she hath lost.

Yet in the first lines of the poem Jonson confesses that he is an "utter stranger to all air of France," and therefore cannot really assess Sylvester's "great pains" in translating the text.

61. All citations of Jonson or Mabbe's text are from *The Rogue, or the Life of Guzmán de Alfarache, Written in Spanish by Mateo Alemán and Done into English by James Mabbe* [1623], ed. James Fitzmaurice-Kelly (New York: Knopf, 1924). Jonson's poem is on 31.

62. This is also the scene where Falstaff states, "Well, I cannot last forever, but it was alway yet the trick of our English nation, if they have a good thing, to make it too common" (213–16).

63. "Pero yo que, aunque parezco padre, soy padrastro de Don Quijote . . . ," Miguel de Cervantes Saavedra, *El ingenioso hidalgo Don Quijote de la Mancha*, ed. Martín de Riquer (Barcelona: Planeta, 1997), 12.

64. Williams suggests that the mock-commendations that preface *Don Quijote* are the model for the "fantastic anthology" of commendatory poems in Thomas Coryate's *Crudities* (1611), including Jonson's ("Commendatory Verses," 11). Given that the publication of the *Crudities* predates Shelton's translation, Jonson may well have known the original Spanish text, although Shelton's translation may of course have circulated in manuscript form. Jonson refers to *Don Quijote* and the Spanish craze for chivalric romances as he mourns his own books in "An Execration upon Vulcan":

Had I compiled from *Amadis de Gaul*,
The *Esplandians*, *Arthurs*, *Palmerins*, and all
The learnèd library of Don Quixote,
And so some goodlier monster had begot . . . (29–32)

65. Thomas Shelton, trans., *The History of the Valorous and Wittie Knight-Errant, Don-Quixote of the Mancha* (London: Edward Blount, 1612), 3r–3v.

66. Cf. also John Florio's epistle dedicatory to his translation of Montaigne, where he describes himself as "at least a fondling-father, having transported [the text] from *France* to *England*; put it in English clothes; taught it to talke our tongue" (Michel de Montaigne, *The essayes or morall, politike and militarie discourses . . .* , trans. John Florio [London: Val. Sims for Edward Blount, 1603], A2).

67. Leonard Digges, "To Don Diego Puede-Ser, and His Translation of Guzman."

68. For a detailed analysis of Mabbe's frequent reliance on the Italian translation in Part II, see Fitzmaurice-Kelly's introduction, xxxii–xxxvi.

69. Jones, 21.

70. For a fascinating vision of the role of clothiers in the making of the English nation, see Thomas Deloney's Elizabethan prose fictions, *Iacke of Newberie* (registered 1597–98) and *Thomas of Reading* (written in 1597–1600). In the latter, Deloney emphasizes that "Among all crafts this was the onely chiefe, for that it was the greatest merchandize, by the which our Countrey became famous through all nations." *The Works of Thomas Deloney*, ed. Francis Oscar Mann (Oxford: Clarendon, 1912), 213. In the same text, the clothiers are instrumental in establishing uniform measures and regularizing the coin of the realm.

71. Barry Supple, *Commercial Crisis and Change in England, 1600–1642* (Cambridge: Cambridge University Press, 1959), 52. For an overview of the causes of the crisis, see also J. D. Gould, "The Trade Depression of the Early 1620s," *Economic History Review* 2nd ser. 8, 1 (August 1954): 81–90.

72. *Commons Debates 1621*, II.75, cited in Supple, 54.

73. Gould, 83; Supple, 58.

74. *Ben Jonson*, ed. C. H. Herford, Percy Simpson, and Evelyn Simpson, 11 vols. (Oxford: Clarendon, 1925–52), 8: 465.

Chapter 2. Knights and Merchants

Epigraph: Nahum Tate, *A Duke and No Duke*, cited in Randall and Boswell, 520.

1. For the particular conditions of the Blackfriars stage, see Tiffany Stern, "Taking Part: Actors and Audience on the Stage at Blackfriars," and Leslie Thomson, "Who's In, Who's Out: *The Knight of the Burning Pestle* on the Blackfriars Stage," in *Inside Shakespeare: Essays on the Blackfriars Stage*, ed. Paul Menzer (Selinsgrove, Pa.: Susquehanna University Press, 2006), 35–53, 61–71.

2. Francis Beaumont, *The Knight of the Burning Pestle*, ed. Sheldon P. Zitner (Manchester: Manchester University Press, 2004), 51. Subsequent references are in the text, by page or line number.

3. J. A. G. Ardila, "The Influence and Reception of Don Quixote in England, 1607–2005," in *The Cervantean Heritage: Reception and Influence of Cervantes in Britain*, ed. Ardila (London: Legenda, 2009), 2–31, citation on 3. For a collection of the more than one thousand allusions to Cervantes's works before 1700 that critics have identified to date, see Dale Randall and Jackson Boswell, *Cervantes in Seventeenth-Century England: The Tapestry Turned* (Oxford: Oxford University Press, 2009).

4. The other literary text was the pastoral romance by Luis Gálvez de Moltalvo, *El pastor de Fílida*, first published in 1600. For a complete list of the texts purchased with this donation, as well as its political and ideological context, see Gustav Ungerer, "The Earl of Southampton's Donation to the Bodleian in 1605," *Bodleian Library Record* 16, 1 (April 1997): 17–41. The entry by John Hales in the Bodleian Benefactors' Register is the first item in Randall and Boswell's catalog (1).

5. Ungerer, 30.

6. Tiffany Stern, "'The Forgery of some modern Author'?: Theobald's Shakespeare and Cardenio's *Double Falsehood*," *Shakespeare Quarterly* 62, 4 (Winter 2011): 555–93, citation on 558.

7. On Burre's strategies to find a market for the published text, see Zachary Lesser, "Walter Burre's *The Knight of the Burning Pestle*," *English Literary Renaissance* 29, 1 (1999): 22–43.

8. Francis Beaumont and John Fletcher, *The Knight of the Burning Pestle*, ed. Herbert Murch (New York: Henry Holt, 1908), xxxiii.

9. Murch, ed., xxxv.

10. These are such classic moments in *Don Quijote* that one could easily argue that even without reading the original Beaumont may well have been aware of these highlights. But of course there is no reason to imagine that he would not have been aware of them at all.

11. Murch, ed., xlii–xliv.

12. Rudolf Schevill, "On the Influence of Spanish Literature upon English in the Early 17th Century." *Romanische Forschugen* 20 (1907): 618, 620.

13. Francis Beaumont, *The Knight of the Burning Pestle*, ed. Michael Hattaway (London: New Mermaids, 1969), 18–19.

14. It is interesting to recall that toward the end of Part II of the novel, Don Quijote also gravitates toward a communal option: forbidden to play a knight any longer, he turns to the pastoral.

15. Donna B. Hamilton, *Anthony Munday and the Catholics, 1560–1633* (Burlington, Vt.: Ashgate, 2005), 80 ff.

16. Hamilton notes that the translation was "announced and entered" in 1580–81, then published repeatedly in 1596, 1602, 1609, and 1616 (81). The romance was first published in Portugal in 1544, by the Portuguese Francisco de Moraes.

17. Janette Dillon, "'Is Not All the World Mile End, Mother?': The Blackfriars Theater, the City of London, and *The Knight of the Burning Pestle*," *Medieval and Renaissance Drama in England: An Annual Gathering of Research, Criticism and Reviews* 9 (1997): 127–48, citation on 127.

18. Ibid., 128.

19. As Jean Howard points out, with a population of 200,000 in 1600, London was far larger than the next nineteen largest English towns put together, which totaled 136,000 people. The second largest city, Norwich, had a population of only 15,000. Howard, *Theater of a City: The Places of London Comedy, 1598–1642* (Philadelphia: University of Pennsylvania Press, 2007), 1.

20. Wendy Wall, *Staging Domesticity: Household Work and English Identity in Early Modern Drama* (Cambridge: Cambridge University Press, 2002), 163.

21. Wall, 187.

22. Howard, 20.

23. Patricia Parker, "Barbers and Barbary: Early Modern Cultural Semantics," *Renaissance Drama* 33 (2004): 201–44. The red beard is the key element in the disguise that the barber adopts in order to lure his friend Don Quijote home. See my *Passing for Spain: Cervantes and the Fictions of Identity* (Urbana: University of Illinois Press, 2003), 23–28.

24. The dream of marrying a princess, or taking her by force if need be, is at the heart of Don Quijote's most prolonged fantasy of social climbing, in Part I, Ch. 21 of Cervantes's novel. In a fascinating exchange with Sancho, Don Quijote worries about the extent to which his lineage will impede his being recognized for his works, however heroic, and allowed to marry the princess he deserves. Some chapters later, when the wealthy farmer's daughter Dorotea is convinced to pretend she is the exotic Princess Micomicona, Sancho

will urge Don Quijote to abandon his fantasies of Dulcinea and seize the immediate advantage in marrying her, to no avail.

25. On the staged representation of gender and conversion, see Jane Degenhardt, *Islamic Conversion and Christian Resistance on the Early Modern Stage* (Edinburgh: Edinburgh University Press, 2010).

26. With her reference to "properer women," Nell reminds us that the so-called Lady is a boy on the English transvestite stage, in one of the many metatheatrical moments in the play.

27. Dillon, 137; Howard, 6.

28. Gurr, "'Within the compass of the city walls': Allegiances in Plays for and About the City," in *Plotting Early Modern London: New Essays on Jacobean City Comedy*, ed. Dieter Mehl, Angela Stock, and Anne-Julia Zwierlein (Burlington, Vt.: Ashgate, 2004), 109–22, citation on 117.

29. "Wee have signified to your Highnesses many tymes heartofore the great inconvenience which we fynd to grow by the Comon exercise of Stage Playes . . . specially beinge of that frame and matter as usually they are, conteining nothinge but prophane fables, lascivious matters, cozeninge devises, & scurrilus beehaviours, which are so set forth as that they move wholie to imitation & not to the avoydinge of those faults & vices which they represent. . . . wee have fownd by th' examination of divers apprentices & other servantes whoe have confessed unto us that the said Staige playes were the very places of theire Randevous appoynted by them to meete with such otheir as wear to joigne with them in theire designes & mutinus attemptes, beeinge allso the ordinarye places for maisterless men to come together & to recreate themselves." Cited in E. K. Chambers, *The Elizabethan Stage*, 4 vols. (Oxford: Clarendon, 1923), 4:321.

30. It is interesting to contrast how martial enterprise, however satirized, elides class difference in the mercantile *Knight of the Burning Pestle*, where Rafe's mock-muster can bring together "gentlemen" and "countrymen" as a matter of course, with the work required to transcend class lines and create an English army in a play like *Henry V* (1599), characterized by its aristocratic and chivalric ethos. Henry explicitly takes on the problem of class difference in his two most famous speeches: "Once more into the breach, dear friends, once more" (3.1.1), he begins, but the fellowship is soon fractured into class lines, so that by the end of the speech he must make a specific (and somewhat taunting) appeal to the yeomen:

> And you, good yeomen,
> Whose limbs were made in England, show us here
> The mettle of your pasture; let us swear
> That you are worth your breeding—which I doubt not,
> For there is none of you so mean and base
> That hath not noble lustre in your eyes. (3.1.25–30)

In the Crispin's Day speech in 4.3, Henry calls forth the famous "We few, we happy few, we band of brothers" (4.3.60), but follows the rousing invocation with a reminder of how exactly the social leveling will work: "For he today that sheds his blood with me

/ Shall be my brother; be he ne'er so vile, / This day shall gentle his condition" (61–63). The reminder of vile condition even as the promise is made to erase it suggests at best an imperfect transformation. Moreover, the occasion for the speech is the fear that there are not enough soldiers on the English side, so that the offer of social leveling has the distinct feel of a transaction offered in a moment of acute need. Dillon notes the echoes of Henry's Agincourt speech in Rafe's lines, but she argues that it "substitutes London for England" (139).

31. Lesser, "Walter Burre's *The Knight of the Burning Pestle*," 37.

32. Lesser, 35–38. Gurr notes, along similar lines, "Beaumont placed his product in a playhouse where he expected the gentry, gallants, and court-followers, to welcome a satire on citizen values" (116).

33. I make a similar argument about the different valences of *A Game at Chess* for different audiences in Chapter 3.

34. Thomas Kyd, *The Spanish Tragedy*, ed. J. R. Mulryne (London: A&C Black, 1989), 1.1.5–7.

35. Kyd, 1.1.1–2.

36. Alexander Legatt notes how money serves to buy the privileged audience of two exactly the play they want, no matter how discontinuous: "The Audience as Patron: *The Knight of the Burning Pestle*," in *Shakespeare and Theatrical Patronage in Early Modern England*, ed. Paul Whitfield White and Suzanne Westfall (Cambridge: Cambridge University Press, 2002), 306. But he misses the Cervantine antecedent to Rafe's refusal to pay for his lodging because the genre of chivalric romance does not allow it (300–301).

37. See Lesser, "Walter Burre's *The Knight of the Burning Pestle*," on the connection between Rafe and the apprentice Face in Jonson's *The Alchemist* as masterful manipulators of dramatic convention.

38. Kathleen Ashleyn and Véronique Plesch. Introduction to *The Cultural Processes of "Appropriation"*, special issue, *Journal of Medieval and Early Modern Studies* 32, 1 (2002): 6.

Chapter 3. Plotting Spaniards, Spanish Plots

1. On English mistrust of the peace, see Paul C. Allen, *Philip III and the Pax Hispanica, 1598–1621: The Failure of Grand Strategy* (New Haven, Conn.: Yale University Press, 2000), 137–38.

2. On Fletcher's zealously protestant family, see Gordon McMullan, *The Politics of Unease in the Plays of John Fletcher* (Amherst: University of Massachusetts Press, 1994).

3. Alexander Samson, "1623 and the Politics of Translation," in Samson, ed., *The Spanish Match: Prince Charles's Journey to Madrid, 1623* (Aldershot: Ashgate, 2006), 91–106, esp. 100–101.

4. For the diplomatic correspondence and court intrigue around the "Spanish match," see Glyn Redworth, *The Prince and the Infanta: The Cultural Politics of the Spanish Match* (New Haven, Conn.: Yale University Press, 2003). Redworth betrays a very English disdain

for Spanish mores, yet underscores the constant Spanish advantage in the negotiations. See also the more balanced collection edited by Sansom.

5. Middleton used several of these pamphlets, including Thomas Scott's *Vox Populi* (1620, 1624) and Reynold's *Vox Coeli* (1624) in his construction of the Black Knight Gondomar. See Jerzy Limon, *Dangerous Matter: English Drama and Politics in 1623/4* (Cambridge: Cambridge University Press, 1986). Tellingly, the full title of the pamphlet is *Vox Coeli, or, Newes from heauen, of a consvltation there held by the high and mighty princes, King Hen. 8, King Edw. 6, Prince Henry, Queene Mary, Queene Elizabeth, and Queene Anne; wherein Spaines ambition and treacheries to most kingdomes and free estates of Europe, are vnmask'd and truly represented, but more particularly towards England, and now more especially vnder the pretended match of Prince Charles, with the infanta Dona Maria; Whereunto is annexed two letters written by Queene Mary from heauen, the one to Count Gondomar, the ambassadour of Spaine, the other to all the Romane Catholiques of England* (London, 1624).

6. Samson, 100.

7. See Claire Jowitt, "Massinger's *The Renegado* (1624) and the Spanish Marriage," *Cahiers Élizabéthains* 65 (2004): 45–54.

8. *Thomas Middleton: The Collected Works*, ed. Gary Taylor and John Lavagnino (Oxford: Oxford University Press, 2007), 1776.

9. I cite here and throughout from *A Later Form of A Game at Chess*, in *Collected Works*.

10. Taylor, 1826.

11. Interestingly, Richard Wilson finds equivocation throughout Marlowe's play: "Much has been written about the Jesuit casuistry of 'lying like truth,' but *The Jew of Malta* may be the first play to highlight 'equivocation' as negotiable currency in modern markets" (Wilson, "Another Country: Marlowe and the Trading Factor," in *Renaissance Go-Betweens: Cultural Exchange in Early Modern Europe*, ed. Andreas Höfele and Werner von Koppenfels [Berlin: Gruyter, 2005], 77–99, citation on 182).

12   A key figure in this improbable link between Machiavelli and Catholicism may have been Tommaso Campanella, the Neapolitan theologian who both denounced Machiavelli and adapted his insights to Counter-Reformation ends. Although Campanella was involved in several plots against Spanish rule in Naples, he also wrote the *Monarchia di Spagna* (1600) in which he offered theological justifications for Spain's universal rule. While a translation of Campanella, that "second Machiavel," into English was not published until 1653, a German translation from 1620 gives some sense of the work's wide circulation. The English and German versions are Edmund Chilead, *Thomas Campanella, an Italian friar and second Machiavel, his advice to the King of Spain for attaining the universal Monarchy of the World* (London, 1659) and *Von der spanischen Monarchy* (Frankfurt, 1620). Middleton himself read Italian, so he may have been acquainted with Campanella's text in the original. It seems likely that Campanella's *Monarchia* is itself an example of equivocation, as Campanella, a committed foe of Spanish rule in Italy, wrote it while in prison. The text that these early English readers seized on as evidence of Spain's universal ambitions may itself be far more slippery than it appears.

13. Arthur F. Marotti, *Religious Ideology and Cultural Fantasy: Catholic and Anti-Catholic Discourses in Early Modern England* (Notre Dame, Ind.: University of Notre Dame Press, 2005), 133.

14. Marotti, 131–32.

15. Reynolds, *Vox Coeli*, 86.

16. James Howell, *Epistolae Ho-Elianae: The Familiar Letters of James Howell*, ed. Joseph Jacobs (London: D. Nutt, 1890), 193.

17. Ann Rosalind Jones, "Italians and Others: The White Devil (1612)," in *Staging the Renaissance: Reinterpretations of Elizabethan and Jacobean Drama*, ed. David Scott Kastan and Peter Stallybrass (New York: Routledge, 1991), 251–62, citation on 251.

18. On the racialization of Spain, see my "The Spanish Race" in *Rereading the Black Legend: The Discourses of Religious and Racial Difference in the Renaissance Empires*, ed. Margaret Greer, Walter Mignolo, and Maureen Quilligan (Chicago: University of Chicago Press, 2007) and Griffin, *English Renaissance Drama and the Specter of Spain*.

19. Richard Dutton, "Thomas Middleton's *A Game at Chess*: A Case Study," in *The Cambridge History of British Theatre*, vol. 1, ed. Jane Milling and Peter Thomson (Cambridge: Cambridge University Press, 2004), 424–38, citation on 435.

20. While the OED uses the publication date 1613, the play is usually dated to 1607. OED, s.v. *plot* 6. *Plat* seems to have been used with the same meaning at the end of the sixteenth century (s.v. *plat*, 3.6).

21. Taylor points to "The Spaniard's Speech in Spanish" (129–39) in Middleton's pageant *The Triumphs of Honour and Industry* (1617) as evidence for the playwright's knowledge of the language (Gary Taylor and John Lavagnino, eds., *Thomas Middleton and Early Modern Textual Culture: A Companion to the Collected Works* [Oxford: Oxford University Press, 2007], 437).

22. As I discuss in greater detail in Chapter 5, in 1994 the self-styled expert Charles Hamilton published *The Second Maiden's Tragedy* as Shakespeare's *Cardenio*. Although the identification was given virtually no credence by serious scholars, it has led to a spate of productions of Middleton's play under the Shakespearean imprimatur and brisk sales of Hamilton's edition.

23. John Reynolds, *The Triumphs of God's Revenge* (1621), History IV. Reynolds locates Alsemero precisely as a Spanish soldier, frustrated by the truce in the Netherlands, and bemoans the immorality of Alsemero and Beatrice-Joanna meeting in a "Popish" church that serves as a "stewes" or brothel (114).

24. For a discussion of the play's authorship, see Douglas Bruster's entry for *The Changeling* in Taylor and Lavagnino, eds., *Thomas Middleton and Early Modern Textual Culture*, 422–23.

25. Swapan Chakravorty, *Society and Politics in the Plays of Thomas Middleton* (Oxford: Clarendon, 1996), 145.

26. In a production in Los Angeles by the Independent Shakespeare Company (October–November 2009), De Flores was played by a swarthy Hispanic actor, Luis Galindo, and Beatrice-Joanna by a fair blonde, Melissa Chalsma. The casting brought out the uneven

"Spanishness" of the play, in which some characters are marked by ethnicity while others are not.

27. It is interesting to juxtapose *The Changeling* to the fascinating contemporaneous play by Lope de Vega, *El perro del hortelano* (*The Dog in the Manger*, pub. 1618). In Lope's play, produced in English as part of the Royal Shakespeare Company's 2004 Spanish Golden Age season, a duchess is tricked into marrying her secretary, a fate she happily accepts, given that she has been in love with him all along. The pretense assumes that the characters recognize the arbitrariness and constructedness of class distinctions.

28. Margot Heinemann, *Puritanism and Theatre: Thomas Middleton and Opposition Drama under the Early Stuarts* (Cambridge: Cambridge University Press, 1980); A. A. Bromham and Zara Bruzzi, The Changeling *and the Years of Crisis, 1619–1624: A Hieroglyph of Britain* (London: Pinter, 1990).

29. Cristina Malcolmson, "'As Tame as the Ladies': Politics and Gender in *The Changeling*," *English Literary Renaissance* 20 (1990): 320–39, citation on 332.

30. *The Spanish Gypsy* is very difficult to attribute correctly, given the number of collaborators and the intense level of collaboration, even within scenes. For purposes of my discussion, however, what is most important is the rich and contradictory vision of Spain that emerges from the use of Spanish materials, not the authorship of any individual scene. Moreover, as Gary Taylor argues, "If the plot/scenario for the play was written primarily by one author, Middleton is the likeliest candidate" (*Thomas Middleton and Early Modern Textual Culture*, 437). For a discussion of the play's authorship, see 433–38.

31. For a comparison of *The Spanish Gypsy* and *A Game at Chess*, see Gary Taylor, "Historicism, Presentism, and Time: Middleton's *The Spanish Gypsy* and *A Game at Chess*," *SEDERI: Journal of the Spanish Society for English Renaissance Studies* 18 (2008): 147–70.

32. For the enduring interest in Spanish materials, see Trudi Darby, "The Black Knight's Festival Book? Thomas Middleton's *A Game at Chess*," in Samson, ed., *The Spanish Match*, 184.

33. Taylor, "Historicism, Presentism, and Time," 151–55.

34. Taylor, 155–56. In setting up this love triangle, Middleton may also be rewriting *Don Quijote* I.42–43, where the young Don Luis is discovered at the inn that he has reached in search of his beloved Clara. Don Fernando, the predatory nobleman who steals Cardenio's Luscinda (as I discuss in Chapter 4), and who seems eager to help Luis in this episode, recalls Roderigo. I am grateful to Walter Cohen for pointing out this connection.

35. In her introduction to the play in the *Collected Works*, Suzanne Gossett links this plot to the others by arguing that it is "also constructed around conflicting filial emotions" (*Thomas Middleton: The Collected Works*, 1724) and that, like Clara, Luis will seek "A noble satisfaction, though not revenge" (3.3.96). Although these echoes certainly contribute to the intricate patterning of the play, they do not really constitute dramatic necessity or a strong plot link.

36. As Taylor points out in his edition, the play takes much of its cant and depiction of the underworld from James Mabbe's *The Rogue* (1622), a translation of the wildly popular

Spanish picaresque *Guzmán de Alfarache*, which I discuss in Chapter 1. What is striking, is how that generic identification is repeatedly refused in the play.

37. See Trudi Darby, "Cervantes in England: The Influence of Golden-Age Prose Fiction on Jacobean Drama, c.1615–1625," *Bulletin of Hispanic Studies* 74 (1997): 425–41; Darby and Alexander Samson. "Cervantes on the Jacobean Stage," and Samson, "'Last Thought upon a Windmill'?: Cervantes and Fletcher," both in *The Cervantean Heritage: Reception and Influence of Cervantes in Britain*, ed. J. A. G. Ardila (London: Legenda, 2009); and Diana de Armas Wilson's two essays on Fletcher's debt to Cervantes, "Contesting the Custom of the Country: Cervantes and Fletcher," in *From Dante to García Márquez: Studies in Romance Literatures and Linguistics*, ed. Gene H. Bell-Villada, Antonio Giménez, and George Pistorius (Williamstown, Mass.: Williams College, 1987), 60–75, and "Of Piracy and Plackets: Cervantes' *La señora Cornelia* and Fletcher's *The Chances*," in *Cervantes for the 21st Century*, ed. Francisco La Rubia Prado (Newark, Del. : Juan de la Cuesta, 2000, 49–60).

38. McMullan, *The Politics of Unease*, 258.

39. James Mabbe, *The Rogue, or the Life of Guzmán de Alfarache, Written in Spanish by Mateo Alemán and Done into English by James Mabbe* [1623], ed. James Fitzmaurice-Kelly (London: Constable, 1924), 29.

40. McMullan, 257.

41. George Walton Williams follows Cyrus Hoy in attributing *Rule a Wife* solely to Fletcher in his edition of the play, in *The Dramatic Works in the Beaumont and Fletcher Canon*, gen. ed. Fredson Bowers, 10 vols. (Cambridge: Cambridge University Press, 1985), 6: 483–605. Subsequent references are to this edition, by act, scene, and line number.

42. Both Fletcher's Spanish sources and his competence in Spanish were convincingly established by Hispanist Edward M. Wilson. See Wilson, "*Rule a Wife and Have a Wife* and *El sagaz Estacio*," *Review of English Studies* 24 (1948): 189–94.

43. Margarita was also the name of the mother of Charles's intended, Princess Maria, and her brother Philip IV of Spain.

44. Hakluyt, ed., *The Principal Navigations*, XI.116.

45. On Drake as a fire-drake, cf. the ravishment of Spanish ships recounted in the contemporaneous play *Dick of Devonshire* (pub. 1626), where piracy and sea-battles are figured as a macabre domestic scene of childbirth:

> when o^r shipps
> carryed such fire drakes in them, that ye huge
> Spanish Galleasses, Galleons, Hulkes & Carrackes,
> being great wth gold, in labour wth some fright,
> were all delivered of fine red cheekt Children
> At Plymouth, Portsmouth, & other English Havens,
> & onely by men midwives: had not Spayne reason
> to cry out, oh Diablos Ingleses?

(James Gilmer McManaway and Mary R. McManaway, eds., *Dick of Devonshire* [London: Malone Society Reprints, 1955], 9–10)

46. Cf. Cervantes's supremely ironic *Exemplary Novels*, the collection from which Fletcher takes his subplot, where enlisting often serves as a cover for picaresque activity.

47. Williams notes in his "Textual Introduction" to the play an 1816 review in *Edinburgh Review* that echoes the striking possessiveness of *Rule a Wife*, which, the review claims, "holds, to this day, undisputed possession of the stage" (485).

48. For an analogous argument on the layered, iterative historiographical and cultural use of central figures, see Kevin M. F. Platt, *Terror and Greatness: Ivan and Peter as Russian Myths* (Ithaca, N.Y.: Cornell University Press, 2011).

CHAPTER 4. *CARDENIO* LOST AND FOUND

Epigraph: Rudolf Schevill, "On the Influence of Spanish Literature upon English in the Early 17th Century," *Romanische Forschugen* 20 (1907): 631.

1. E. K. Chambers, *William Shakespeare: A Study of Facts and Problems*, 2 vols. (Oxford: Clarendon, 1930), 2:343.

2. *Double Falshood; or The Distrest Lovers. A play, as it is acted at the Theatre-Royal in Drury-Lane. Written originally by W. Shakespeare; and now revised and adapted to the stage by Mr. Theobald, the author of* Shakespeare Restor'd (London: J. Watts, 1728). David Scott Kastan notes the irony of Shakespeare's "restorer" revising and adapting *Double Falshood*, a dichotomy that exemplifies the two approaches that he finds contemporaneously in the eighteenth century: "But in the single figure of Lewis Theobald can be seen the era's schizophrenic relation to Shakespeare—always admiring, but, in one mode, presumptuously altering his plays for success on the stage, while, in another, determinedly seeking the authentic text in the succession of scholarly editions that followed Rowe's" (*Shakespeare and the Book* [Cambridge: Cambridge University Press, 2001], 93). See also Michael Dobson, *The Making of the National Poet: Shakespeare, Adaptation and Authorship, 1660–1769* (Oxford: Clarendon, 1992) and James Marino, *Owning Shakespeare* (Philadelphia: University of Pennsylvania Press, 2011).

3. G. Harold Metz, ed., *Sources of Four Plays Ascribed to Shakespeare* (Columbia: University of Missouri Press, 1989), 257.

4. Dobson, *The Making of the National Poet*, 131n.

5. For the most recent skeptical account of Theobald's role, see Tiffany Stern, "'The Forgery of some modern Author'?: Theobald's Shakespeare and Cardenio's *Double Falsehood*," *Shakespeare Quarterly* 62, 4 (Winter 2011): 555–93.

6. In a letter "To the Author of the British Gazetteer," *Weekly Journal or the British Gazetteer*, February 10, 1728, 142, cited in Metz, 261.

7. "The Modern Poets," *Gentlemen's Magazine* 111 (November 1731): 493; cited in Metz, 261.

8. For a full account of the acrimony between Pope and Theobald, and the cultural

capital at stake, see Brean Hammond, *Double Falsehood, or The Distressed Lovers* (London: Arden Shakespeare, 2010), 66–70, 307–19.

9. Howard Marchitello, "Finding *Cardenio*," *English Literary History* 74 (2007): 957–87, citation on 979.

10. *Double Falshood; or The Distrest Lovers. A play, as it is acted at the Theatre-Royal in Drury-Lane. Written originally by W. Shakespeare; and now revised and adapted to the stage by Mr. Theobald, the author of Shakespeare Restor'd. The second edition* (London: J. Watts, 1728), Preface.

11. Theobald, my emphasis.

12. Hammond, ed., 92.

13. John Freehafer, "Cardenio, by Shakespeare and Fletcher," *PMLA* 84 (1969): 507.

14. Kenneth Muir, *Shakespeare as Collaborator* (London: Methuen, 1960), 160.

15. Stephan Kukowski, "The Hand of John Fletcher in *Double Falsehood*," *Shakespeare Survey* 43 (1991): 84.

16. Kukowski, 89. Theobald seems to have been unaware of the entry in the Stationers' Registry that ascribed the play to both Shakespeare and Fletcher.

17. Marchitello, "Finding *Cardenio*," 961.

18. William Shakespeare and John Fletcher, *Henry VIII (All Is True)*, ed. Gordon Mc-Mullan (London: Arden, 2000), 181. On collaboration, see also Jeffrey Masten, *Textual Intercourse: Collaboration, Authorship, and Sexualities in Renaissance Drama* (Cambridge: Cambridge University Press, 1997).

19. Leah Marcus, *Puzzling Shakespeare: Local Reading and its Discontents* (Berkeley: University of California Press, 1988), 44.

20. For Pope's vicious emphasis on this line, see Hammond, ed., *Double Falsehood*, 322–24.

21. Richard Wilson, "Unseasonable Laughter: The Context of Cardenio," in *Shakespeare's Late Plays: New Readings*, ed. Jennifer Richards and James Knowles (Edinburgh: Edinburgh University Press, 1999): 193–209.

22. *Double Falshood*, 5.2, p. 59.

23. *William Shakespeare: The Complete Works*, 2nd ed., ed. Stanley Wells and Gary Taylor (Oxford: Clarendon, 2005); *The Norton Shakespeare, Based on the Oxford Edition*, 2nd ed., ed. Stephen Greenblatt, Walter Cohen, Jean E. Howard, and Katharine Eisaman Maus (New York: Norton, 1997, 2008), vi. *Love's Labours Won* receives similar treatment (837), although the evidence for that play is much scanter than for *Cardenio*. Greenblatt's slight revision of the Oxford entry on *Cardenio* carries a whiff of optimism, with much more *Cardenio* on the horizon. Whereas the 2005 Oxford edition concludes: "Though [*Double Falshood*] deserved its limited success, it is now no more than an interesting curiosity" (1245), Greenblatt's revision for the Norton, published just three years later, is more open-ended: "Theobald's play stands as a tantalizing reminder of what has been lost" (3117).

24. Jonathan Gil Harris, "Recent Studies in Tudor and Stuart Drama," *SEL Studies in English Literature 1500–1900* 51, 2 (2011): 465–513, citation on 501–2.

25. Hammond, ed., 81–84.

26. Hammond, ed., "General Editors' Preface," xvi.

27. Ibid., 3.

28. Ibid., 6.

29. Bernard Richards, "Now am I in Arden," Rev. of *Double Falsehood, or The Distressed Lovers*, ed. Brean Hammond, *Essays in Criticism* 61, 1 (2011): 79–88.

30. Trudi Darby and Alexander Samson, "'Cervantes on the Jacobean Stage" and Alexander Samson, "'Last Thought upon a Windmill'?: Cervantes and Fletcher," in *The Cervantean Heritage: Reception and Influence of Cervantes in Britain*, ed. J. A. G. Ardila (London: Legenda, 2009).

31. Stern, 580–83. The full title of the novella is *The Adventures on the Black Mountains; A Tale, Upon which the Plan of a Posthumous Play, call'd Double Falsehood, was written Originally by W. Shakespeare* (Samuel Croxall, ed., *Select Collection of Novels and Histories*, 6 vols. [London, 1729], 1:311–38). Shakespearean "originality" here masks Cervantine origins. Stern argues, moreover, that the Arden Shakespeare publication of *Double Falsehood* "has obliged its excellent editor, Brean Hammond, to avoid the bits of the Theobald story that relate to Fletcher (there is no mention in the Arden edition that Theobald was a Fletcher editor) or *Don Quixote* (there is no mention in the Arden that Theobald was a Cervantes fanatic, or that he worked with, and perhaps wrote or translated, a novel based on the Cardenio story)" (592–93).

32. See Dale B. J. Randall and Jackson C. Boswell, eds., *Cervantes in Seventeenth-Century England: The Tapestry Turned* (Oxford: Oxford University Press, 2009) and Ardila, ed, *The Cervantean Heritage*.

33. For a more suspicious reading of Jonson's praise, see Marino, *Owning Shakespeare*, 134–35.

34. Dobson, 5. Dobson makes a fascinating case for the construction of Shakespeare both as a national deity and as cultural capital for export in the eighteenth century. As my reading of Jonson suggests, I see some of the same dynamics much earlier.

35. On landscape as property in early modern drama, see Garrett Sullivan, *The Drama of Landscape: Land, Property, and Social Relations on the Early Modern Stage* (Stanford, Calif.: Stanford University Press, 1998).

36. Theobald, *Double Falshood*, Prologue.

37. On eighteenth-century efforts to make Shakespeare conform to neoclassical norms, see Kastan.

38. Margreta de Grazia, *Shakespeare Verbatim* (Oxford: Clarendon, 1991), 44–45.

39. Hammond, ed., 60.

40. See Christine Gerrard, *The Patriot Opposition to Walpole: Politics, Poetry, and National Myth, 1725–1742* (Oxford: Clarendon, 1994), esp. Chapter 6, "Political Elizabethanism and the Spenser Revival," 150–84, citations on 157. Theobald may have absorbed some of his own jingoism from Jacobean texts. Stern notes that, when offered a benefit night by the Drury Lane company, Theobald chose to present *Rule a Wife and Have a Wife*, which I discuss in Chapter 3.

41. Lewis Theobald, *Memoirs of Sir Walter Raleigh* (London: W. Mears, 1719).

42. Ibid., 5, 7.

43. Ibid., 20.

44. Ibid., 26.

45. Gerrard.

46. Cited in Dobson, 201.

47. See John Loftis, "English Renaissance Plays from the Spanish Comedia," *English Literary Renaissance* 14, 2 (Spring 1984): 230–48, reprised in his *Renaissance Drama in England and Spain: Topical Allusion and History Plays* (Princeton, N.J.: Princeton University Press, 1987).

48. Barbara Mowat, "The Theater and Literary Culture," in *A New History of Early English Drama*, ed. John D. Cox and David Scott Kastan (New York: Columbia University Press, 1997), 213–30.

49. Cohen's disappointment at the relative formalism of the studies is evident in his afterword to *Comedias del Siglo de Oro and Shakespeare*, ed. Susan L. Fischer (Lewisburg, Pa.: Bucknell University Press, 1989), 142–51.

50. Aside from the Cohen and Loftis monographs and Fischer's collection, there are two volumes of conference proceedings on the topic: *Parallel Lives: Spanish and English National Drama, 1580–1680*, ed. Louise and Peter Fothergill-Payne (Lewisburg, Pa.: Bucknell University Press, 1991) and *Vidas paralelas: el teatro español y el teatro isabelino, 1580–1680*, ed. Anita K. Stoll (London: Támesis,1993). A more promising recent bilingual collection, *Between Cervantes and Shakespeare: Trails Along the Renaissance*, ed. Zenón Luis Martínez and Luis Gómez Canseco (Newark, Del.: Juan de la Cuesta, 2006), includes some essays under "Crossroads" but far more under "Parallel Paths."

51. Valerie Wayne, "The *Don Quixote* Effect on Early Modern Drama," in the program for the RSC *Cardenio: Shakespeare's Lost Play Re-imagined* (2011) and "*Don Quixote* and Shakespeare's Collaborative Turn to Romance," forthcoming in Gary Taylor and David Carnegie, eds., *The Quest for Cardenio*. I am grateful to Professor Wayne for sharing the unpublished essay with me.

52. See Catherine Boyle and David Johnston, eds., with Janet Morris, *The Spanish Golden Age in English: Perspectives on Performance* (London: Oberon, 2007).

53. Catherine Boyle, "Perspectives on Loss and Discovery: Reading and Reception," in Boyle and Johnston, eds., 61–74, citation on 61–62. Boyle is citing Susannah Clapp, "Putting Shakespeare in His Place," *The Observer*, April 25, 2004. In an interview with David McGrath in Boyle and Johnston's volume, director Jonathan Munby claims, "We should absolutely be looking to our own forgotten works at the same time as bringing Golden Age into the repertoire. There are many, many plays that I want to do, contemporaries of Shakespeare and so on, but at the moment I simply cannot get a production of them in a professional context" (133–40, citation on 138). What Munby fails to note is how many of those plays might lead back to Spain.

Chapter 5. *Cardenios* for Our Time

Epigraph: Antonio Machado, "El mañana efímero," in *Campos de Castilla (1907–1917)*, ed. Geoffrey Ribbans (Madrid: Cátedra, 2006), 213–14.

1. The play has also been recreated by Gary Taylor, whose *The History of Cardenio* produced in Wellington, New Zealand, in May 2009, is an attempt to "unadapt" *Double Falshood*, and by Bernard Richards, whose *Cardenio*, produced in March 2009 at Queen's College, Cambridge, added six scenes by Richards to *Double Falshood*. See Hammond, ed., *Double Falshood*, 124–30.

2. Stephen Greenblatt, "Theatrical Mobility," in Greenblatt et al., eds. *Cultural Mobility: A Manifesto* (Cambridge: Cambridge University Press, 2010), 75–95.

3. "Cardenio: Greenblatt Interview," YouTube, http://www.youtube.com/watch?v=SRxd2Q0-UXc, consulted March 31, 2009.

4. Greenblatt, "Theatrical Mobility," 78.

5. "About the (Re)making Project," http://www.charlesmee.org/html/about.html, consulted March 31, 2009.

6. Interview by Ryan McKittrick, http://www.amrep.org/articles/6_4/como.html, consulted March 31, 2009.

7. I am grateful to Professor Greenblatt for making available to me a late draft of the play, which is now available online at http://www.fas.harvard.edu/~cardenio/us-script.html

8. Greenblatt, "Theatrical Mobility," 85.

9. See David Quint, *Cervantes's Novel of Modern Times* (Princeton, N.J.: Princeton University Press, 2003) on how to read the interpolated novellas in relation to the main plot.

10. Greenblatt, "Theatrical Mobility," 84.

11. See A. S. Rosenbach, "The Curious-Impertinent in English Dramatic Literature before Shelton's Translation of *Don Quijote*," *MLN* 17, 6 (June 1906): 179–84, and William Peery, *The Plays of Nathaniel Field* (Austin: University of Texas Press, 1950).

12. Theatre Communications Group—New Plays Website, http://www.tcg.org/tools/newplays/details.cfm?ShowID=1.

13. On the canonization of Shakespeare, see Michael Dobson, *The Making of the National Poet: Shakespeare, Adaptation and Authorship, 1660–1769* (Oxford: Clarendon, 1992).

14. *The Life and Complete Works in Prose and Verse of Robert Greene*, ed. Alexander. B. Grosart, 15 vols. (London, 1881–86), XII.144. See Loewenstein, *Ben Jonson and Possessive Authorship*, 84–89.

15. *Boston Globe*, May 10, 2008.

16. Charles Hamilton, *William Shakespeare and John Fletcher: Cardenio or the Second Maiden's Tragedy* (Lakewood, Colo.: Glenbridge, 1994), 1.

17. See Hamilton, Chapter 3, "Shakespeare and Cervantes: Collaborators." The title aside, Hamilton sets out to chart the "vast disparity between their literary talents, with Shakespeare far outshining his Spanish counterpart" (187). Despite such tendentiousness,

Hamilton's bizarre edition continues to sell; such is the power of the Shakespearean imprimatur.

18. Greenblatt, "Theatrical Mobility," 90.

19. Interestingly, in his *Cardenio entre Cervantes et Shakespeare: Histoire d'une pièce perdue* (Paris: Gallimard, 2011), Roger Chartier notes the early modern cultural mobility of Cervantes's Cardenio, adapted on the Spanish stage by Guillén de Castro and on the French by a certain Pichou.

20. See, for example, the front-page article by Reshmi Sengupta, "Shakespeare, Found via Tagore," which notes, "Shakespeare is said to have written *Cardenio* inspired by an episode from Cervantes's *Don Quixote*, where the character Cardenio tests the chastity of his wife by asking his friend to seduce her" (*Telegraph*, Calcutta, Thursday January 4, 2007), or the subsequent review in the same paper (March 24, 2007), "Finding El Dorado," in which Ananda Lai deems *Cardenio* the "El Dorado of Shakespearean texts" and explains the plot of *Jaha Chai*: "As in Cervantes' episode, a husband (Goutam Halder) foolishly decides to test the virtue of his wife (Sohini Sengupta-Halder) by persuading his best friend (Debsankar Halder) to try to seduce her," http://www.telegraphindia.com/1070324/asp/opinion/story_7552011.asp, consulted August 3, 2011.

21. E-mail communication from Stephen Greenblatt to Jesús Eguía Armenteros, July 2, 2007. I am grateful to Jesús Eguía Armenteros for making these materials available to me.

22. E-mail from Greenblatt to Eguía Armenteros, July 17, 2007.

23. Letter from Stephen Greenblatt, "To whom it may concern," October 11, 2007.

24. E-mail between Greenblatt and Eguía Armenteros, July 24–25, 2007.

25. It is striking that the sole press announcement of the play included on Greenblatt's website describes it as "una propuesta nacional para un proyecto internacional" [a national proposal for an international project], http://www.fas.harvard.edu/~cardenio/spain-press.html, consulted August 17, 2011.

26. E-mail between Stephen Greenblatt and Jesús Eguía Armenteros, July 24, 2007.

27. Personal communication with Eguía Armenteros, August 16, 2011.

28. Jesús Eguía Armenteros, *The Cardenio Project*, http://www.fas.harvard.edu/~cardenio/spain-script.html, downloaded August 8, 2011, 3–4.

29. Eguía Armenteros, *The Cardenio Project*, trans. Teresa Álvarez-Garcillán and Karen Velásquez, http://www.fas.harvard.edu/~cardenio/spain-script.html, downloaded August 8, 2011, 3–5.

30. Personal communication with Eguía Armenteros, August 16, 2011.

31. Eguía Armenteros, *The Cardenio Project*, 63.

32. Eguía Armenteros, *The Cardenio Project*, trans. Álvarez-Garcillán and Velásquez, downloaded August 8, 2011, 82–83.

33. "The Cardenio Project," http://www.fas.harvard.edu/~cardenio/spain-production.html, consulted August 17, 2011.

34. Greenblatt, "Theatrical Mobility," 91.

35. "The Cardenio Project," consulted August 3, 2011.

36. *Double Falshood* was staged at the Union Theater in London in January 2011, directed by Phil Willmott, and by the Classic Stage Company in New York in March–April, 2011, directed by Brian Kulick. Both productions attributed the play to Shakespeare, although CSC attempted to hedge its bets, with a publicity campaign that placed the onus on the spectator: "Shakespeare's long lost play? Decide for yourself."

37. http://www.rsc.org.uk/whats-on/cardenio/, consulted August 17, 2011.

38. *Cardenio: Shakespeare's "Lost Play" Re-Imagined* (London: Nick Hern, 2011), unpaginated.

39. Ibid.

40. Ibid., 5.

41. Ibid., 6.

42. http://www.rsc.org.uk/whats-on/cardenio/qa-doran.aspx, consulted August 18, 2011.

43. Ibid.

44. The website for *Cardenio*'s publisher, Nick Hern Books, puts yet another spin on matters, listing Doran and Álamo as "editors," and Shakespeare and Fletcher as authors, http://www.nickhernbooks.co.uk/?isbn=9781848421806, consulted August 18, 2011. On editorship and copyright, see James Marino, *Owning Shakespeare: The King's Men and Their Intellectual Property* (Philadelphia: University of Pennsylania Press, 2011).

45. Hammond, ed., 131, citing a private communication with Gregory Doran, July 23, 2007.

46. Gregory Doran, private communication, August 31, 2011.

47. On the construction of Spain as non-European or exotic, see my *Exotic Nation: Maurophilia and the Construction of Early Modern Spain* (Philadelphia: University of Pennsylavnia Press, 2009), and José Colmeiro, "Exorcising Exoticism: *Carmen* and the Construction of Oriental Spain," *Comparative Literature* 54, 2 (2002): 127–43.

48 Doran, "Week Four Already," February 25, 2011, http://www.rsc.org.uk/explore/blogs/entry/week-four-already/, consulted August 18, 2011.

49. In his now classic *Time and the Other: How Anthropology Makes Its Object*, Johannes Fabian identifies the "denial of coevalness" that places "*the referent(s) of anthropology in a Time other than the present of the producer of anthropological discourse*" (New York: Columbia University Press, 1983, 2nd. ed. 2002), with a new foreword by Matti Bunzl, 31, emphasis original. While the RSC *Cardenio* is by no means anthropological, its construction of Spain emphasizes its timeless otherness.

50. Gregory Doran, "Introduction," *Cardenio: Shakespeare's "Lost Play" Re-Imagined*, 6–7.

51. Doran, "Pancake Tuesday," March 18, 2011, http://www.rsc.org.uk/explore/blogs/reimagining-cardenio/pancake-tuesday/, consulted August 22, 2011.

52. Marvin Carlson, *The Haunted Stage: The Theater as Memory Machine* (Ann Arbor: University of Michigan Press, 2001), 8.

53. Doran, "Serenatas in Spain," January 21, 2011, http://www.rsc.org.uk/explore/blogs/reimagining-cardenio/serenatas-in-spain/, consulted August 22, 2011.

54. Charles D'Avillier, *Spain*, illus. Gustave Doré, trans. J. Thomson (London: Bickers & Son, 1881), 8.

55. Ibid., 134.

56. "The Escorial," January 26, 2011, http://www.rsc.org.uk/explore/blogs/entry/the-escorial/, consulted August 18, 2011.

57. Michael Billington, "Cardenio—Review." *The Guardian*, April 28, 2011, http://www.guardian.co.uk/stage/2011/apr/28/cardenio-review, consulted August 5, 2011.

58. Charles Spenser, "Cardenio, RSC, Stratford-upon-avon, Review," *Daily Telegraph*, April 28, 2011, http://www.telegraph.co.uk/culture/theatre/theatre-reviews/8479816/Cardenio-RSC-Stratford-upon-avon-review.html, consulted August 5, 2011.

59. Paul Taylor, "Shakespeare with a Stylish Spanish Twist," *Independent*, May 2, 2011, http://www.independent.co.uk/arts-entertainment/theatre-dance/reviews/cardenio-swan-theatre-stratforduponavon–2277636.html, consulted August 5, 2011.

60. Jonathan Thacker, "History of Performance in English," in *The Spanish Golden Age in English: Perspectives on Performance*, ed. Catherine Boyle and David Johnston with Janet Morris (London: Oberon, 2007), 15–30, citation on 21–22.

61. "El Papa, en Madrid: Los incidentes registrados en la manifestación laica ensombrecen la llegada del Papa," *El País*, August 17, 2011, http://politica.elpais.com/politica/2011/08/17/actualidad/1313607443_608832.html, consulted August 22, 2011; Raúl Salazar, "Madrid, plagada de confesionarios portátiles," http://www.unrespetoalascanas.com/2011/madrid-plagada-de-confesionarios-portatiles, consulted August 22, 2011.

62. Personal communication with Eguía Armenteros, August 16, 2011.

63. "The Spanish Golden Age," season brochure, ed. Royal Shakespeare Company, June 2004, cited in Kathleen Jeffs, "Golden Age Page to Stratford Stage: Rehearsing and Performing the Royal Shakespeare Company's Spanish Season," D.Phil Thesis, University of Oxford, 2009, 1. I am grateful to Dr. Jeffs for sharing her work with me. The RSC's metaphor is the same as in Felix Schelling's 1923 account of Spanish sources: "The coffers of Spanish drama, thus opened, continued to afford English playwrights their treasures." Having surveyed multiple foreign sources, Schelling asks, in a kind of literary-historical mercantilism: "What was there left that was native after all this use of the coin of other realms?" His confident answer: "Nearly everything is left" (Schelling, *Foreign Influences in Elizabethan Plays* [New York: Harper, 1923], 123, 138).

64. Perhaps unsurprisingly, even the "discovery" of Golden Age Spanish theater by British companies leads to chauvinistic coverage. In response to the much vaunted RSC Spanish Golden Age season in 2004, and their performance in Madrid of Lope de Vega's *El perro del hortelano* (The Dog in the Manger), directed by Boswell, Dominick Cavendish recounts in *The Telegraph* "How the RSC Gave Spain a Lesson in Teatro," November 1, 2004. In an interview with David Johnston, Boswell is far more cautious and modest about the enterprise, recognizing the wariness about appropriation: "There are always issues around ownership. We were nervous because it would be very easy to say that we were doing something inappropriate, that Lope should be performed by Spanish actors. We really had very little idea as to how classical Spanish theatre worked in contemporary

Spain." In Boyle and Johnston, eds., *The Spanish Golden Age in English*, 148–54, citation on 151.

   65. Ibid., 153. Boswell has since directed a production of Lope's *Fuenteovejuna* both at the Canadian Stratford Shakespeare Festival (2008), where his own translation of the text was used, and in both Madrid and Alcalá (2009).

   66. Jeffs, 24.

Bibliography

About the (Re)making Project. http://www.charlesmee.org/html/about.html, consulted March 31, 2009.

Akenside, Mark. "The Remonstrance of Shakespeare." 1749.

Alemán, Mateo, and James Mabbe. *The Rogue: Or, the Life of Guzman de Alfarache*. London: Constable, 1924.

Allen, Paul C. *Philip III and the Pax Hispanica, 1598–1621: The Failure of Grand Strategy*. New Haven, Conn.: Yale University Press, 2000.

Andrews, Kenneth. "North and Northwest." In *Trade, Plunder and Settlement: Maritime Enterprise and the Genesis of the British Empire, 1480–1630*. Cambridge: Cambridge University Press, 1984.

Ardila, J. A. G., ed. *The Cervantean Heritage: Reception and Influence of Cervantes in Britain*. London: Legenda, 2009.

———. "The Influence and Reception of *Don Quixote* in England, 1607–2005." In *The Cervantean Heritage: Reception and Influence of Cervantes in Britain*, ed. J. A. G. Ardila. London: MHRA and Maney, 2009. 2–31.

Armstrong, T. E. "The Arctic." In *The Hakluyt Handbook*, ed. D. B. Quinn. 2 vols. London, 1974. 1: .254–60.

Ashley, Kathleen and Véronique Plesch. Introduction to *The Cultural Processes of "Appropriation"*, special issue, *Journal of Medieval and Early Modern Studies* 32, 1 (2002): 1–15.

Baffin, William. *The Voyages of William Baffin, 1612–1622*. Ed. Clements R. Markham. London: Printed for the Hakluyt Society, 1881.

Bearden, Elizabeth. "Sidney's 'Mongrell Tragicomedy' and Anglo-Spanish Exchange in the *New Arcadia*." *The Spanish Connection*, special issue, *Journal of Early Modern Cultural Studies* 10, 1 (Spring/Summer 2010), ed. Barbara Fuchs and Brian Lockey. 29–51.

Beaumont, Francis. *The Knight of the Burning Pestle*. Ed. Sheldon P. Zitner. New York: Manchester University Press, 2004; Ed. Michael Hattaway. London: New Mermaids, 1969.

Beaumont, Francis, and John Fletcher. *The Coxcomb* (1609). London, 1647.

———. *The Knight of the Burning Pestle*. Ed. Herbert Murch. New York: Henry Holt, 1908.

Beecher, Donald. "The Legacy of John Frampton: Elizabethan Trader and Translator." *Renaissance Studies* 20, 3 (2006): 320–39.

Billington, Michael. "Cardenio—Review." *The Guardian*, April 28, 2011.

Blank, Paula. *Broken English: Dialects and the Politics of Language in Renaissance Writings.* London: Routledge, 1996.

Boyle, Catherine. "Perspectives on Loss and Discovery: Reading and Reception." In *The Spanish Golden Age in English: Perspectives on Performance*, ed. Catherine Boyle and David Johnson. London: Oberon, 2007. 61–74.

Boyle, Catherine and David Johnston, eds., with Janet Morris. *The Spanish Golden Age in English: Perspectives on Performance.* London: Oberon, 2007.

Bromham, A. A. and Zara Bruzzi. *The Changeling and the Years of Crisis, 1619–1624: A Hieroglyph of Britain.* London: Pinter, 1990.

Brownlee, Marina, ed. *Intricate Alliances: Early Modern Spain and England.* Special Issue of *Journal of Medieval and Early Modern Studies* 39, 1 (2009).

Burke, Peter. "The Renaissance Translator as Go-Between." In *Renaissance Go-Betweens: Cultural Exchange in Early Modern Europe*, ed. Andreas Höfele and Werner von Koppenfels. Berlin: Gruyter, 2005. 17–31.

Burke, Peter and Ronnie Po-Chia Hsia, eds. *Cultural Translation in Early Modern Europe.* Cambridge: Cambridge University Press, 2007.

Campanella, Tommaso. *Monarchia di Spagna.* 1600. Trans. Edmund Chilead, *Thomas Campanella, an Italian friar and second Machiavel, his advice to the King of Spain for attaining the universal Monarchy of the World.* London, 1659.

"Cardenio." *Nick Hern Books.* http://www.nickhernbooks.co.uk/?isbn=9781848421806, consulted August 18, 2011.

"Cardenio." *Royal Shakespeare Company Website.* http://www.rsc.org.uk/whats-on/cardenio/, consulted August 17, 2011.

Cardenio: Greenblatt Interview. YouTube, http://www.youtube.com/watch?v=SRxd2Qo-UXc, consulted March 31, 2009.

The Cardenio Project. http://www.fas.harvard.edu/~cardenio/spain-production.html, consulted August 3–17, 2011.

Carew, George. *The Excellency of the English Tongue* (c. 1595). In William Camden, *Remaines Concerning Britain.* London: John Legatt for Simon Waterson, 1614.

Carlson, Marvin. *The Haunted Stage: The Theater as Memory Machine.* Ann Arbor: University of Michigan Press, 2001.

Cave, Terence. *The Cornucopian Text: Problems of Writing in the French Renaissance.* Oxford: Oxford University Press, 1979.

Cavendish, Dominick. "How the RSC Gave Spain a Lesson in Teatro." *Telegraph*, November 1, 2004.

Cervantes Saavedra, Miguel de. *The History of the Valorous and Wittie Knight-Errant, Don-Quixote of the Mancha.* Trans. Thomas Shelton. London: Edward Blount, 1612.

———. *El ingenioso hidalgo Don Quijote de la Mancha.* Ed. Martín de Riquer. Barcelona: Planeta, 1997.

———. *Novelas ejemplares.* 1613. Ed. Marín F. Rodríguez. Madrid: La Lectura, 1914.

Chakravorty, Swapan. *Society and Politics in the Plays of Thomas Middleton.* Oxford: Clarendon, 1996.

Chambers, E. K. *William Shakespeare: A Study of Facts and Problems.* 2 vols. Oxford: Clarendon, 1930.

Chartier, Roger. *Cardenio entre Cervantès et Shakespeare: Histoire d'une pièce perdue.* Paris: Gallimard, 2011.

Clapp, Susannah. "Putting Shakespeare in His Place." *The Observer*, April 25, 2004, 133–40.

Cohen, Walter. "Afterword." In *Comedias del Siglo de Oro and Shakespeare*, ed. Susan L. Fischer. Lewisburg, Pa.: Bucknell University Press, 1989. 142–51.

Colmeiro, José. "Exorcising Exoticism: *Carmen* and the Construction of Oriental Spain." *Comparative Literature* 54, 2 (2002): 127–43.

Corro, Antonio de. *The Spanish Grammar.* Trans. John Thorius. London: J. Wolfe, 1590.

Coryate, Thomas. *Coryats Crudities.* London: William Stansby, 1611.

Croxall, Samuel, ed. *The Adventures on the Black Mountains; A Tale, Upon which the Plan of a Posthumous Play, call'd Double Falsehood, was written Originally by W. Shakespeare. Select Collection of Novels and Histories.* 6 vols. London: John Watts, 1729. 1:311–38.

Daniel, Samuel. *Musophilus* (1599). In *Samuel Daniel: The Complete Works in Verse and Prose*, ed. Alexander B. Grosart, 5 vols.,1. New York: Russell and Russell, 1963 [1885–1896].

Darby, Trudi L. "The Black Knight's Festival Book? Thomas Middleton's *A Game at Chess.*" In *The Spanish Match: Prince Charles's Journey to Madrid, 1623*, ed. Alexander Samson. Burlington, Vt.: Ashgate, 2006. 173–187.

———. "Cervantes in England: The Influence of Golden-Age Prose Fiction on Jacobean Drama, c. 1615–1625." *Bulletin of Hispanic Studies* 74 (1997): 425–441.

Darby, Trudi L. and Alexander Samson. "Cervantes on the Jacobean Stage." In *The Cervantean Heritage: Reception and Influence of Cervantes in Britain*, ed. J. A. G. Ardila. London: Legenda, 2009. 206–22.

D'Avillier, Charles. *Spain.* Illus. Gustave Doré, trans. J. Thomson. London: Bickers & Son, 1881.

De Grazia, Margreta. *Shakespeare Verbatim: The Reproduction of Authenticity and the 1790 Apparatus.* Oxford: Clarendon, 1991.

Degenhardt, Jane. *Islamic Conversion and Christian Resistance on the Early Modern Stage.* Edinburgh: Edinburgh University Press, 2010.

Dekker, Thomas. *The Shoemaker's Holiday* (1599). London, 1600. Ed. R. L. Smallwood and Stanley W. Wells. Manchester: Manchester University Press, 1979.

Deloney, Thomas. *The Works of Thomas Deloney.* Ed. Francis Oscar Mann. Oxford: Clarendon, 1912.

Dick of Devonshire. 1626. Facsimile ed. James Gilmer McManaway and Mary R. McManaway. London: Malone Society, 1955.

Dillon, Janette. "'Is Not All the World Mile End, Mother?': The Blackfriars Theater, the City of London, and *The Knight of the Burning Pestle.*" *Medieval and Renaissance Drama in England: An Annual Gathering of Research, Criticism and Reviews* 9 (1997): 127–48.

Dobson, Michael. *The Making of the National Poet: Shakespeare, Adaptation and Authorship, 1660–1769.* Oxford: Clarendon, 1992.

Doran, Gregory. "The Escorial." *Reimagining Cardenio: Royal Shakespeare Company Blog.* January 26, 2011. http://www.rsc.org.uk/explore/blogs/entry/the-escorial/, consulted August 18, 2011.

——. "Introduction." *Cardenio: Shakespeare's "Lost Play" Re-Imagined.* London: Nick Hern, 2011.

——. "Pancake Tuesday." *Reimagining Cardenio: Royal Shakespeare Company Blog.* March 18, 2011. http://www.rsc.org.uk/explore/blogs/entry/week-four-already/, consulted August 22, 2011.

——. "Reconstructing Cardenio." *Royal Shakespeare Company Website.* http://www.rsc.org.uk/whats-on/cardenio/qa-doran.aspx, consulted August 18, 2011.

——. "Week Four Already." *Reimagining Cardenio: Royal Shakespeare Company Blog.* February 25, 2011. http://www.rsc.org.uk/explore/blogs/entry/week-four-already/, consulted August 18, 2011.

Double Falshood; or The Distrest Lovers. A play, as it is acted at the Theatre-Royal in Drury-Lane. Written originally by W. Shakespeare; and now revised and adapted to the stage by Mr. Theobald, the author of Shakespeare Restor'd. London: J. Watts, 1728.

Dutton, Richard. "Thomas Middleton's *A Game at Chess*: A Case Study." In *The Cambridge History of British Theatre*, vol. 1, ed. Jane Milling and Peter Thomson. Cambridge: Cambridge University Press, 2004. 424–38.

"El Papa, en Madrid: Los incidentes registrados en la manifestación laica ensombrecen la llegada del Papa." *El País*, August 17, 2011.

Eldred, Jason. " 'The Just will pay for the Sinners': English Merchants, the Trade with Spain, and Elizabethan Foreign Policy, 1563–1585." *Journal for Early Modern Cultural Studies* 10, 1, ed. Barbara Fuchs and Brian C. Lockey (Spring/Summer 2010): 5–28.

Enciso, Martín Fernández de. Suma de geographia. Trans. John Frampton as *A Briefe Description of the Portes, Creekes, Bayes and Havens conteyned in the West India, the originall whereof was Dedicated to the mightie Kinge, Charles the V Kinge of Castile.* London: Henry Bynneman, 1578.

Enríquez, José. "En la estela de Shakespeare y Cervantes." Rpt. *Cardenio Project Website.* http://www.fas.harvard.edu/~cardenio/spain-press.html, consulted August 17, 2011.

Eguía Armenteros, Jesús. " *The Cardenia Project,* Script." *The Cardenia Project.* Trans. Teresa Álvarez-Garcillán and Karen Velásquez. http://www.fas.harvard.edu/~cardenio/spain-script.html, accessed August 8, 2011.

Ercilla y Zúñiga, Alonso de. *La Araucana.* 1569. Ed. Isaías Lerner. Madrid: Cátedra, 1993. Trans. George Carew as *The Historie of Aravcana written in verse by Don Alonso de Ercilla translated out of the spanishe into Englishe prose allmost to the Ende of the 16 Canto.* Transcr. with intro. and notes Frank Pierce. Manchester: Manchester University Press, 1964.

Fabian, Johannes. *Time and the Other: How Anthropology Makes its Object.* 2nd ed., foreword Matti Bunzl. New York: Columbia University Press, 1983.

Field, Nathaniel. *The Plays of Nathaniel Field.* Ed. William Peery. Austin: University of Texas Press, 1950.

Fletcher, John. *To Rule a Wife and Have a Wife.* (1624). Ed. George Walton Williams in *The*

Dramatic Works in the Beaumont and Fletcher Canon, gen. ed. Fredson Bowers. 10 vols. Cambridge: Cambridge University Press, 1985. 6:483–605.

Florio, John. *A Worlde of Wordes, Or Most copious and exact Dictionarie in Italian and English*. London: Arnold Hatfield for Edward Blount, 1598.

Fothergill-Payne, Louise and Peter Fothergill-Payne, eds. *Parallel Lives: Spanish and English national drama, 1580–1680*. Lewisburg, Pa.: Bucknell University Press, 1991.

Frampton, John. *The Arte of Navigation, wherein is contained all the rules, declarations, secrets & advises, which for good Navigation are necessarie & ought to be knowen & practised*. London, 1581.

Freehafer, John. "Cardenio, by Shakespeare and Fletcher." *PMLA* 84, 3 (1969): 501–513.

Fuchs, Barbara. *Exotic Nation: Maurophilia and the Construction of Early Modern Spain*. Philadelphia: University of Pennsylvania Press, 2009.

———. *Mimesis and Empire: The New World, Islam, and European Identities*. Cambridge: Cambridge University Press, 2001.

———. *Passing for Spain: Cervantes and the Fictions of Identity*. Urbana: University of Illinois Press, 2003.

———. "The Spanish Race." In *Rereading the Black Legend: The Discourses of Religious and Racial Difference in the Renaissance Empires*, ed. Margaret Greer, Walter Mignolo, and Maureen Quilligan. Chicago: University of Chicago Press, 2007.

———. "Traveling Epic: Translating Ercilla's *La Araucana* in the Old World." *Journal of Medieval and Early Modern Studies* 36, 2 (Spring 2006): 379–95.

Fuchs, Barbara and Brian C. Lockey, eds. *The Spanish Connection*. Special issue of *Journal of Early Modern Cultural Studies* 10, 1 (Spring/Summer 2010).

Fuller, Mary. *Voyages in Print: English Travel to America, 1576–1624*. Cambridge: Cambridge University Press, 1995.

Gálvez de Moltalvo, Luis. *El pastor de Fílida*. Madrid: L. Sánchez, 1600.

Gerrard, Christine. *The Patriot Opposition to Walpole: Politics, Poetry, and National Myth, 1725–1742*. Oxford: Oxford University Press, 1994.

Goethe, Johann Wolfgang von. *Conversations with Eckermann, 1823–1832*. Trans. John Oxenford. San Francisco: North Point, 1984.

Gossett, Suzanne. Introduction to "*The Spanish Gypsy*." In *Thomas Middleton: The Collected Works*, ed, Gary Taylor, John Lavagnino, and MacDonald P. Jackson. Oxford: Clarendon, 2007. 1723–27.

Gould, J. D. "The Trade Depression of the Early 1620's." *Economic History Review* 2nd ser. 8, 1 (August 1954): 81–90.

Greenblatt, Stephen. "Learning to Curse: Aspects of Linguistic Colonialism in the Sixteenth Century." In *Learning to Curse: Essays in Early Modern Culture*. New York: Routledge, 1990. 16–39.

———. "Theatrical Mobility." In *Cultural Mobility: A Manifesto*, ed. Stephen Greenblatt et al. Cambridge: Cambridge University Press, 2010. 75–95.

Greenblatt, Stephen and Charles Mee. "*Cardenio* (United States), Script." *Cardenio Project*. http://www.fas.harvard.edu/~cardenio/us-script.html.

————. Interview with Ryan McKittrick. American Repertory Theater. http://www.amrep
.org/articles/6_4/como.html, consulted March 31, 2009.

Greene, Robert. *The Life and Complete Works in Prose and Verse of Robert Greene.* Ed. Alexander B. Grosart. 15 vols. New York: Russell and Russell, 1964.

Greene, Roland. *Unrequited Conquests: Love and Empire in the Colonial Americas.* Chicago: University of Chicago Press, 1999.

Griffin, Eric. *English Renaissance Drama and the Specter of Spain: Ethnopoetics and Empire.* Philadelphia: University of Pennsylvania Press, 2009.

Guazzo, Stefano. *The Civile Conversation.* Trans. George Pettie. London: Richard Watkins, 1581.

Gurr, Andrew. "'Within the compass of the city walls': Allegiances in Plays for and about the City." In *Plotting Early Modern London: New Essays on Jacobean City Comedy,* ed. Dieter Mehl, Angela Stock, and Anne-Julia Zwierlein. Burlington, Vt.: Ashgate, 2004. 109–22.

Gutiérrez de la Vega, Luis. *A Compendious Treatise entitled* De Re Militari. Trans. Nicholas Lichfield. London: Thomas East, 1582.

Hakluyt, Richard. *The Principal Navigations, Voyages, Traffiques and Discoveries of the English Nation* [1589/1600]. 12 vols. Glasgow: Maclehose and Sons, 1903. "The Epistle Dedicatory to Sir Robert Cecil" [1599], I. lxvi.

Hamilton, Charles. *William Shakespeare and John Fletcher:* Cardenio *or the* Second Maiden's Tragedy. Lakewood, Colo.: Glenbridge, 1994.

Hamilton, Donna B. *Anthony Munday and the Catholics, 1560–1633.* Burlington, Vt.: Ashgate, 2005.

Hammond, Brean, ed. *Double Falsehood, or The Distressed Lovers.* Arden Shakespeare 3. London: Arden Shakespeare, 2010.

Harris, Jonathan Gil. "Recent Studies in Tudor and Stuart Drama." *Studies in English Literature 1500–1900* 51, 2 (2011): 465–513.

Hart, Jonathan. *Representing the New World: The English and French Uses of the Example of Spain.* New York: Palgrave, 2000.

Heinemann, Margot. *Puritanism and Theatre: Thomas Middleton and Opposition Drama under the Early Stuarts.* Cambridge: Cambridge University Press, 1980.

Helgerson, Richard. *Forms of Nationhood: The Elizabethan Writing of England.* Chicago: University of Chicago Press, 1992.

————. "Language Lessons: Linguistic Colonialism, Lingustic Postcolonialism, and the Early Modern English Nation." *Yale Journal of Criticism* 11, 1 (1998): 289–99.

Hesiod. *The Georgicks of Hesiod, by George Chapman, translated elaborately out of the Greek.* . . . London: H. Lounes for Miles Partrich, 1618.

Heywood, Thomas. *The Four Prentices of London.* (1594). *The Dramatic Works of Thomas Heywood,* 6 vols. London: J. Pearson, 1874.

Höfele, Andreas and Werner von Koppenfels, eds. *Renaissance Go-Betweens: Cultural Exchange in Early Modern Europe.* Berlin: Gruyter, 2005.

Holland, Philemon. *The Historie of the World, Commonly called, The Naturall Historie of C. Plinius Secundus. Translated into English by Philemon Holland, Doctor in Physycke, The First Tome.* London: Adam Islip, 1601.

Howard, Jean. *Theater of a City: The Places of London Comedy, 1598–1642.* Philadelphia: University of Pennsylvania Press, 2007.

Howell, James. *Epistolae Ho-Elianae. The Familiar Letters of James Howell.* 2 vols. Ed. Joseph Jacobs. London: D. Nutt, 1890.

Huarte de San Juan, Juan. *Examen de ingenios para las ciencias.* (1575). Ed. Guillermo Serés. Madrid: Cátedra, 1988. Trans. Richard Carew as *Examen de ingenios: The examination of mens wits: in which by discouering the varietie of natures, is shewed for what profession each one is apt, and how far he shall profit therein.* London: Adam Islip for Richard Watkins, 1594.

Hulse, Clark. *Elizabeth I: Ruler and Legend.* Urbana: University of Press, 2003.

James, Heather. *Shakespeare's Troy: Drama, Politics, and the Translation of Empire.* Cambridge: Cambridge University Press, 1997.

Jeffs, Kathleen. "Golden Age Page to Stratford Stage: Rehearsing and Performing the Royal Shakespeare Company's Spanish Season." D.Phil. Thesis, University of Oxford, 2009.

Johns, Adrian. *Piracy: The Intellectual Property Wars from Gutenberg to Gates.* Chicago: University of Chicago Press, 2009.

Jones, Ann Rosalind. "Italians and Others: The White Devil (1612)." In *Staging the Renaissance: Reinterpretations of Elizabethan and Jacobean Drama,* ed. David Scott Kastan and Peter Stallybrass. New York: Routledge, 1991. 251–62.

Jones, Richard Foster. *The Triumph of the English Language.* Stanford, Calif.: Stanford University Press, 1953.

Jonson, Ben. *Ben Jonson.* Ed. C. H. Herford, Percy Simpson, and Evelyn Simpson. 11 vols. Oxford: Oxford University Press, 1925–52.

Jonson, Ben. "On the Author, Work, and Translator." In *The Rogue, or the Life of Guzmán de Alfarache, Written in Spanish by Mateo Alemán and Done into English by James Mabbe* [1623], ed. James Fitzmaurice-Kelly. New York: Knopf, 1924.

Jonson, Ben. *Timber, or Discoveries,* in *Ben Jonson's Literary Criticism.* Ed. James D. Redwine, Jr. Lincoln: University of Nebraska Press, 1970.

Jowitt, Claire. *The Culture of Piracy, 1580–1630: English Literature and Seaborne Crime.* Burlington, Vt.: Ashgate, 2010.

———. "Massinger's *The Renegado* (1624) and the Spanish Marriage." *Cahiers Élizabéthains* 65 (2004): 45–54.

Kagan, Richard L. "Prescott's Paradigm: American Historical Scholarship and the Decline of Spain." *American Historical Review* 101 (1996): 423–46.

———. *Spain in America: The Origins of Hispanism in the United States.* Urbana: University of Illinois Press, 2002.

Kastan, David Scott. *Shakespeare and the Book.* Cambridge: Cambridge University Press, 2001.

Keats, John. "On First Looking into Chapman's Homer." 1816. In *Complete Poems,* ed. Jack Stilinger. Cambridge Mass.: Harvard University Press, 1982.

Kukowski, Stephan. "The Hand of John Fletcher in *Double Falsehood*." *Shakespeare Survey* 43 (1991): 81–89.

Kyd, Thomas. *The Spanish Tragedy.* Ed. J. R. Mulryne. London: A&C Black, 1989.

Legatt, Alexander. "The Audience as Patron: *The Knight of the Burning Pestle*." In *Shakespeare and Theatrical Patronage in Early Modern England*, ed. Paul Whitfield White and Suzanne Westfall. Cambridge: Cambridge University Press, 2002.

Lesser, Zachary. "Walter Burre's *The Knight of the Burning Pestle*." *English Literary Renaissance* 29, 1 (1999): 22–43.

Limon, Jerzy. *Dangerous Matter: English Drama and Politics in 1623/4*. Cambridge: Cambridge University Press, 1986.

Lockey, Brian. *Law and Empire in English Renaissance Literature*. Cambridge: Cambridge University Press, 2008.

Loewenstein, Joseph. *The Author's Due: Printing and the Prehistory of Copyright*. Chicago: University of Chicago Press, 2002.

———. *Ben Jonson and Possessive Authorship*. Cambridge: Cambridge University Press, 2002.

Loftis, John. "English Renaissance Plays from the Spanish Comedia." *English Literary Renaissance* 14, 2 (Spring 1984): 230–48; rpt. in *Renaissance Drama in England and Spain: Topical Allusion and History Plays*. Princeton, N.J.: Princeton University Press, 1987.

Lopes de Castanheda, Fernão. *The first booke of the historie of the discouerie and conquest of the East Indias, enterprised by the Portingales, in their daungerous nauigations, in the time of King Don Iohn, the second of the name. . . .* Trans. Nicholas Lichfield. London, 1582.

Mabbe, James, trans. *The Rogue, or the Life of Guzmán de Alfarache, Written in Spanish by Mateo Alemán and Done into English by James Mabbe*. 1623. Ed. James Fitzmaurice-Kelly. London: Constable; New York: Knopf, 1924.

MacLure, Millar. *George Chapman: A Critical Study*. Toronto: University of Toronto Press, 1966.

Malcolmson, Cristina. "'As Tame as the Ladies': Politics and Gender in *The Changeling*." *English Literary Renaissance* 20 (1990): 320–39.

Marchitello, Howard. "Finding *Cardenio*." *English Literary History* 74 (2007): 957–87.

Marcus, Leah. *Puzzling Shakespeare: Local Reading and Its Discontents*. Berkeley: University of California Press, 1988.

Marino, James J. *Owning William Shakespeare: The King's Men and Their Intellectual Property*. Philadelphia: University of Pennsylvania Press, 2011.

Marotti, Arthur F. *Religious Ideology and Cultural Fantasy: Catholic and Anti-Catholic Discourses in Early Modern England*. Notre Dame, Ind.: University of Notre Dame Press, 2005.

Martínez, Zenón Luis and Luis Gómez Canseco, eds. *Between Cervantes and Shakespeare: Trails along the Renaissance*. Newark, Del.: Juan de la Cuesta, 2006.

Masten, Jeffrey. *Textual Intercourse: Collaboration, Authorship, and Sexualities in Renaissance Drama*. Cambridge: Cambridge University Press, 1997.

McMullan, Gordon. *The Politics of Unease in the Plays of John Fletcher*. Amherst: University of Massachusetts Press, 1994.

Mendoza, Bernardino de. *Theorique and Practise of Warre, Written to Don Philip Prince of Castil, by Don Bernardino de Mendoza. Translated out of the Castilian tonge into Englishe, by Sr. Edwarde Hoby, Knight. Directed to Sr. George Carew*. London, 1597.

Metz, G. Harold ed. *Sources of Four Plays Ascribed to Shakespeare*. Columbia: University of Missouri Press, 1989.

Mexía, Pedro de. *Silva de varia lección*. 1540. Ed. Antonio Castro Díaz. 2 vols. Madrid: Cátedra, 1989–90. Trans. *The Treasury of Ancient and Modern Times*, London, 1613.

Middleton, Thomas. *Thomas Middleton: The Collected Works*. Ed. Gary Taylor, John Lavagnino, and MacDonald P. Jackson. Oxford: Clarendon, 2007.

"The Modern Poets," *Gentlemen's Magazine* i, ii (November 1731): 493.

Monardes, Nicolás. *Joyfull Newes out of the Newe Founde Worlde wherein is declared the rare and singular vertues of diverse and sundrie hearbes, trees, oyles, plants and stones, with their applications, as well for phisicke as chirurgerie*. Trans. John Frampton. London: William Norton, 1577.

Montaigne, Michel de. *The essayes or morall, politike and militarie discourses. . . .* Trans. John Florio. London: Val. Sims for Edward Blount, 1603.

Montemayor, Jorge de. *Diana of George of Montemayor: translated out of Spanish into English by Bartholomew Yong of the Middle Temple Gentleman*. London: Bollifant, 1598.

Morini, Massimiliano. *Tudor Translation in Theory and Practice*. Burlington, Vt.: Ashgate, 2006.

Mowat, Barbara. "The Theater and Literary Culture." In *A New History of Early English Drama*, ed. John D. Cox and David Scott Kastan. New York: Columbia University Press, 1997. 213–30.

Munday, Anthony, trans. *The Honorable, Pleasant and Rare Conceited Historie of Palmendos Sonne to the Famous and Fortunate Prince Palmerin d'Oliua, Emperour of Constantinople and the queene of Tharsus*. London, 1589.

Muir, Kenneth. *Shakespeare as Collaborator*. London: Methuen, 1960.

Lai, Ananda. "Finding El Dorado." Rev. of *Cardenio*. *The Telegraph*, Calcutta, March 24, 2007. http://www.telegraphindia.com/1070324/asp/opinion/story_7552011.asp, consulted August 3, 2011.

Nebrija, Antonio de. *Gramática castellana*. Ed. Miguel Ángel Esparza and Ramón Sarmiento. Madrid: Fundación Antonio de Nebrija, 1992.

Nocera, Carmela. "George Pettie and his *Preface* to *The Civile Conversation* (1581)." In *Thou Sittest at Another Boke. . . : English Studies in Honour of Domenico Pezzini*, ed. Giovanni Iamartino, Maria Luisa Maggioni, and Roberta Facchinetti. Monza, Italy: Polimetrica, 2008. 75–84.

Notestein, Wallace, Frances H. Relf, and Hartley Simpson, eds. *Commons Debates, 1621*. New Haven, Conn.: Yale University Press, 1935.

Parker, Patricia. "Barbers and Barbary: Early Modern Cultural Semantics." *Renaissance Drama* 33 (2004): 201–44.

Perceval, Richard. *Bibliotheca Hispanica*. London, 1591.

Perceval, Richard and John Minsheu. *A Spanish grammar, first collected and published by Richard Perciuale Gent. Now augmented and increased with the declining of all the irregular and hard verbes in that toong, with diuers other especiall rules and necessarie notes for all such as shall be desirous to attaine the perfection of the Spanish tongue. Done by Iohn*

Minsheu professor of languages in London. Hereunto for the yoong beginners learning and ease, are annexed speeches, phrases, and prouerbes, expounded out of diuers authors, setting downe the line and the leafe where in the same bookes they shall finde them, whereby they may not onely vnderstand them, but by them vnderstand others, and the rest as they shall meete with them. London: Bollifant, 1599.

Peterson, Richard S. *Imitation and Praise in the Poems of Ben Jonson.* New Haven, Conn.: Yale University Press, 1981.

Platt, Kevin M. F. *Terror and Greatness: Ivan and Peter as Russian Myths.* Ithaca, N.Y.: Cornell University Press, 2011.

The Pleasaunt Historie of Lazarillo de Tormes a Spaniarde wherein is Conteined His Marueilous Deedes and Life. With the Straunge Aduentures Happened to Him in the Seruice of Sundrie Masters. Drawen out of Spanish by Dauid Rouland of Anglesey. London: Jeffs, 1586.

Quint, David. *Cervantes's Novel of Modern Times.* Princeton: Princeton University Press, 2003.

Randall, Dale. *The Golden Tapestry: A Critical Survey of Non-Chivalric Spanish Fiction in English Translation (1543–1657).* Durham, N.C.: Duke University Press, 1963.

Randall, Dale and Jackson Boswell. *Cervantes in Seventeenth-Century England: The Tapestry Turned.* Oxford: Oxford University Press, 2009.

Reynolds, John. "History IV." *The Triumphs of God's Revenge.* London: Felix Kyngston, 1621.

Redworth, Glyn. *The Prince and the Infanta: The Cultural Politics of the Spanish Match.* New Haven, Conn.: Yale University Press, 2003.

Reynolds, John. *Vox Coeli, or, Newes from heauen, of a consvltation there held by the high and mighty princes, King Hen. 8, King Edw. 6, Prince Henry, Queene Mary, Queene Elizabeth, and Queene Anne; wherein Spaines ambition and treacheries to most kingdomes and free estates of Europe, are vnmask'd and truly represented, but more particularly towards England, and now more especially vnder the pretended match of Prince Charles, with the infanta Dona Maria; Whereunto is annexed two letters written by Queene Mary from heauen, the one to Count Gondomar, the ambassadour of Spaine, the other to all the Romane Catholiques of England.* London, 1624.

Richards, Bernard. "Now am I in Arden." Rev. of *Double Falsehood, or The Distressed Lovers,* ed. Brean Hammond. *Essays in Criticism* 61, 1 (2011): 79–88.

Rojas, Fernando de. *La Celestina.* 1499. Trans. John Rastall as *Calisto and Melebea,* London, c. 1530; trans. James Mabbe as *The Spanish Bawd, Represented in Celestina,* London, 1631.

Rosenbach, A. S. "The Curious-Impertinent in English Dramatic Literature Before Shelton's Translation of *Don Quijote.*" *MLN* 17, 6 (June 1906): 179–84.

Salas Barbadillo, Alonso Jerónimo de. *El sagaz Estacia marido examinado.* Madrid: Juan de la Cuesta, 1620.

Salazar, Raúl. "Madrid, plagada de confesionarios portátiles." *Un respeto a las canas.* http://www.unrespetoalascanas.com/2011/madrid-plagada-de-confesionarios-portatiles, consulted August 22, 2011.

Samson, Alexander. "1623 and the Politics of Translation." In *The Spanish Match: Prince Charles's Journey to Madrid, 1623*, ed. Alexander Samson. Aldershot: Ashgate, 2006. 91–106.

Samson, Alexander. "'Last Thought upon a Windmill'?: Cervantes and Fletcher." In *The Cervantean Heritage: Reception and Influence of Cervantes in Britain*. London: Legenda, 2009. 223–33.

Schelling, Felix. *Foreign Influences in Elizabethan Plays*. New York: Harper, 1923.

Schevill, Rudolf. "On the Influence of Spanish Literature upon English in the Early 17th Century." *Romanische Forschugen* 20 (1907): 604–34.

Scott, Thomas. *An Experimentall discoverie of Spanish practises, or, The Counsell of a well-wishing souldier, for the good of his prince and state wherein is manifested from known experience, both the cruelty, and policy of the Spaniard, to effect his own ends*. London, 1623.

———. *Narrative of the wicked plots carried on by Seignior Gondamore for advancing the popish religion and Spanish faction*. London, 1679.

———. *Second Part of Vox Populi / Gondomar appearing in the likenes of Matchiauell in a Spanish parliament, wherein are discouered his treacherous & subtile practises to the ruine as well of England, as well as the Netherlands*. London,1624.

———. *A Second part of Spanish practises, or, A Relation of more particular wicked plots, and cruell, inhumane, perfidious, and vnnaturall practises of the Spaniards with more excellent reasons of greater consequence, deliuered to the Kings Maiesty to dissolue the two treaties both of the match and the Pallatinate, and enter into warre with the Spaniards*. London, 1624.

———. *Vox Populi, or Newes from Spayne translated according to the Spanish coppie. . . .* London, 1620.

Sengupta, Reshmi. "Shakespeare, Found Via Tagore." *The Telegraph*. Calcutta, January 4, 2007.

Shakespeare, William. *The Norton Shakespeare, Based on the Oxford Edition*. 2nd ed. Ed. Stephen Greenblatt, Walter Cohen, Jean E. Howard, and Katharine Eisaman Maus. New York: Norton, 1997, 2008.

———. *William Shakespeare: The Complete Works*. 2nd ed. Ed. Stanley Wells and Gary Taylor. Oxford: Clarendon, 2005.

Shakespeare ,William and John Fletcher. *Henry VIII (All Is True)*. Ed. Gordon McMullan. London: Arden, 2000.

Sidney, Philip. *The Defence of Poesie* (1579). London: William Ponsonby, 1595.

Spenser, Charles. "Cardenio, RSC, Stratford-upon-Avon, Review." *Daily Telegraph*. April 28, 2011.

Stern, Tiffany. "'The Forgery of some modern Author'?: Theobald's Shakespeare and Cardenio's *Double Falsehood*," *Shakespeare Quarterly* 62, 4 (Winter 2011): 555–93.

———. "Taking Part: Actors and Audience on the Stage at Blackfriars." In *Inside Shakespeare: Essays on the Blackfriars Stage*, ed. Paul Menzer. Selinsgrove, Pa.: Susquehanna University Press, 2006. 35–53

Stoll, Anita K., ed. *Vidas paralelas: el teatro español y el teatro isabelino, 1580–1680*. London: Támesis, 1993.

Sullivan, Garrett. *The Drama of Landscape: Land, Property, and Social Relations on the Early Modern Stage*. Stanford, Calif.: Stanford University Press, 1998.

Supple, Barry. *Commercial Crisis and Change in England, 1600–1642*. Cambridge: Cambridge University Press, 1959.

Taylor, Gary. "Historicism, Presentism, and Time: Middleton's *The Spanish Gypsy* and *A Game at Chess*." *SEDERI: Journal of the Spanish Society for English Renaissance Studies* 18 (2008): 147–70.

Taylor, Gary and John Lavagnino, eds. *Thomas Middleton and Early Modern Textual Culture: A Companion to the Collected Works*. Oxford: Clarendon, 2007.

Taylor, Paul. "Shakespeare with a Stylish Spanish Twist." Rev. of *Cardenio*. *Independent*, May 2, 2011. http://www.independent.co.uk/arts-entertainment/theatre-dance/reviews/cardenio-swan-theatre-stratforduponavon–2277636.html, consulted August 5, 2011.

Thacker, Jonathan. "History of Performance in English." In *The Spanish Golden Age in English: Perspectives on Performance*, ed. Catherine Boyle and David Johnston, with Janet Morris. London: Oberon, 2007. 15–30.

Theatre Communications Group—New Plays. http://www.tcg.org/tools/newplays/details.cfm?ShowID=1.

Theobald, Lewis. *Memoirs of Sir Walter Raleigh*. London: W. Mears, 1719.

Thomson, Leslie. "Who's In, Who's Out: *The Knight of the Burning Pestle* on the Blackfriars Stage." In *Inside Shakespeare: Essays on the Blackfriars Stage*, ed. Paul Menzer. Selinsgrove, Pa.: Susquehanna University Press, 2006. 61–71.

"To the Author of the British Gazetteer." *Weekly Journal or the British Gazetteer*, February 10, 1728, 142.

Tucker, T. G. *The Foreign Debt of English Literature*. London: Bell and Sons, 1907.

Uman, Deborah and Belén Bistué. "Translation as Collaborative Authorship: Margaret Tyler's The Mirrour of Princely Deedes and Knighthood." *Comparative Literature Studies* 44, 3 (2007): 298–323.

Ungerer, Gustav. "The Earl of Southampton's Donation to the Bodleian in 1605." *Bodleian Library Record* 16, 1 (April 1997): 17–41.

Valdés, Francisco de. *A Dialogue of the Office of a Sergeant Major*. Trans. John Thorius. London, 1590.

Vega, Félix Arturo Lope de. *El perro del hortelano*. Ed. Adrienne L. Martín and Esther Fernández Rodríguez. Newark: Juan De La Cuesta, 2011.

Wall, Wendy. *Staging Domesticity: Household Work and English Identity in Early Modern Drama*. Cambridge: Cambridge University Press, 2002.

Wayne, Valerie. "*Don Quixote* and Shakespeare's Collaborative Turn to Romance." In *The Quest for Cardenio*, ed. Gary Taylor and David Carnegie, forthcoming.

———. "The *Don Quixote* Effect on Early Modern Drama." In the program for *Cardenio: Shakespeare's Lost Play Re-imagined*.

Whibley, Charles. *Literary Studies*. London: Macmillan, 1919.

Williams, Franklin. "Commendatory Verses: The Rise of the Art of Puffing." In *Studies in Bibliography: Papers of the Bibliographical Society of the University of Virginia* 19, ed.

Fredson Bowers and L. A. Beaurline. Charlottesville: University Press of Virginia, 1966.

———. *Index of Dedications and Commendatory Verses in English Books Before 1641*. London: Bibliographical Society, 1962.

Wilson, Diana de Armas. *Cervantes, the Novel and the New World*. Oxford: Oxford University Press, 2000.

———. "Contesting the Custom of the Country: Cervantes and Fletcher." In *From Dante to García Márquez: Studies in Romance Literatures and Linguistics*, ed. Gene H. Bell-Villada, Antonio Giménez, and George Pistorius. Williamstown, Mass.: Williams College, 1987. 60–75.

———. "Of Piracy and Plackets: Cervantes' *La señora Cornelia* and Fletcher's *The Chances*." In *Cervantes for the 21st Century*, ed. Francisco La Rubia Prado. Newark, Del.: Juan de la Cuesta, 2000. 49–60.

Wilson, Edward M. "*Rule a Wife and Have a Wife* and *El sagaz Estacio*." *Review of English Studies* 24 (1948): 189–94.

Wilson, Richard. "Another Country: Marlowe and the Trading Factor." In *Renaissance Go-Betweens: Cultural Exchange in Early Modern Europe*, ed. Andreas Höfele and Werner von Koppenfels. Berlin: Gruyter, 2005. 177–99.

———. "Unseasonable Laughter: The Context of Cardenio." In *Shakespeare's Late Plays: New Readings*, ed. Jennifer Richards and James Knowles. Edinburgh: Edinburgh University Press, 1999. 193–209.

Index

Acknowledgments

I have been fortunate to have found a series of wonderful interlocutors in the study of Spain and England, from Roland Greene, Patricia Parker, and Stephen Orgel, who fostered my earliest work on the topic, to my dear friend Edmund Campos, to the wonderful colleagues and students who explored the Spanish connection with me at the Folger and at Penn, including Elizabeth Bearden, Larissa Brewer-García, Brian Lockey, and Miguel Martínez. Along the way, Marshall Brown reinforced my conviction that comparatists make magnificent mentors. I dedicate this book to him as a small measure of my appreciation. My UCLA writing group—Christine Chism, Caroline Ford, Hannah Landecker, Zrinka Stahuljak, and Sarah Stein—provided valuable feedback on several chapters. I owe thanks also to the friends who generously commented on various sections: Karina Galperín, J. K. Barret, Eric Griffin, and Paul Saint-Amour. Walter Cohen, who read the manuscript for Penn Press with an eagle eye, made invaluable suggestions for which I am truly grateful. I have been fortunate to work with very fine research assistants, now valued colleagues—Cyrus Mulready, Emily Weissbourd, and Sara Torres—on different aspects of this project, as well as with the gracious Tamar Boyadjian, who helped with Latin translations. As an early modernist, it is rare that I have the privilege of engaging with contemporary practitioners, and I am grateful to Jesús Eguía Armenteros and Gregory Doran for discussing their respective productions with me. Stephen Greenblatt graciously provided me with an early copy of the *Cardenio* that he wrote with Charles Mee. Katherine Jeffs and Carla della Gatta shared with me their work on the representation of Spain on the English stage, and their infectious enthusiasm for the topic. Early versions of some of the arguments in this book first appeared in *Modern Philology*, the *Journal for Medieval and Early Modern Studies*, the *Oxford Handbook to Thomas Middleton*, edited by Gary Taylor, and *Laureations: Essays in Memory of Richard Helgerson*, edited by Roze Hentschell and Kathy Lavagnino. I am grateful to the various editors and readers for their suggestions. My research was supported by two generous grants from the UCLA Academic Senate. For kindly granting permissions for images, I owe thanks to the Huntington Library, the Shakespeare Birthplace Trust, the Art Institute of Chicago, the UK National Portrait Gallery, and the American Repertory Theater. Jesús Eguía, Burt Sun, and Raúl Salazar also graciously facilitated images. Jerry Singerman, at Penn Press, has been as responsive and constructive as ever. I am fortunate to have him as my editor and my friend. As always, I thank my family for their patience and support, including everything from traipsing to Stratford to helping me collate versions of *Cardenio*. It is a pleasure to share with them my love for what I do.